THE FIRST WORLD PRESIDENCY

The First World Presidency

George H. W. Bush, 1989–1993

Eric E. Otenyo and Nancy S. Lind

<teneo> // press

Youngstown, New York

Copyright 2009 Eric E. Otenyo and Nancy S. Lind

All rights reserved
Printed in the United States of America

ISBN: 978-1-934844-09-0

No part of this publication may be reproduced, stored in or introduced into a retrieval system, or transmitted, in any form, or by any means (electronic, mechanical, photocopying, recording, or otherwise), without the prior permission of the publisher.

Requests for permission should be directed to:
permissions@teneopress.com, or mailed to:
Teneo Press
PO Box 349
Youngstown, New York 14174

To Allan M. Winkler and Ryan J. Barilleaux
                              —*Eric E. Otenyo*

To DeeDee Sharkey and Isabelle Stelmahoske
                              —*Nancy S. Lind*

  For your encouragement over the years

Table of Contents

Preface	xi
Acknowledgments	xiii
Introduction	1
Chapter 1: The Setting: America as a Great Power	11
The United States as a Great Civilization	15
American Fears	16
The Fall of the Soviet Empire	18
Chapter 2: Being a U.S. President	25
Chapter 3: The Making of President George H. W. Bush	37
Modern Republicans and the Making of the Bush Presidency	45
The Bush Vision	51
The 1988 Campaign and the Election of President Bush	52
Chapter 4: Bush and the Gulf War of 1991	61
The United States and Iraq in the Reagan-Bush Era	63
The Gulf War and the Vietnam Syndrome	71
The Bush Plan Receives Congressional Backing	74
World Protests: Bush and Iraqgate	77
Chapter 5: Security, Trade, and Democracy in Latin America and Asia	91
Latin America and Monroe's Ghost	92
Friends or Foes?	93
Trade Worries	93

National Security Reform Directives	96
Narco-Politics and Promotion of Democracy	96
Concerns in the Pacific Rim and Asia	99
China	100
Cambodia	102
Taiwan	103
Korea	104
India and Pakistan Turn Nuclear on Bush's Watch	105

Chapter 6: Standing Up for the Voiceless in Africa — **111**

Bush's History With Africa and the Cold War Legacy	112
Operation Restore Hope: The Last Bush Act	115
Neo-Isolationism as Another Policy Orientation	119
Of Democracy: "We Know What Works, Freedom Works. We Know What's Right: Freedom Is Right" (Bush)	123

Chapter 7: A New World Order? — **133**

America Inspiring the World	135
Criticisms of the New World Order	136
African Americans Raise Questions About the New World Order	143
Buchanan's Attack	145

Chapter 8: At Home — **151**

Bush and Minority Politics	156
Health Politics	162
Education and the President	163
The Savings and Loan Scandal	165
Budget Problems Revisited	167
The Environmental President	169
The Wetlands	171

Chapter 9: The Reelection Debacle   **181**

Chapter 10: The Bush Legacy and Conclusions   **197**
    Shaping a New World Order and Democratic Globalism   198
    Reforming International Institutions
       and Reasserting Global Power   201
    Kinder and Gentler Home Front   203
    Reevaluating President Bush's Leadership   205
    Bush and Trade Agreements   208

Selected Bibliography   **215**

Index   **231**

About the Authors   **243**

PREFACE

This book provides a critical analysis of George H. W. Bush, whose administration evolved in response to world events and changes in the politics and policies of globalization from 198 to 1993. It focuses on how Bush's vision and actions influenced international peace and development during his administration and after. Bush, the forty-first president of the United States of America, was in office when America surpassed the Soviet Union in the decades-long race for world political supremacy. Before now, not much academic scrutiny explained the making of this leader or examined his long-lasting contributions to America and the global community.

Although America has been viewed as a superpower since World War II, the political changes after 1989, including the fall of the Berlin Wall and the beginning of the end of communist rule in Eastern Europe, presented the world with an opportunity to more closely analyze the unfolding global realignments. While these changes are well documented, a rigorous examination of Bush's presidency requires further exploration of the ramifications of his stances on domestic and foreign policy issues.

After examining the president's public record, evidence suggests that historical facts were often distorted, which has led to misperceptions of Bush's administration. This research of Bush's intense focus on internationalism in response to advances in international communications and emerging globalization is evidence that Bush's administration, an institution that included the most powerful head of state who was no longer threatened by any other national leader as a potential superpower, was the first world presidency.

In many respects, the presidency of Bush was a watershed presidency, particularly because he was the first president who did not have to deal with a united Soviet Union. The legacy of Bush's decisions, proclivities, character, and policies has persisted through the presidencies of William Jefferson Clinton and George W. Bush—and will likely continue to exercise a formative influence on future U.S. presidents. It is the conclusion of the present study that George H. W. Bush was better at developing "the new world order" than either he or most students of politics hitherto supposed.

ACKNOWLEDGMENTS

We acknowledge indebtedness to several authors and persons who were cited or interviewed in this work. We also acknowledge the scholars who provided book endorsements, particularly David T. Canon, James Pfiffner, and Charles Walcott.

Eric E. Otenyo is deeply grateful to Professors Allan M. Winkler and Ryan J. Barilleaux of Miami University, Ohio, "The two know that I owe them more than a book dedication." Eve C. Paludan was generous in editing the manuscript, and she did it diligently. Finally, to my children, Jane and Marvin, thank you.

Nancy S. Lind thanks her friends from the "regular Sunday suppers" for providing the time to unwind and refocus for the next week. These include Joy Barnard; Greg and Louise Darnall; Thom and Jayne DelForge; Bill, Alex, Alyssa, and Chelsea Dryer; Allene Gregory; Mary and Molly Munson; Edna and Sharon Schnittker; Sydney and David Stiles; and Royce Womack.

To the many colleagues who advised and supported the project, including Shailer Thomas, Manfred Steger, Lane Crothers, Ken Panfilio, Jamal Nassar, Ali Riaz, Mary Munson, Charles Walcott, Sandra Metts, Sue Sprecher, and Bill Tolone—thank you. As is usual, we, the authors, remain responsible for all errors herein.

The First World Presidency

INTRODUCTION

The First World Presidency: George H. W. Bush, 1989–1993 is based on three assertions. First, America's rise to world superpower status is an affirmation of the quality and character of its political leaders. Second, American political leaders are products of the historical forces surrounding them. Third, the actions of U.S. presidents are of interest to Americans and non-Americans by virtue of the dominant unchallenged status of the United States since 1989.

Scholars of the American presidency engage in the exercise of rating presidents by using terms such as *weak* or *strong, courageous* or *cowardly, conservative* or *liberal*, and so on.[1] Some scholars evaluate the presidency in terms of normative models derived from biblical and cultural metaphors. For example, Nelson's models of the presidency as satan, savior, or Samson are particularly intriguing.[2] Nelson posited that the savior school is applicable when a president is negotiating with Congress to win major policy concessions. The satanic model depicts a powerfully dangerous presidency that responds recklessly to domestic or international crises. The third model, Samsonic, may be the imperiled or tethered presidency. It is based on the reality that presidents cannot deliver all they promise to their constituents. These models are heuristic devices for understanding the important institution of the presidency.

Most commentaries on the performance of U.S. presidents measure presidential leadership in a comparative framework. This scrutiny is done against the background of presidential performance in the domestic and international arenas. This last criterion is particularly useful since presidential conduct outside the United States has received surprisingly little attention.

Evaluating presidents is particularly useful for comparisons across different eras. Cronin and Genovese questioned why the average American continues to evaluate presidents using imprecise standards.[3] Cronin and Genovese made an important contribution by explaining how and why the expectations from the public have varied with changing times. In the nineteenth century, the evaluation criteria were different from criteria used to evaluate today's postmodern presidency. Many writers posit that presidential popularity may have little correlation with overall policy successes or failures. The paradox is that presidents are held accountable for the quality of domestic and international policy outcomes during their terms.

An additional model for evaluating presidents is provided by Ryan Barilleaux, who examined the issue of presidential performance in foreign affairs through a series of comparative case studies.[4] Barilleaux noted that scholars do not have an agreed-upon set of criteria for assessments of presidential performance, but he identified five common standards that dominate evaluations of presidential performance in foreign affairs. These standards are policy design and direction, organization and staffing, management and oversight, consensus building, and achievements and outcomes.[5] This study employs the last three criteria to examine George H. W. Bush, whose presidency was marked by historic reconfigurations in global power and politics.

With respect to global power, presidential performance can be evaluated on how well a president manages crises and articulates his vision in consensus building. A president's policy outcomes can be ascertained using a continuum from success to failure. Barilleaux stated,

> The president's performance in foreign affairs is to be judged according to the outcome he achieves. The criterion is a central one for most observers, whether scholars, commentators, or the general public. It is a judgment based not on outputs, on what the president and his administration do, but on outcomes: the results and consequences of presidential policy making.[6]

The First World President: America and George H. W. Bush, 1989–1993 is an evaluation drawn from international sources. Attention is focused on presidential actions that affect the lives of millions of people across the globe. This study recognizes the interrelatedness between the presidency as an institution and the president as a person and draws out the linkages.

Historically, American presidents are elected with specific policy and political agendas. For example, Franklin D. Roosevelt promised the New Deal, Lyndon B. Johnson promised the Great Society, and Ronald W. Reagan promised to roll back the federal bureaucracy, cut taxes, and re-establish the military supremacy of the United States in global affairs. The significance of presidential agendas is well covered by several scholars, including Paul Light, John Kingdon, Lydia Andrade, and others.[7] Charles Jones stated that Bush assumed the presidency when expectations were very low, and Bush had a limited agenda.[8] On the home front, Bush had to carry the burdens inherited from the Reagan years, such as a massive budget deficit. In the international arena, this volume examines Bush's initiatives in the context of America's world leadership.

Much inspiration is drawn from Clinton Rossiter's seminal work that concluded the U.S. presidency is about world leadership.[9] Rossiter's sentiment is expressed in numerous additional works on American presidential leadership. For example, Aaron Wildavsky contended that the United States has two presidencies—one for domestic affairs and the other for defense and foreign affairs.[10] The Bush presidency is characterized by caution with an occasional dash of boldness, search for consensus, heavy reliance on personal contacts, and a proclivity for surprise.[11] Bush also had a more hands-on policy than the previous chief executives of this generation.

Bush demonstrated these attributes in different situations. For example, his consensus-building strategy worked in dealings with America's North Atlantic Treaty Organization (NATO) allies. He cooperated with Germany's Helmut Kohl and France's François Mitterrand to transform NATO. Bush worked with allied leaders to reduce military hardware in Europe and to pave the way for the redefinition of NATO's operations. This was widely considered to be President Bush's first foreign policy victory.[12]

It is fitting to contextualize President Bush's agenda in light of America's overall position and standing in world affairs. From the outset, no pretense is made that this study is a comprehensive commentary on the influence of the president's personal character on his foreign policy conduct. The central thesis is that President Bush's upbringing and value systems influenced his actions and dispositions. The leadership style of President Bush points to one observation, that is, he wished to translate his inner personality and predispositions into the American political landscape. In this book, it is argued that Bush moderated his views on extremely thorny issues without compromising his ideals.

The first chapter contends that at the time Bush assumed the presidency, the United States had overtaken its closest rival in terms of world political, economic, and military leadership. This superpower status added more responsibilities to U.S. political leadership, especially the presidency. The increased role of U.S. leadership was to be provided within the parameters of a declining economy at home.

The second and third chapters give a sense of what being a U.S. president entails and how President Bush rose to become leader of the world's premier economic and military power. The chapters demonstrate how these qualities helped develop Bush into the first leader in the U.S.-led world order. The title of this book, *The First World Presidency: George H. W. Bush, 1989–1993*, reinforces this theme. For the first time, American leadership over the United Nations (UN) appeared to be undisputed.

Bush was presented with an unprecedented opportunity to shape world politics. The concept of "first" is used in a metaphorical sense because, being the global center for world politics, the United States is the leader among the family of nations. By extension, the U.S. head of state is the first in the pecking order of power.

Presidential power is a function of the incumbent's personal motivation and characteristics. This power thesis is well documented by Neustadt's *Presidential Power and the Modern Presidents*.[13] An alternative argument is found in Dean K. Simonton's book titled *Why Presidents Succeed: A Political Psychology of Leadership*, a political psychologist's view of power motivation.[14] Bush, it is suggested, made a number of important domestic and foreign policy decisions based on psychological considerations. This text examines Bush's decision to use persuasion and force when demanded by political exigencies. Quite predictably, his early life and service in the U.S. Marines and the CIA had a bearing on his evident extroversion. The current analysis brings out the connections between President Bush's biographical data—his values, attitudes, and so on—and his use of power.

There is also a deliberate effort to relate his perceived weaknesses to the same set of criteria. This is partly an offshoot of Neustadt's observation that a president's authority and status give him great advantages in dealing with people he wished to persuade.[15] Each "power" is a vantage point for the president in the degree that others have use of his authority.[16] In addition, presidential advantages are greater than a mere listing of powers.[17] In cases where negotiation is required, presidents are involved in a game of give and take with Congress or, at times, a foreign power. Therefore, if outcomes are not as expected by U.S. citizens, a president's power to successfully persuade is limited. Ordinarily, a president must be perceived to have sufficient powers to effectively discharge his or her duties. Without the power to bargain, Bush could not have been successful as the first leader of what emerged as a new world order.

The first three chapters in this book are efforts to prepare the reader to understand the psychological and theoretical preparations of the principal player in U.S. politics between 1989 and 1993. The key assumption is that one cannot understand U.S. political processes under the Bush administration without some background information on what shaped Bush's predispositions.

The fourth, fifth, sixth, and seventh chapters build on the salience of foreign policy making by the American presidency. These chapters shed light on important moments in President Bush's international agenda. Chapter 4 describes internationalism as a value that Bush adopted from the Nixon administration. Specifically, it is a commentary about the Gulf War in 1991. Bush's leadership in important areas of American interest in Asia and Latin America are outlined in chapter 5. Chapter 6 describes the promotion of democracy in Africa and President Bush's role in restoring hope in Somalia as key elements of the administration's mission to promote freedom and demonstrate compassionate conservatism abroad. The thesis is that President Bush, more than any other president since Woodrow Wilson, championed democratization of the world by employing diplomatic methods.

While it is appreciated that forces used were borne out of specific domestic needs of these countries, initiatives provided by the Bush administration cannot be disputed. The policies and events of the Bush years after 1990 demanded that one-party dictatorships must initiate reforms. Leading scholars on U.S.-African relations, including Larry Diamond[18] and Peter Schraeder,[19] agreed that Bush's leadership was significant.

Bush used his leadership to usher in his signature doctrine, the New World Order. This is the primary content of chapter 7, which debates and presents opposing views and conceptualizations of the rhetorical concept. The term *new world order* is deconstructed and placed in the perspective of changes that were taking place in world politics and affairs.

Chapter 8, "At Home," supplements the earlier chapters on "Being a U.S. President" and "The Making of President Bush" by addressing some of the specific problems and issues of interest to Americans at home. In this chapter, a number of actual policy decisions by the president are addressed, including his handling of minority politics, health policy, education, the budget, and the environment. It becomes clear that Bush was more focused on international than domestic affairs throughout much of his term.

Moderate conservatism defined President Bush's outlook on domestic policy agendas. The emerging changes supported by Bush's philosophy are discussed in chapter 9. The arguments explain the fundamental reasons for the president's failure to join the ranks of two-term presidents such as Wilson, Dwight Eisenhower, and Reagan. Chapter 9 is a brief attempt at explaining Bush's failed bid for re-election. Chapter 10 evaluates the enduring legacy of President Bush's policies.

Bush provided leadership to America and the world at a time when the Berlin Wall collapsed. Bush was a moderate conservative at a time when right-wing conservatism was permeating the American fabric, causing unprecedented division between what were later coined the *blue* and *red* states. Bush attempted to reduce the excesses of *Reaganomics* and the growth of right-wing Republicans whose influence changed the core values of the American experiment.

Bush must be studied for his poorly articulated vision of the New World Order, a policy that informed the twenty-first century's neoliberal globalization agenda. This book is one piece of the global debate on America's leadership on the world stage. While the Reagan presidency created conditions for the collapse of widespread Communism, the succeeding George H. W. Bush administration was the first world presidency. For the first time in recent world history, a head of state utilized an almost unprecedented opportunity to shape world politics.

Notes

1. D. A. Lonnstrom and T. O. Kelly II, "Rating the Presidents: A Tracking Study," *Presidential Studies Quarterly* 27, no. 3 (summer 1997): 591–598.
2. Michael Nelson, *The Presidency and the Political System* (Washington, DC: Congressional Quarterly Press, 1998), 3–8.
3. Thomas Cronin and M. A. Genovese, *The Paradoxes of the American Presidency* (New York: Oxford University Press, 1998).
4. Ryan J. Barilleaux, "Presidential Conduct of Foreign Policy," *Congress and the Presidency* 15, no. 1 (spring 1988): 1–22.
5. Ibid., 2.
6. Ibid., 3.
7. S. A. Warshaw, *The Domestic Presidency Policy Making in the White House* (Boston: Allyn & Bacon, 1997); Paul Light, *The President's Agenda: Domestic Choice From Kennedy to Carter* (Baltimore: Johns Hopkins University, 1982); John Kingdon, *Agendas, Alternatives, and Public Choices* (Boston: Little, Brown, 1984); Charles O. Jones, *The Presidency in a Separated System* (Washington, DC: Brookings Institution Press, 1994), 164–181; L. Andrade and G. Young, "Presidential Agenda Setting: Influences on the Emphasis of Foreign Policy," *Political Research Quarterly* 49 (1996): 591–605.
8. Jones, *The Presidency in a Separated System*, 180.
9. Clinton Rossiter, *The American Presidency* (New York: A Mentor Book, 1962), 14–40.
10. Aaron Wildavsky, "Two Presidencies," *Transaction* 4, 2 (1966): 237–250, reproduced in Stella Z. Theodoulou and M. A. Cahn, *Public Policy: The Essential Readings* (Englewood Cliffs, NJ: Prentice Hall, 1995).
11. B. Kellerman and Ryan Barilleaux, *The President as World Leader* (New York: St. Martin's, 1991).
12. Ibid., 212.
13. Richard Neustadt, *Presidential Power and the Modern Presidents: The Politics of Leadership From Roosevelt to Reagan* (New York: The Free Press, 1990), 15.
14. Dean K. Simonton, *Why Presidents Succeed: A Political Psychology of Leadership* (New Haven, CT: Yale University Press, 1987), 97–109.
15. Neustadt, *Presidential Power and the Modern Presidents: The Politics of Leadership From Roosevelt to Reagan*, 15.
16. Ibid., 30–31.

17. Ibid., 32.
18. Larry Diamond, "Promoting Democracy in Africa: United States and International Policies in Transition," in *The United States and Africa From Independence to the End of the Cold War*, ed. Macharia Munene, Korwa Adar, and Joshua Nyunya (Nairobi, Kenya: East African Educational Publishers, 1995), 193–219. Also see Korwa Adar, "The Wilsonian Conception of Democracy and Human Rights: A Retrospective and Prospective," *African Studies Quarterly* 2, no. 2 (September 25, 1998), http://Africa.ufl.edu/asq.
19. Peter J. Schraeder, "Removing the Shackles? U.S. Foreign Policy Toward Africa After the End of the Cold War," in *Africa in the New International Order: Rethinking State Sovereignty and Regional Security*, ed. E. J. Keller and Donald Rothchild (Boulder, CO: Lynne Rienner Publishers, 1996), 187–204.

CHAPTER 1

THE SETTING: AMERICA AS A GREAT POWER

Only America can head the world. America remains the only global, universal civilization in the history of mankind.
—Newt Gingrich*

Political scientists and historians have long been interested in understanding the dynamics of global power. The rise and fall of power within the world offers an opportunity to examine the roles of the president in providing global leadership.

In June 1991 *The Forum*, a journal of informed commentary on American politics, proclaimed that

> the stature of Washington, D.C. was recently elevated as the end of Cold War politics ushered in a new international order, essentially affirming the political superiority of the United States throughout the world. The whole world now listens to what Washington, D.C. has to say.[1]

This chapter describes the setting in which the American presidency occurs in relation to global power. Despite the emergence of U.S. domination in world affairs, the tendency to compare and contrast dominant powers in a historical perspective informs the setting for evaluating the abilities and performance of the leaders at the helm of their countries. Since President George H. W. Bush assumed the role of world leader at a time when cold war rivalries ended, the analysis in this chapter situates the presidency at a crossroads in world history. The position of the United States as a dominant global power provides a unique lens to assess the presidency of Bush.

Bush was the first U.S. president to take office after the end of the bipolar cold war, at the beginning of America's ascendancy to unipolar superpower. This unprecedented fart, as jointly affirmed by Bush and Mikhail Gorbachev at the Malta Summit in December 1989, is critical to understanding the actions and inactions of President Bush and assessing his presidency. A popular approach to the study of the American presidency developed by Clinton Rossiter argues that historical significance of a presidency ought to be judged by the expanded responsibilities that a president assumes beyond those that have been constitutionally mandated or conferred on him by precedent.[2] Rossiter saw George Washington's eminence as a product of the events and epoch of revolutionary times.[3] Abraham Lincoln was essentially judged in regard to the Civil War of 1861–1865, Woodrow Wilson was judged against the events that precipitated World War I, and Franklin D. Roosevelt against the Great Depression.

In this study of President Bush, we have joined the popular "indoor sport of history-minded Americans"[4] that rank presidents using a wide array of criteria. William E. Carleton noted that even presidents of the United States like to play this popular game of ranking the presidents.[5] Using one of the more popular ranking schemes, Arthur Schlesinger Jr. evaluated Bush and arrived at the conclusion that President Bush was just an "average performer." He evaluated presidents and placed them into one of six categories—great, near great, high average, average, below average, and failure. Of interest is the placement of Bush among the likes of James Madison, John Quincy Adams, William Henry Harrison, Bill Clinton, Martin Van Buren, William Howard Taft, Rutherford B. Hayes, Ronald Reagan, Jimmy Carter, and Gerald Ford.[6]

This volume will not attempt the ranking methodology applied in the Sigmund Freud and William Bullitt[7] assessment of Wilson's presidency, as that study was later classified as flawed and devoid of rigor. This study of President Bush, instead, focuses on documentary resources available worldwide, particularly those obtained from USIS centers and the U.S. State Department. This volume highlights the president's role as manager of the U.S. political system in greater detail than the short-term approaches taken in studies conducted by Colin Campbell and others.[8] They discussed the question, "How is the president doing within the American political system?" and then proceeded to render descriptive accounts of how Bush performed in the first two years of his presidency. While Campbell, Rockman, and others evaluate mainly domestic angles of presidential conduct, this book extends their orientation to allow for greater scrutiny of presidential leadership overseas. The framework applied in our assessment is one drawn from Mansfield's scholarship on presidential leadership.[9]

Mansfield's observation that the American president was neither a revived Roman dictator nor a moderated British monarch was pertinent to a study of the president during the eventful period of 1989–1993. The United States resembled in many dimensions the Roman Empire, and it is not surprising that U.S. ambassadors in third-world countries during the Bush era became active partners in the governance of their respective host countries under Bush. An example was Smith Hempstone's tenure in Nairobi, Kenya. Hempstone, a Bush nominee and confirmed political appointee as U.S. ambassador to Kenya, was hailed as a champion of the Kenyan opposition leaders for playing a key role in forcing the one-party dictatorial regime to accept multiparty politics in 1991 to 1992. The result was that half of all voters in the first multiparty elections in Kenya since 1966 voted for opposition parties. Bush's appointee was, therefore, hailed as a defender of U.S. ideals of democracy, a key motivation in U.S. foreign policy since Wilson's Fourteen Points of 1918.

What makes scholars such as Paul Kennedy argue that the United States epitomized a new Roman Empire? Two arguments have been popularized. First, a study of U.S. civilization leaves observers with little doubt that the country is the richest and most powerful nation on earth. The second reason is the collapse of the Soviet empire and the subsequent end of hostilities between the two superpowers followed by America's propensity to act as world sovereign. The most obvious similarity between the Bush administration and the Roman Empire is overwhelming military strength. P. Kennedy stated that from the outset, America has been an imperial and conquering nation, just as the Romans tried to conquer every corner of the world.[10]

Charles Beard and Mary Beard have narrated a similar rise in American civilization.[11] Ancient Rome was established by use of force in 509 BCE, and the United States was established by force through the American War of Independence from 1775 to 1783.[12] Rome began to decline with cracks in its republic inflicted by a civil war in 49 BCE. This last factor scares Americans from drawing a parallel between themselves and Rome—the Roman Empire declined and fell.

Historians record that Emperor Augustus attempted to restore the Roman republic and undertook to build a middle class through which he recruited administrators, financiers, and civil servants. Augustus succeeded in establishing a system that combined democratic traditions and freedom from the "insolence of tyranny."[13] Interestingly, Augustus preferred to be called "princeps" (i.e., "first citizen") or "president," signaling his disdain for the monarchical imperator or commander in chief. Paradoxically, Nicolson noted that the decline of the Roman Empire had much to do with the emperor having abolished true democracy without ever desiring to do so.[14] Perhaps more than anything else, Rome's succession of imperial and absolute dictatorships—including Tiberius, Claudius, Nero, and others—was the path to self-destruction. The center could not hold the provinces and colonies together. In the end, Rome gradually ceased to be the center of the civilized world. Drawing parallels with the Roman Empire, it would seem a priori that the fall of the United States would one day arrive. This prediction of the eventual fall of the United States leads to a discussion of the fears of Americans.

THE UNITED STATES AS A GREAT CIVILIZATION

The United States has been a great civilization for over two hundred years. Since its independence from Britain in 1776, the United States has developed important institutions, traditions, and social conditions to distinguish it from other civilizations. A historian would identify some of these as its Constitution adopted in 1789, its application of the theory of separation of powers, its unique liberal democratic traditions, its corporatism, and its entry into the postindustrial "age of high mass consumption" attained a few decades after 1860.

In spite of the industrial successes and consumerism that Christopher Lasch and others described, America was not a bed of roses. A study by Edward Greenberg[15] not only cast doubts on the U.S. political system but also argued that U.S. democracy was a farce in the sense that the conventional instruments of the system in ensuring democratic accountability failed because of the power of corporations and other moneyed social groups.[16] Despite the powerful arguments raised by Greenberg, as well as racial imperfections described by Gunnar Myrdal,[17] the core values of American civilization placed U.S. civilization at the top of human achievements. According to Max Lerner, the United States was considered the most urbane, mature, and rational society on earth.[18]

The United States was on top of the world not only because of its military superiority and techno-industrial advances but also because of its cultural advances. In an unpublished paper, a scholar from the developing world argued that less-developed areas would find it difficult to retain their cultures if they equated modernization to Americanization.[19] Nonetheless, as a state projecting its power abroad, the United States provides a yardstick for other nations to measure their progress.

As argued by power theorists such as Robert Dahl and Hans Morgenthau, power is a process of controlling behavior and exercising domination. Their analysis provides evidence that at the global level, the relationships between America and other parts of the world are unequal. The United States has greater resources to project its values than do other countries. Over the years, the United States developed a capacity to affect other players in the international system in a controlling and dominant position. The United States assumed power and leadership over variables such as the use of global resources, management of the democratic order, and stabilization of the global order. In old parlance, the United States assumed the role of establishing global "balance of power" structures and leadership. No other power on the global scale has been able to utilize positive and negative sanctions and persuasion to achieve its core interests. In countries where human rights abuses have run rampant, no embassy receives as many petitions for assistance as does the American embassy. In cases of drought, cyclones, tsunamis, and other natural disasters, it is the United States that is expected to provide expertise and material support. It follows, therefore, that the conduct of the American president is unique and often determines the well-being of the lives of people worldwide.

AMERICAN FEARS

The rise of American fears is the second argument to explain the international setting and context of the Bush presidency. Numerous books pose the argument that U.S. civilization was under siege and its powers were declining relative to its immediate past. Some diplomatic historians traced the United States' qualification as a world power to as early as 1776.[20] Several scholars observe that American eminence in world affairs can be traced back to the years 1898 and 1899 when the U.S. militarily defeated Spain, the world's maritime leader.[21] After 1945, with Truman's order to use the atomic bomb, American expansionism and world leadership was no longer in doubt. As Paterson argued, the United States had the "prime instrument of destruction, the atomic bomb, and the prime weapon of reconstruction" development—wealth not hitherto possessed by any other nation.[22] Marxist scholars announced that the United States had become the organizer and leader of the imperialist system.[23] The United States took it upon itself to build a network of countries with similar economic and social systems. By 1955 it became obvious that U.S. military and economic successes were threatened by the Marxist-Leninist Soviet Union (USSR). The United States and the Soviet Union were viewed as global superpowers.

Cold war politics did not deter American leadership from enhancing development on the domestic front. The United States continued to modernize rapidly and reached out with abundant aid programs to friendly but poor nations. For example, an African nationalist observed that U.S. government aid since 1946 was £33.5 billion—or US$97.6 billion—to foreign nations.[24] The Marshall Plan after World War II was the key aid program. Giving huge amounts of aid implied economic power and relative affluence within the United States. John F. Kennedy's plan to "create a Peace Corps using the skills of dedicated Americans to help people abroad"[25] was a testimony to the level of prosperity the United States had attained.

Doubts concerning U.S. leadership emerged after America began to reduce many of its past aid programs, especially with the emergence of the "Reagan Revolution" and the rise in conservatism. Throughout the 1980s, Americans raised concerns over declining welfare programs. An assessment of the Reagan administration, for example, raised questions about America's social policies.[26] General consensus was that American culture and material progress as evidenced by the relative disintegration of the economy, as well as high budget deficits, in the Reagan years led to a sense of frustration by many citizens.

Even though Bush[27] was quoted to have expressed pride and faith in capitalism by asserting that Gorbachev's socialist Soviet Union was a nonworking system, many other commentators did not think the U.S. system was doing any better. James Fallows examined the Japanese model, which many Americans had been suggesting should be emulated to get America back to its known leadership position, and found that Americans could "rise to their best" and take back the number one position in all human endeavors.[28] Fallows posited that the United States would not fall to the barbarians as the Romans did. The key message was that signals of U.S. decline were evident, but there would be a chance to redress the decline. Michael Aho further observed that America could avoid decline.[29]

From the observations discussed, the decline of America was relative to itself, and America had to create conditions for its resilience. Apart from Japan, the united Germany seemed to have grown as an important world leader, at least at the level of using nonmilitary instruments for penetrating weak states. Regardless, America's main challenger up to 1989 was the former Soviet Union; its demise leads us to discuss the third view—the collapse of the Soviet empire and the new rise of America.

THE FALL OF THE SOVIET EMPIRE

Even though Japan and Germany were economically progressive states, the two could not assume military leadership after the collapse of the Berlin Wall. Moreover, "Project Europe"—emanating from the Maastricht Treaty—was not a strong military rival to the United States in the immediate future. At the economic level, European integration was widely viewed as diminishing U.S. economic power. Scholars such as Leonhard Gleske regarded the European community as joining the United States and Japan to lead a tripolar world economy.[30] However, the combined economy of the European Union (EU) was, by 1992, larger than that of the United States.[31] Regardless of the promise of an expanded EU, China posed another threat. The persistent fear was that China's growth in the post–Mao era would create a new power in the East. Although China has achieved considerable economic progress, its ability to project power on the international stage is still lower than that of the United States. As Patrick Buchanan observed,

> Is China a strategic threat as great as was the former Soviet Union in the Cold War? Certainly, it was not yet. Moscow had an army and armoured forces larger than the United States, a navy of submarines and surface ships that prowled the world's oceans, and bombers and missiles that could have delivered thousands of

nuclear warheads on American soil. China has nothing remotely comparable today.[32]

U.S. superiority in the military sense was still intact due to the demise of the Soviet Union's and United States' advances in science and technology. The fall of the Soviet Union began around 1985 with the Soviet flag at the Kremlin falling on December 25, 1991. Several reasons have been advanced to explain the decline of the Soviet Union. One author argued that the Soviet Union declined primarily because of ethnic nationalism. Ethnic nationalism did not begin in the Soviet Union, but it had been a common feature in the Central and Eastern European nations. It had spread to Eurasia and ushered in a new era of international chaos and relative disorder. The disorder and anarchy led the Soviet Union to disintegrate into fifteen independent but unstable political enclaves, or nation-states. A journalist, Anatoly Gladilin, explained the same phenomenon when he noted,

> The Cold War was won by the U.S. economy and the American way of life—the government had nothing to do with it. As far as foreign policy was concerned, the Soviet Union kept gaining points, the Soviets kept pressing, while America quietly retreated. Then suddenly, and absolutely unexpectedly for all, the Soviet Union collapsed of its own weight, due to its own internal cause.[33]

The decay of the old Soviet empire overwhelmed doctrinaire Communists in rendering obsolete their centralized planning and controlled economies. Ethnicity as an ideology was a potent force, more lethal than Marxist materialism and dialectics. As a result, there were questions of whether C. B. Macpherson's categorization of the nonliberal version of democracy ever applied to the Soviet Union.[34] Events unfolding in the Soviet Union since Gorbachev's rule point to highly repressive regimes and lack of a proletariat with a consciousness that transcended ethnic barriers. For more than seven decades, the system failed to assimilate over one hundred ethnic nationalities through its industrialization and economic strategies. Russia, the largest state of the former Soviet Union, did not demonstrate political development—defined by Lucian Pye as the existence of responsible and rational government behavior, that is, avoidance of reckless actions that undermine the vested interests of significant components of the society[35]—and was unable to resolve rebellions from Chechnya, among other entities. The collapse of the Soviet Union and the end of the cold war meant new responsibilities for the United States.

One of the most important components of the leadership responsibilities bestowed upon the United States dealt with its control of vast arsenals of nuclear weapons. President Bush moved to the White House when the security of Central and Eastern Europe was threatened by ethnic wars. America's responsibility in this regard also required continuing negotiations with Russia over the safety of its nuclear warheads and assisting Eastern Europe in making a smooth transition to democracy and free markets.

As commander in chief of the only remaining superpower, Bush was expected to exhibit the highest level of moral guardianship. However, Dahl criticized this guardianship and expected the U.S. leadership to exercise caution in formulating a nuclear weapons elimination policy.[36] Bush was president of a country expected to provide leadership in handling weapons of mass destruction—clearly an affirmation of its position as world leader. Was Bush, a product of a democratic system, successful in providing guidance in this field, or was he without the skills to discharge the expected moral leadership and guardianship? To answer this question, we explore the preparation and making of the Bush presidency and his handling of foreign policy decisions in the next chapter.

NOTES

* *Daily Nation*, February 10, 1995, 6.
1. Newsletter, *The Forum* 7, no. 2 (fall 1991): 24.
2. Clinton Rossiter, *The American Presidency* (New York: A Mentor Book, 1962), 138.
3. Ibid.
4. Ibid., 137 and Arthur M. Schlesinger Jr., "Rating of Presidents: Washington to Clinton," *Political Science Quarterly*, 112, no. 2 (summer 1997): 179–190.
5. William G. Carleton, "A New Look at Woodrow Wilson," in *Taking Sides: Clashing Views on Controversial Issues in American History*, II, ed. Eugene Kuzirian and Larry Madaras (Guilford, CT: The Dushkin Group, 1987), 251.
6. Schlesinger Jr., "Rating of Presidents: Washington to Clinton," 180.
7. Sigmund Freud and William Bullitt, *Thomas Woodrow Wilson: A Psychological Study* (Boston: Houghton Mifflin, 1967), cited in *Taking Sides*, ed. Eugene Kuzirian and Larry Madaras, 251.
8. Colin Campbell and Bert A. Rockman, eds., *The Bush Presidency: First Appraisals* (Chatham, NJ: Chatham, 1991).
9. Harvey Mansfield Jr., *Taming the Prince: The Ambivalence of Modern Executive Power* (New York: Free Press, 1989). Also see Marcia Lynn Whicker, "Policy Making in the White House: The Best Books on the Presidency in 1991," *Public Administration Review* 51, no. 1 (January/February 1991): 74.
10. Paul Kennedy, *The Rise and Fall of the Great Powers* (New York: Vintage, 1989).
11. Charles Beard and Mary Beard, *The Rise of American Civilization* (1930; repr., Kila, MT: Kessinger Publishers, 2005).
12. Burton F. Beers, *World History, Patterns of Civilization* (Englewood Cliffs, NJ: Prentice Hall, 1988), 273.
13. Harold Nicolson, *Kings, Courts and Monarchy* (New York: Simon & Schuster, 1962), 66.
14. Ibid.
15. Edward S. Greenberg, *The American Political System: A Radical Approach* (New York: Scott Foresman, 1989), 130.
16. Ibid., 130–145.
17. Gunnar Myrdal, *An American Dilemma* (New York: Harper and Row, 1962).

18. Max Lerner, *America as a Civilization* (New York: Simon & Schuster, 1957), 58.
19. Eric E. Otenyo, "Can Developing Countries Preserve Their Traditional Cultures? Should They Want To? A Case Study of Kenya" (unpublished conference paper, Kenyatta University Cultural Week, Nairobi, Kenya, December 5, 1994).
20. John M. Blum et al. *The National Experience, A History of the USA Up to 1877* (New Haven, CT: Harcourt, Brace & World, 1963), 273.
21. Ibid., 79.
22. Richard W. Leopold, *The Emergence of America as a World Power: Some Second Thoughts*, in *Taking Sides*, ed. Eugene Kuzirian and Larry Madaras (Guilford, CT: Dushin/A Division of McGraw-Hill, 1987), 223.
23. Ibid. Also see Stephen Saunders Webb, "Five Centuries of American Empire 1584–2084," in *Democratic Governance: America in the 21st Century, The 9th Annual Donald S. MacNaughton Symposium Proceedings, November 8–9, 1989* (Syracuse, NY: Syracuse University Press, 1990), 175–193. The thrust of his paper was that America, like Britain, has evolved into an empire.
24. Tom Mboya, *Freedom and After* (Nairobi, Kenya: Heinemann, 1963), 241.
25. Ralph G. Martin, *A Hero for Our Time* (Boston: Ballantine Books, 1983).
26. John L. Palmer and Isabel V. Sawhill, *The Reagan Record: An Urban Institute Study* (Cambridge, MA: Ballinger, 1984).
27. James Fallows, *More Like Us: Making America Great Again* (Boston: Houghton Mifflin, 1989), vii.
28. Ibid.
29. C. Michael Aho, "Can America Avoid Decline," in the 9th D. S. MacNaughton Symposium Proceedings, *Democratic Governance: America in the 21st-Century* (Syracuse, NY: Syracuse University Press, 1990), 57–68.
30. Leonhard Gleske, "The Opportunities and Perils for the United States of European Integration," in *The Future of U.S-European Relations in Search of a New World Order*, ed. Henry Brandon (Washington, DC: Brookings Institution Press, 1992), 103.
31. Patrick J. Buchanan, *Where the Right Went Wrong: How Neoconservatives Subverted the Reagan Revolution and Hijacked the Bush Presidency* (New York: St. Martin's Press, 2004), 135–136.
32. Anatoly Gladilin, "Will America Save the World?," *Moscow News* 38 (October 2–8, 1997): 4.
33. Ibid.

34. C. B. Macpherson, *The Real World of Democracy* (New York: Oxford University Press, 1966), 12–22.
35. Lucian W. Pye, *Aspects of Political Development* (Boston: Little, Brown and Co., 1966).
36. Robert Dahl, *Controlling Nuclear Weapons: Democracy Versus Guardianship* (Syracuse, NY: Syracuse University Press, 1985), 33–44.

CHAPTER 2

BEING A U.S. PRESIDENT

> ...*The President would have to be a dull clod indeed to regard himself without a feeling of awe. The atmosphere of the White House is calculated to instill in any man a sense of destiny. He literally walks in the footsteps of hallowed figures—of Jefferson, of Jackson, of Lincoln.*
>
> —George Reedy*

Greenberg and other American governmental and political scholars see the presidency as "the pre-eminent institution in the national government of the USA."[1] In the previous chapter, we singled out the U.S. Constitution as one of the key signposts of American civilization. The vital office of the U.S. president is established under article II, section I of the Constitution. It stipulates that the executive power shall be vested in the president. The requirements are that he or she must be a natural-born citizen of the United States or a citizen of the United States at the time of adoption of the Constitution. The president of the United States serves as commander in chief of the army, navy, air force, and of the national militia stationed in all states of the union. The president's job includes making treaties and appointing ambassadors and other key administrators with U.S. Senate confirmation.

Although a study of U.S. constitutionalism and the Constitution itself is a fairly basic enterprise, the study of the U.S. presidency can be a complex matter. As Robert DiClerico stated, "There is an extraordinary dearth of students of the Presidency. The Presidency is in many ways the most difficult of the three national institutions to investigate with some degree of rigour."[2] Even though we attempt to "peek into" the White House, DiClerico's caution is still timely. His assertion that the White House discussions leading to presidential decisions are not public hearings makes the process of studying presidents quite difficult and leads to speculations and rumors.[3] Even though freedom-of-information laws permit scholars to examine presidential records, the process of declassification can take several years. All that is known about U.S. presidents is, for the most part, through secondary sources. But presidential scholars cannot fail to see the actions of U.S. presidents. These are easily observable on a daily basis on television, Internet blogs, and Web sites. One authority on this subject asserts that U.S. presidents appear as "big men" in relation to the other branches of the federal government.[4] An example of this phenomenon is seen in Theodore Roosevelt's adherence to the dictum, "speak softly and carry a big stick,"[5] which he applied when he had a dispute with Congress over sending troops to protect American businessmen on the high seas.[6] To his credit, T. Roosevelt won the dispute.

The war power enjoyed by U.S. presidents has been problematic and controversial. The vast discretion available to the president in wartime is certainly above his ability to leverage policy in the conduct of peaceful foreign affairs and in providing leadership in domestic, economic, and social issues. This leaves most scholars to imagine that the U.S. president is what George Reedy called the American monarchy.[7] An American president is more or less a king. In fact, several decades ago, Reedy observed what is now commonplace—that the "aura of majesty begins to envelop him the moment it becomes apparent that the electorate has decided upon its next president."[8] In the context of America in

1988, when Bush succeeded Reagan as president, may we speak of King George Bush I? Perhaps historians will make a case that the legacy of the Bush family, with his son George W. Bush elected as the forty-third president, raises the question even more profoundly. This argument is reinforced by our previous assertion that the United States is the only superpower or empire in military and economic might.

As president of the world's major power, Bush's character and strength were of concern not only to Americans but also to the entire world. The twentieth century mass communication advances made U.S. presidents into household names in remote villages in countries such as Afghanistan, Bangladesh, and Uganda. To the American, the office is the only one in the land whose occupier is elected by the whole nation. The incumbent must, therefore, deliver—and if possible, strive to make the country better than he found it. Essentially, that was the same motto used by the Greek rulers of antiquity.

Most U.S. presidents worry about their legacy and imprint in history, perhaps more than other world leaders. In this vein, there may be some exceptions. Some commentators do not think Warren G. Harding or Calvin Coolidge, presidents 1921–1923 and 1923–1929, respectively, made any great impact on U.S. civilization. Perhaps they did not care about their legacies or, alternatively, were simply incompetent. The assertion assumes that the institution provides opportunities for the incumbent to make an imprint on global history. According to Reedy, the office of the U.S. president merely "provides a stage upon which all his personality traits are magnified and accentuated."[9] Building on this assertion, one could argue that Bush was not a Harding- or Coolidge-type president. Bush's character and resolve in handling important U.S. foreign policy missions are extensive and enduring. The lessons of the "mother of all battles" with Saddam Hussein, the decisions on Somalia's disintegration, and the difficult, if not tormenting, confirmation of his Supreme Court appointee Clarence Thomas, along with Bush's record on civil rights, are all unique. Bush referred to Chief of Police Gates as a "top cop" in spite of his poor record of handling minority rights in the greater Los Angeles area, particularly the Rodney King beating.

In American history, presidents must present an image of using immense presidential powers to the advantage of their personal or party interests. This eventuality affects or, is impacted by, the individual leader's character. For example, Reagan was charismatic, even though his brand of economic policy—christened as "Reaganomics"—never improved the American budget deficit. On the other hand, Bush failed to recapture the presidency, yet he claimed to embrace compassionate conservatism, which on the surface might have endeared him to groups that rejected him.

It may well be that Bush, unlike Reagan, bargained too much to affect his likeability and survival in the second race to the White House. According to Peter W. Sperlich, "The president who would always govern by bargaining may soon not govern at all."[10] If the bargaining trait was evident in Bush's presidency, then the study of U.S. presidents must necessarily sharpen its psychological focus and observe these considerations.

In a political sense, the U.S. presidency, symbolically powerful as head of state and government, is a crucial instrument in foreign and domestic policymaking. Today, it is probably the most prestigious office on earth. To paraphrase President Taft's words, it is an embodiment of American people's dignity.[11]

Besides the frustrations and burdens of office, as president of the world's key economic and military powerhouse, the man or woman in the White House has the moral responsibility to ensure the national security of the United States and be, as John Hughes pointed out, a global peacemaker.[12]

The U.S. president should demonstrate a certain level of comprehension of the barriers present in American society's quest for domestic harmony and, particularly, the sensitive area of liberties and civil rights. For example, Lyndon B. Johnson was considered to be "very strong in the area of civil rights, perhaps as strong as you can expect a president to be," to use the words of a spokesman for the Urban League.[13] Since the discussion is about Bush, from a comparative point of view, evidence should be examined to assess his responses to the civil rights agenda either as a Republican Party nominee or a successor to Reagan, considered in many circles to be the foremost conservative statesman in modern history. Alternatively, it is appropriate to examine Bush's record as a flexible individual who sought to reach out to members of the less fortunate communities. The manner in which U.S. presidents handled the age-old race dilemma is an important part of discerning his ability to play good politics—considering that politics is what Harold Lasswell called the art of managing a polity to determine "who gets what, how, and when." It could be argued that President Bush performed a public relations gesture in bashing the Louisiana gubernatorial candidate in 1990–1991, the controversial Klan activist David Duke. The question then is whether that was enough, or was Bush simply playing the politics of race? Looking back to history, President Truman[14] was basically able to sidestep the Klan issue, but it is not obvious that Reagan did the same. Reagan received support from right-wing groups, even though he rejected it.[15] However, as his successor, Bush avoided race-sensitive issues much like Truman and often exhibited a moderate position on race issues.

Perhaps Bush's undoing in the 1992 election can be largely attributed to his failure to manage domestic issues, which included the erosion of the legendary American middle class. On the economic front, the Bush administration never enjoyed a sustainable high rating as it did on the international scene. One way of examining Bush's public record is through scrutinizing the president's decisions with regard to domestic issues, especially those with moral and public service dimensions. This is a perspective that is most popular in domestic press editorials.[16] The extension of these criteria is that a U.S. president has to be close to "a faithful and economical public servant."[17] In this sense, we interpret the term *economical* in a broader sense and measure faithfulness in terms of the ethical dimensions of his tenure. Bush certainly did not face Nixon's Watergate-type of scandal, but his administration had a number of hurdles with which to grapple.

It might not be prudent at this juncture to discuss in detail the attributes of a U.S. president. Nevertheless, any assessment of the performance of a U.S. president does not miss searching for elements of statesmanship and service to the country. By extension, evidence of courage in decision making places the president in good standing. While courage is a difficult trait to measure, there is no doubt that President Lincoln, in preserving the Union, demonstrated it. Allan Nevis expressed this idea in clear terms, "The President of America requires courage to nationalize the policies of the great Conglomerate nation. While courage might be a sensible virtue, historically, some presidents like Andrew Johnson, and Woodrow Wilson, were broken partly for their very courage."[18] This also applies to J. F. Kennedy. One may benefit from understanding J. F. Kennedy's vision of courage:

> The President of the United States is not subject to quite the same test of political courage as a Senator. His constituency is not sectional, his losses in popularity with one group or section may be offset on the same issue by his gains from others and his power and prestige normally command a greater political security than that afforded by a Senator. But…even the president feels the pressures of constituents and special interests.[19]

At the bottom of this assertion by J. F. Kennedy is the truism that U.S. presidents must be ready to make decisions that require courage, and such decisions can immensely lower the president's popularity. According to J. F. Kennedy, even President Washington was once accused of "being an enemy of America, and subject to the influence of a foreign country."[20] Modern presidential scholars know that Washington courageously withstood the test of time and emerged as a great leader in spite of the allegations. Bush also had his tribulations, but one cannot ignore, particularly, his foreign policy successes. It is possible to consider Bush as having a fair amount of courage in making foreign policy decisions with far-reaching ramifications.

This brings us to yet another question: Did Bush qualify to be what *The Economist* called the "perfect president"?[21] According to this journal, history judges presidents by their performance in two respects—in particular, "their ability to cope with the unexpected, and their ability to bring about the unexpected."[22] F. D. Roosevelt dealt with the depression; Truman, the end of World War II and use of atomic bombs; and J. F. Kennedy, the discovery of Soviet missiles in neighboring Cuba. Other modern presidents too had their share of issues, as Nixon had to cope with the repercussions brought about by the Watergate tapes. Carter had the nightmare of Americans held hostage by Iranians. Reagan had to cope with several crises, including threats to American oil tankers by Iranians fifty miles northeast of Bahrain in the Gulf Sea.[23] While we shall not delve into how each president resolved their specific problems or issues, it is important to know that President Bush's predecessor, Reagan, was considered a decisive leader. Reagan had to quickly respond to the Libyan "terrorist" threat.

On the other hand, Bush met his day in the gulf region. *The Economist* argued that a U.S. president does not require great intelligence to deal with such issues, but he certainly "needs a cool head, enough education to be able to ask the right questions, the intelligence to understand the answers and the shrewdness to have appointed good advisers to provide them."[24] Bush was tested on all those levels.

To a large degree, Bush also brought about the unexpected. Those living in the third world, particularly in Africa, credit his stewardship for the upsurge of democracy on the continent. Many Americans may find this conclusion surprising. However, according to *The Economist*, "The achievements of great men are won by easing, squeezing, shaping or leveraging events in such a manner that history moves their way, not the way of their antagonists."[25] The Bush administration got Africa out of the final vestiges of doctrinaire apartheid after de Klerk and Mandela agreed to end hostilities in South Africa. While credit for the successful handing over of power to the African people in South Africa is attributed to their sacrifices, the occurrence of the transition and stewardship of the global movement toward freedom and democracy in sub-Saharan Africa took place under Bush's watch. Bush's diplomatic initiatives proved pivotal in raising the tempo of the democratic moment. Several Bush ambassadors in Africa joined in the democratization processes in their host countries, forcing dictatorships to crumble. Thanks to Bush, the activities of the United Nations (UN), at least for a short while, gave

Somalia a new lease on life following the disintegration of the state after the overthrow of Siyad Barre. According to *The Economist*, Bush "certainly made diplomatic capital out of the military buildup."[26] From Reagan, Bush had inherited the goodwill and opportunity to pursue an internationalist agenda that included rejuvenating the Wilsonian aspiration of spreading democracy abroad.

The purpose of this chapter is to discuss elements of presidential qualities. While there is substantial literature that identifies key presidential attributes, there is no agreed-upon set of the most important considerations. One variable that seems to be commonplace is political skill, that is, the ability of the leader to direct his subordinates toward the attainment of a prescribed goal. This has a great deal to do with each leader's vision. Other commentaries seem to suggest ideal types and link personality traits with the attributes of the presidents. The latter model includes works by James Barber, who identifies character traits such as active-positive, active-negative, passive-positive, and passive-negative personalities.[27] The attributes, as Campbell noted, are disputable but have some heuristic merit to the extent that they can apply in selected situations.[28] From the Barber lens, the Bush presidency was articulate in its bid to consolidate American leadership at the global level, and hence, Bush demonstrated an active personality. This was confirmed by President Bush's personal skills in bargaining, cooperating, and arm twisting of other major players in international politics.

Other important attributes include providing moral leadership and avoiding scandalous dealings. A president that provides vision in terms of a principled doctrine, charting out a map for his nation's growth, stands to gain respect. Also important is a president's ability to provide leadership that is accountable when in the wrong. In the American system, accountability and ability to strike a rapport and cooperation with Congress in policymaking and implementation is an important yardstick by which success can be measured. At a more complex level, it is useful to evaluate a president's performance in terms of how he satisfies all public demands. Terms used in the huge volume of literature on this issue include parameters such as the president's ability to promote harmony and government legitimacy, success of public goal attainment, or simply how he measures up as a "political manager."

Thus, presidential leadership on the domestic front counts a great deal toward shedding light on an incumbent's successes. Since a lot of policy success depends on the president's ability to work amicably with Congress, presidential performance becomes a function of how well this relationship is translated to meeting the demands of the American people. The presidential agenda is best pursued when he is able to win congressional support. Once elected to the presidency, the leader needs skills to win congressional support to succeed in achieving the administration's agenda.

Also, the leader's personality counts, particularly in the campaigns. In the example of Reagan, it is evident he enjoyed more public goodwill than his policies or party. The ability of a president to project himself as an expressive leader counts a great deal in his overall strategies. This constitutes our starting point in assessing the Bush presidency at its epoch. Media pundits have coined this term the *likeability factor*. Some candidates just do not have it, regardless of their skills and public service experience.

In conclusion, being a U.S. president is a complicated matter. In our efforts to study the Bush presidency, the basic premise was summarized in Peter Calvert's words, "To sum up, therefore, though the presidential office is an awe inspiring and powerful one, it is a human institution and amenable to the same treatment as any other form of leadership."[29] It is in this direction that we continue, in greater detail, to shed some light on understanding the Bush edition of the U.S. presidency.

Notes

* George E. Reedy, *The Twilight of the Presidency* (New York: New American Library, 1970), 15.
1. Edward S. Greenberg, *The American Political System: A Radical Approach* (New York: Scott Foresman and Company, 1989), 228.
2. Robert E. DiClerico, *The American President* (Englewood Cliffs, NJ: Prentice Hall, 1983), 3.
3. Ibid., 4. A federal judge has also recently declared null and void an agreement that gave Bush the control of computerized records of his presidency. However, Judge Charles Richey's ruling did not make it any easier to access the records. *The East African Standard* (March 1, 1995), 10.
4. Emmet John Hughes, *The Living Presidency: The Resources and Dilemmas of American Presidential Office* (New York: Coward, McCann & Geoghegan, 1973), 220.
5. Greenberg, *The American Political System: A Radical Approach*, 239.
6. Ibid.
7. Reedy, *The Twilight of the Presidency*, 3–7.
8. Ibid., 9.
9. Ibid., 18–19.
10. Peter W. Sperlich, "Bargaining and Overload: An Essay on Presidential Power," in *Perspectives on the Presidency*, ed. Aaron Wildavsky (Boston: Little, Brown, 1975), 426.
11. Greenberg, *The American Political System: A Radical Approach*, 234.
12. Hughes, *The Living Presidency: The Resources and Dilemmas of the American Presidential Office*, 213.
13. Lee Rainwater and William L. Yancey, *The Moynihan Report and Politics of Controversy: A Trans-Action Social Science and Public Policy Report* (Cambridge, MA: The MIT Press, 1967), 189. Also see Seymour M. Lipset and Earl Raab, *The Politics of Unreason: Right Wing Extremism in America, 1790–1970* (New York: Harper and Row, 1970), 500–508. Lipset and Raab convincingly argued that the American population is highly vulnerable to political extremism and so is its political system. The U.S. president cannot ignore extremism in the form of racial politics.
14. Jonathan Daniels, *The Man of Independence* (London: Victor Gollancz, 1951), 124. This assertion applies to his prepresidential campaign strategies but was also sustained during his leadership.

15. Reagan is cited, in Lucius J. Barker, ed., *New Perspectives in American Politics* (New Brunswick, NJ: Transaction, 1989), 398, as having rejected the endorsement of the KKK in his quest for the presidency in 1980 and 1984. However, we must caution that Lipset and Raab noted that the Ku Klux Klan Society is only slightly known to many people. Lipset and Raab, *The Politics of Unreason*, 325.
16. Daniels, *The Man of Independence*, 125.
17. Ibid.
18. Allan Nevis, as cited in the foreword to John F. Kennedy's *Profiles in Courage* (New York: Harper and Row, 1961), xix–xx.
19. J. F. Kennedy, *Profiles in Courage*, 232.
20. Ibid.
21. "The Perfect President," *The Economist* (October 17, 1987): 13.
22. Ibid.
23. Russell Watson and John Barry, "A U.S. Ambush in the Gulf, New Tactics Produce Small But Satisfying Victory as Iran Is Trapped in the Act of Laying Mines," *Newsweek*, October 5, 1987, 24–25.
24. "The Perfect President," *The Economist*, 13.
25. Ibid.
26. Ibid.
27. James D. Barber, *The Presidential Character: Predicting Performance in the White House* (Englewood Cliffs, NJ: Prentice Hall, 1972).
28. Colin Campbell, "The Let's Deal President," in *The Bush Presidency: First Appraisals*, ed. Colin Campbell and Bert Rockman (Chatham, NJ: Chatham, 1991), 185–222.
29. Peter Calvert, "Studying the American Presidency," in *The American Way: Government and Politics in the United States*, ed. Lynton Robins (London: Longman, 1985), 111.

CHAPTER 3

THE MAKING OF PRESIDENT GEORGE H. W. BUSH

In short, Bush is by and large a politician without a political identity.

—Margaret Warner*

This chapter discusses the making of a president from a different perspective than Theodore H. White's 1960 framework in *The Making of the President*. White's work is an analysis of J. F. Kennedy's victory over the Republican Party. The current framework considers the emergence of Bush in the context of the sociopolitical environment that conditioned his four-year presidency. Several factors shaped Bush's vision and subsequent performance as president of the world's leading power, including his patrician upbringing, his competitive character, and his socialization in party and public service career opportunities. We add his election victory in 1988 as a key element in the making of the president.

First, President Bush's background includes social class and psychological elements that factored into his leadership. Second, the vice presidency was a succession factor, and third, the salience of issues connected with the republicanism of the 1970s to the 1980s all played a role in building Bush's character.

Fortunately, interdisciplinary approaches help shed light on Bush's emergence as a leader. Whereas sociology assumes environmental factors determine behavior, psychology personality theorists argue that behavior is primarily shaped by the person's predisposition. Motivation is an important focus in their analysis. In the psychologist's scheme, motivation is an internal process that can be traced to one's traits. Psychologists measure an individual's personality traits, dynamics of motivation, and processes of social development to give us a clue as to how an individual became presidential. For example, Harold Lasswell argued that the essence of political psychology stems from the contention that a great deal of political behavior is a function of the interaction between one's environment and one's predispositions or values. In many cases, scholars argued that a leader's personality, his childhood, his relationship with parents and siblings, and major incidents in his life had a bearing on his psychological imprint. On the other hand, political sociologists study the interaction between societal factors—including the family, religion, and education, and the processes of power acquisition and socialization. The latter approach to understanding politics entails discerning developmental processes through which persons acquire political orientations and norms of conduct.

All of these tools of analysis are incorporated into this account. There is a strong correlation between Bush's personality and his upbringing. In the absence of rigorous psychological and historical anthropological insights, anecdotal comments are relied upon, albeit cautiously. Our assumptions are based on content analysis and data of professional journalists and political scientists who watched Bush closely.

Bush was born in 1924 in New England. His parents, Prescott and Dorothy Walker Bush, were religious. The family, starting with his grandfather Walker, was immensely wealthy. The Bush children, including George, were subsequently raised in the best environment as befitted their father's social standing. Apparently, the religious trait in his family partly explained Bush's motivation to enter politics. This is evident from his confession that he "felt fascinated, believed in the country, in its strength, in helping people."[1]

The second important trait in the making of the president was traced back to the competitive spirit imbued by the elder Bush. The elder Bush taught George the virtues of integrity, fairness, and sportsmanship.[2] When George was in prep school, Andover Greenwich County Day School, around 1939, and also later at Yale in 1948, he was encouraged to participate in tennis and baseball. The fact that at Yale he was captain of the baseball team is an indication that Bush was a potential leader. Bush was seen by his teammates as competitive, a unifier, and of modest temperament, hence his election as team captain. As one author observed, Bush exemplified the unifying leadership function through his actions "after winning the presidential election of 1988."[3] John Gardner cited Bush's reconciliation with Jack Kemp and Robert Dole, who had rivaled him for the Republican nomination, and his meeting with Jesse Jackson and Coretta Scott King, both of whom had been against his election, as signs of pragmatic and inclusive leadership.[4] In fact, Kemp was offered a ministerial position to be secretary of housing and urban development while Senator Dole's wife, Elizabeth H. Dole, was given the position of secretary of labor in Bush's first cabinet.[5]

In "Bush Battles the Wimp Factor," Margaret Garrard Warner detailed some of the inner traits that made the six-feet-two man a president.[6] According to her narrative, when Bush was growing up under his parents, it was family law that taught Bush to be a team player. If a Bush child burst into the house to say he had hit a home run that day, Dorothy would sweetly reply, "How did the team do, dear?"[7] The Bush family discouraged self-important individualism. The family emphasized and encouraged sharing—"have half"—and were not enthralled with the virtues of wealth. In their home, there was genuine concern for others.[8]

The making of Bush can also be traced to his family background in a politically active family. Bush's father served as senator from Connecticut for ten years. This is important in that Bush undoubtedly learned the rudiments of politics at home. His service as congressman for two terms, beginning in 1966, was a remarkable accomplishment and gave him an advantage over his rivals in the campaign for the 1988 presidential election.

A third factor that shaped the president was inner motivation, personal drive, and the desire to achieve. When Bush was asked why he chose to join politics, besides the "civic duty" argument, he embraced politics to face challenges.[9] In a treatise on the dynamics of motivation, prominent psychologists, including Wortman, Barone, and others, observed that people with a desire to achieve tend to set challenging goals.[10] Barone, a staffer at *The Washington Post*, used psychoanalytic terminology to argue that Bush derived motivation from his successful father. From early childhood, Bush appeared to have been an achiever who placed great value on success. No doubt Bush had the virtues of courage and confidence inculcated in his formative years. Bush's "school days were not a time of political or philosophical awakening but rather of preparing to succeed."[11] Indeed, one of his Yale classmates saw him as an achiever.[12]

The view is in sharp contrast to the argument that some presidents are accidental. In the larger scheme, political competition allows for persons of weak character and spirit to be elected. Further, being a patrician does not necessarily bestow upon an individual the respect and skills to rise to high office. Notions of "accidental presidents," as suggested in Dean Keith Simonton's work, can be misleading and are inappropriate when one considers an impressive résumé such as that of President Bush.[13] While Bush may not have been a scientist like Benjamin Franklin, there are similarities in terms of achievement and motivation. Franklin was born in Boston but made his fortune in Philadelphia. Bush was born in Maine but made his fortune in West Texas, where he established a booming oil business including the Zapata Petroleum Corporation.[14] Much like Franklin, Bush was a diplomat. Franklin served in France whereas Bush served in China. Bush surprised many people by being pragmatic and opting not to join his Ivy League classmates by working on New York's Wall Street but, instead, venturing into the oil lease trading business.

The characterization of Bush as a wimp by the media was certainly not rooted in a careful observation of the president's public record. The notion of wimp was more specific to political campaigning and was enlarged by the dominance of modern-day electronic media. Greenberg asserted that "it is the nature of television as a medium to convey short bursts of information, to ignore historical and contextual material, and to focus on personalities and celebrities."[15] Bush was a victim of media framing, especially since the wimp factor was given so much publicity in the campaigns.[16] Bush was perceived by the press to not be strong enough for the challenges of the Oval Office. The wimp factor also was overplayed in relation to the glorification of Reagan, his predecessor. Undeniably, Reagan was a superb orator and a charming image maker. The trivialization of U.S. politics opened Bush to harsh criticisms, even to the point of several commentators dismissing his voice as "tight and twangy which under stress…lacks power."[17] It is hard to regard these formulations as reinforcing his leadership qualities.

Additionally, Bush, at age eighteen in 1942, served as a naval aviator and was later hailed a war hero having bravely served his country in World War II. Bush flew fifty-eight combat missions and was nearly killed on one occasion.

Bush's run for the U.S. Senate at President Nixon's urging in 1970 was an indication that Bush was aiming for higher callings. Although he lost to Democrat Lloyd Bentsen, his star had not been dimmed. In 1970 Nixon appointed him as U.S. ambassador to the UN. However, while here, Bush was overshadowed by Henry Kissinger's high-profile diplomatic style. There were often points of disagreement in the style and content of foreign policy decision making. For example, Bush put forward a strong case for Taiwan's recognition in the UN but opposed Nixon-Kissinger's efforts to court China and enhance U.S.-Chinese relations.

Regardless of the difference of opinion and style, President Nixon was considered Bush's mentor. In 1972 Nixon gave him his next national assignment—chairman of the Republican National Committee (RNC). While serving on the RNC, Bush suffered from the Watergate attack on Nixon. Bush did not criticize Nixon but was devastated by the fact that

Nixon lied in his bid to exonerate himself from the scandal.[18] Nixon's fall in 1973, after the Watergate hearings, provided Vice President Ford with an opportunity to serve as commander-in-chief.

President Ford appointed Bush as U.S. ambassador to China in 1974, and shortly thereafter, Bush served as the Central Intelligence Agency director. As director 1975–1976, Bush spent most of his energies trying to mollify angry lawmakers who sharply restricted CIA missions.[19] Bush resigned this position in 1979 to compete for the post of U.S. president but backed out when he realized that the Republican Party faithful preferred Reagan's nomination. Reagan subsequently won the presidential election against incumbent Carter.

In 1980 Bush became the vice president of the United States under Reagan in spite of having challenged Reagan for the Republican nomination earlier. Bush's strong voter rating, experience, competence, and credentials worked in his favor. Jules Witcover saw Bush as a jack-of-all-trades, an affirmation of his numerous abilities.[20]

In discussing the making of Bush the president, one identifies the home factors, especially his upbringing. No single factor accounts for his model of politics as much as his upbringing. President Bush's sister, Nancy, eloquently stated, "George is absolutely the product of his upbringing."[21] Being born into a political family was an added advantage, for it gave him name recognition. Regardless, his personal achievements, including service as congressman, UN ambassador, Republican Party chief, China envoy, CIA director, and vice president, were no scant achievements. One does not rise to all these positions without a world vision. Although Bush has been described as lacking a political identity, the forty-first president had experience that profoundly endeared him to internationalism.[22] Bush's career in politics created some important virtues that he articulated, albeit poorly, as he admitted that he lacked adequate communication skills to articulate his vision clearly.[23]

Goldstein, in an in-depth study on the modern American vice presidency, posited that the position had been regarded as a political graveyard. Goldstein argued that its occupant only becomes president at the resignation or death of the incumbent. George Bush became Vice President in January 1980 upon the victory of Reagan. It is believed that Bush had been matched as Reagan's running mate in the 1980 campaign because of his experience in Washington, D.C. matters.[24]

Goldstein continued, "A presidential candidate who is a Washington outsider often appears to select an insider as a running mate."[25] Although this rule may not always apply, there was evidence that Bush's selection was a Republican strategy to retain the presidency, especially because Bush had challenged Reagan in the primaries and attempted to win the Republican nomination.[26] Moreover, Bush had denied he would accept the vice presidency and had even publicly attacked Reagan's plan to balance the U.S. budget deficit by reducing taxes and simultaneously increasing defense spending as "voodoo economics."[27] Reagan confided in a friend his "strong" reservations on the Texan's abilities.[28] When Reagan was making his decision to select Bush as his running mate, he dropped popular names such as Jim Baker, Paul Laxalt, Donald Rumsfeld, Bill Simon, Richard Lugar, Guy Jagt, and Kemp. A former president, Ford, had been a possible candidate, but some political activists were uncomfortable with Ford's stature as a possible "co-president."[29] Although Bush had been periodically depicted as a political weakling, his selection as vice president could be interpreted as disapproval of this misconception.[30] For example, Bush demonstrated that he was up to the challenge by initially running against Reagan for the Republican nomination. In fact, Reagan had remarked, "Bush had shown some toughness in the primaries."[31] Secondly, Bush was a strong voice in the Reagan campaign against the Carter-Mondale Democratic ticket that lost the presidency.

Bush had some inherent advantages of his own. His turnabout to back the very "voodoo economics" he had admonished was a reflection of his commitment to mainstream republicanism. Bush as vice president fully supported Reagan and his policies.[32] Likewise, Bush was to expect his vice president, Dan Quayle, to "fully and enthusiastically" support his decisions "whether he made those recommendations or not."[33] Although

Reagan departed from the White House as a relatively popular president, Vice President Bush did not seem to receive similar acclaim. At the end of Reagan's presidency, *The Economist* wrote,

> Yet as Mr. Reagan's Loyal Lieutenant Mr. Bush should at least be able to take credit for the successes of the past 8 years. It seems, therefore, that Bush's total support to Reagan gave him the exposure and insider position in the White House. He became part of Reagan's winning team.[34]

Although Bush religiously served Reagan and was viewed by some Democrats as a vice president who "does nothing but deliver fulsome praise of the president, a thing which the public does not respect,"[35] Bush proved to be his own man in the management of Reagan's crisis committee known as the Special Situations Group. And, when John Hinckley shot President Reagan during late March 1981, Bush acted in a most presidential manner, calming both the American people and world in general. Bush's coolness restored calm to the center of U.S. power when other administration officials appeared to suggest a power vacuum could emerge. For example, Bush did not behave in an assertive manner as did Secretary of State Alexander Haig, who declared prematurely that "he was in charge," thereby upsetting some officials.

Although President Bush was America's forty-first president, statistically there is no important correlation between being vice president and becoming president in the sense that more than half of the forty presidents before him—about twenty-six—were never vice presidents.[36] At a more general level, though, the making of President Bush was, perhaps, enhanced by his performance as vice president. Bush helped reshape Reagan's vision on the new internationalism and toned down the radical conservatism in the Republican administration represented by Kemp and others.

As vice president, Bush presided over the Senate with diligence, creating an enabling environment that strengthened Reagan's rapport with Congress. That is not unusual in history. Historians record that Albin Barkley—vice president to Truman, 1949–1953—and John C. Calhoun—vice president to Adams (1825–1829) and Andrew Johnson (1829–1833) respectively—proved to be extremely useful to the presidents as links to the House of Representatives and Senate.[37]

By comparison, Nixon fared badly as vice president to President Dwight Eisenhower, but he was still judged as qualified for president.[38] Nixon was "easily the most useful vice president within memory."[39] Bush understood well the limits of the vice presidency. This is not surprising, as after Nixon, Americans generally saw a potential president in a vice president. In fact, "neither party would nominate a man to the second office who had not been considered seriously for the first."[40] Bush met these criteria. If presidential historians believe that "the vice presidency is generally what the president chooses to make it,"[41] Reagan made it a training ground for the Bush presidency. That perhaps explains why Bush was seen in some quarters as a status quo president. The downside was that Bush, like Truman, had to take the high office from an immensely popular statesman. Truman, vice president to F. D. Roosevelt in 1945, was to become the world's first president to blow a nuclear bomb whistle and usher the United States into a nuclear armed conflict to protect its foreign policy objectives. In a sense, this was a new global order that was to provide the conditions under which the presidency would function. Bush presided over a regime that saw the demise of an international system marked with cold war rivalries.

Modern Republicans and the Making of the Bush Presidency

In the wake of Johnson's apparent frustrations over the Vietnam War and the subsequent defeat of the Democratic Party's candidate, Vice President Hubert Humphrey, in 1969, republicanism reemerged as the driving force in the American presidency. By the early 1970s, Nixon was at the helm of the White House. Republicans broke the Democrats' grip on the U.S. presidency from the F. D. Roosevelt years. Nixon's reemergence in 1969 as president revived the spirit of conservatism with its antiliberal fervor that included a reversal of F. D. Roosevelt's New Deal successes, such as privatizing the Tennessee Valley Authority (TVA) and making contributions to social security voluntary. Nixon's agenda included countering the successes of the impressive J. F. Kennedy record, as well as its successor, the "Great Society" initiatives by Johnson's administration.

The Nixon era began a new shift to the right in American politics. Nixon proclaimed a vague "New American Revolution" in January 1971 and imposed wage and price reductions in the Keynesian tradition. Nixon championed the return to traditional values and morality and attempted to appoint to the Supreme Court justices with a conservative agenda. Nixon, particularly after his landslide re-election in 1972, took an abrupt turn against the civil rights achievements of the Johnson administration. Nixon gave rhetorical support for less government and espoused the doctrine of new federalism "to reverse the flow of power and resources from the states and communities to Washington."[42] The idea was to emphasize local solutions for local problems. New federalism meant reducing the big government syndrome popularized by Democratic administrators. Nixon's major influence on the subsequent Republican administration of Bush could be traced to Nixon's assertion that the principal business of an American president was to handle foreign affairs. "I have always thought this country could run itself domestically without a president"—to quote his campaign words before assuming the presidency.[43] Bush, as the record demonstrated, literally applied this Nixon philosophy.

However, the downside was that with Nixon's fall in 1974, the Republicans appeared to have been humiliated. Although Nixon had dented the image of the presidency through his administration's Watergate scandals, his successor, Ford, coming to office through a constitutional requirement rather than the election process, attempted damage control for his party. However, Ford was not strong enough to stop the Democrats from returning to the White House in 1976.

In 1976 Carter's leadership did not get a strong mandate to steer America through the increasing turmoil in world events and the growing economic downturn right after his first term in office. Carter's failure to handle the American hostage saga in Iran led to his undoing and subsequent failure during the 1980 elections. These elections were, by and large, a referendum on his leadership.[44] However, it may be unfair to blame Carter entirely for the Iranian hostage saga. If the thesis that the Reagan-Republican campaign colluded with Iranian terrorists to delay the release of the American hostages until after the election was over, it would be safe to conclude that U.S. politics, particularly Republican realism, was essentially Machiavellian.[45] Sick revealed that Reagan's campaign chairman, William J. Casey, met with an Iranian cleric, Hojatolislam Mehdi Karrubi, in a Madrid hotel in July 1980. Casey became the CIA director in Reagan's administration. Casey's discussion with Karrubi was intended to persuade Iran to hold the fifty-two American hostages until after Reagan took the oath of office. Bush, then vice president, had been speaking of the "October surprise" to warn of the possible use of the hostage issue by the Carter administration to win votes. The Reagan-Casey plan was that if the deal worked, the Iranians would be given back their frozen assets and be supplied with military equipment and spare parts through an Israel conduit. Sick's evidence also implicated Bush and charged that there was a possibility that Bush attended at least one of the meetings in which the deal was organized. Although Bush and Reagan denied the charges, many Americans were skeptical. It is unlikely that the truth will be known until after all of Reagan's documents are declassified. Casey, the key strategist, died and never gave sufficient evidence against his political bosses.

Reagan became president after crushing Carter in the 1980 elections. Reagan was, in addition to his personal popularity, advantaged by post–New Deal republicanism. Republicans have for many years controlled a larger geographical base than the Democrats.[46] Reagan enjoyed the support of anti-abortionists, big defense spenders, and supply-side economists. At the end of the Reagan era, many commentators hailed him a success. *The Economist* argued that "many factors have played a part in the transformation of American politics over the past quarter-century. One of the biggest of them was Mr. Reagan."[47]

Reagan's record as "a crazed anti-communist"[48] and "the high priest and chief rhetorician of the Republican doctrinaire conservatism" was equally telling.[49] According to many ordinary Americans, Reagan had a magical charm.

George F. Will contended that President Reagan changed America drastically.[50] In Will's assessment, Reagan lived to the anachronistic Greek idiom, "We shall leave this city better than we found it," by leaving the country better than he found it. Although disputed by many interest groups, such as the civil rights movement, Reagan changed the temperament of government business. To quote a leading scholar, Reagan "slowed the progress on the civil rights movement."[51] Lucius J. Barker asserted that "as expected and given his constituency base, President Reagan gave little support to African-Americans and pro-civil rights interests…His legislative agenda and budget priorities brought about a total redefinition of racial equality."[52] The Reagan administration was not committed to affirmative action programs and used litigation to overturn policies favorable to African American interests. Ironically, "the Reagan era saw an increase in the number of elected African American officials,"[53] but even these elected officials could not achieve their goals for lack of funds precipitated by Reagan's economic policies.

Reagan's policies, shaped by economic gurus such as Milton Friedman, focused on tackling inflation, using less taxation, and reducing government regulatory intervention, as well as lowering government spending on social services.[54] Reagan's key strategy was to spend on defense at the expense of everything else. Reagan's policies meant there were more and more market-driven decisions rather than government decisions. For some pundits, Reagan's economic policies produced impressive results and were the best of any modern president.[55] Supporters insisted, "America's GNP increased six fold–three times the rate of its population growth" and resulted in greater production of goods and services.[56]

Reagan, according to Will, was to be placed by historians "in the front rank of the second rank of American Presidents."[57] Reagan gave America a new sense of optimism and self-confidence and saved capitalism by liquidating the cold war.[58] He enhanced patriotism, produced national cohesion, and championed freedom of all peoples of the world.

Reagan earned unswerving support from conservatives for making "work better than welfare." His supporters contended that the United States became more competitive than it was under Carter. But Reagan's supporters failed to point out that he bullied small countries like Grenada and promoted guerrilla violence against the leftist Sandinistas in El Salvador. Reagan's militarism was also criticized after he sent troops to Benghazi and Tripoli, Libya, to threaten and bomb Kaddafi in April 1986. At that time, the CIA machinery believed Kaddafi was plotting to kill Reagan.

Reagan's huge defense spending created an environment that produced smart weapons that reinforced the militarist nature of the American psyche and positioned the country to its unassailable lead in the production of weapons of mass destruction. Many Americans saw this breakthrough, including the Star Wars program, as evidence of their manifest destiny or special redemptive destiny in world politics.

So idolized was Reagan that some historians have recorded the occurrence of a Reagan Revolution. Will acknowledged that Reagan's revolution was a truism in that it was a post–F. D. Roosevelt attack on the role of government."[59] Reagan continuously promoted the old Republican rhetoric that big government was the problem and not the solution to U.S. problems. Overall, there is little evidence that what "Reagan did is comparable to what Franklin Delano Roosevelt did in the mid 1930s."[60] F. D. Roosevelt can be considered as a true revolutionary for altering, "irrevocably, the relationship between citizens and the federal government in the USA."[61] F. D. Roosevelt made government assume responsibility for managing the economy to avert the depression.

For Will, if Reagan repealed those federal responsibilities, he would have staged a coup and qualified as a real revolutionary. He did not, and therefore, his policies only achieved peripheral revolutionary significance.

Irving S. Shapiro's[62] analysis saw no such thing as a Reagan Revolution in the making. To Shapiro, the first American Revolution was the political independence struggle for freedom; the second, the Industrial

Revolution; and the third, unnamed but emanating from the 1930s struggles for equality and justice.

But what were the lessons for Bush in the Reagan game plan in the making of the Bush presidency? First, for the first time in many years, a U.S. president left the White House more popular than when he entered it. More than ever, the presidency epitomized America's position as the number one power in the world. Second, Reagan had set immediate standards for Bush, particularly in Republican eyes. According to an influential journalistic commentary, "Reagan made it respectable to be a Right Wing Republican."[63] Third, Bush thought of the United States in global militaristic terms. His regime was more outward looking than that of his predecessors. Regardless, his mix of foreign and domestic issues became a key issue in his bid to return to the White House in 1992. Will's message was that while foreign policy was the most important subject, it is of secondary importance in terms of consequence and is rarely an election-turning issue.[64]

Historians know that Bush did not completely ignore the domestic issues at hand. The president, in one of his question and answer sessions with the press, made this his vision—"A kinder, gentler America as part of a more peaceful, democratic world"[65]—in response to the question, "Have you thought about what you hope your legacy will be in four or eight years?"[66]

The fourth factor has to do with what Bush inherited from the Reagan era. There is no doubt that Reagan did not solve all the problems America faced in the difficult period of 1980–1988. New challenges were created by the Reagan team. Insofar, as these problems had to be tackled by the incoming Bush team, they not only helped Bush set his agenda for the presidency but also provided him with an orientation and framework from which to provide his leadership.

The alleged Reagan success was transient in nature. A gamut of problems awaited Bush before he settled into the White House in January 1989. A reasonable list of these daunting problems was drawn up in *Newsweek*.[67] It included international and domestic problems, as these are not mutually exclusive. The major problems inherited were the budget deficit; high tax levels; declining educational standards; the war on drugs; environmental concerns; high medical costs, that is, Medicare and Medicaid programs; the future of U.S. defense policy in a unipolar world; and possibly the role of the North Atlantic Treaty Organization (NATO). A question was whether the problems were created by increasing third-world debt, international terrorism, or the strategic arms control issues, including the proliferation of nuclear weapons for newer players, on the international scene? While this is not an exhaustive list of the key issues the Bush administration was determined to tackle, it is fair to argue that Bush faced more problems than Reagan. It is also fair to assert that probably only Truman faced similar geopolitical problems as did Bush.[68] Similar to F. D. Roosevelt, Bush was required to provide answers to questions such as "How much military means is necessary to achieve real world geopolitical goals?"[69]

THE BUSH VISION

Bush was fully aware of the magnitude of the challenges ahead of him between 1989 and 1993. In his initial proclamations, Bush offered only marginal departures from Reagan, and even his advisors, like Pete Teeley, saw him as having few principles of his own.[70] Bush lacked a natural political base and "uncomfortably embraced Reagan's policies of the 1980s."[71] Many Republicans felt that the Reagan shoes would be too large for Bush to fill. As Will stated, "As the 1988 election approaches, the Republican Party does not feel as good about itself as it did in 1981."[72] Republicans were worried that Reagan's policies that proved popular among the major groups such as traditional Southern Democrats, Irish and Italian ethnics, blue-collar workers, and so on would not be sustained with the less-fanatic Bush. Kevin P. Phillips warned that republicanism was fading after having a stronghold on the presidency for the past twenty years.[73] Bush knew the problems facing the country, and he had his priorities and vision. As former *New York Times* correspondent Robin Toner noted, "Simply put, George Bush is not Ronald Reagan."[74]

For example, during the 1988 campaign against Michael Dukakis, Bush talked of wanting to be the education president, to tame the environmental pollution menace, and to push forward with cuts in the capital gains tax, as well as to lead the world in enhancing global security in the wake of the emergence of a new world order.

The 1988 Campaign and the Election of President Bush

We have previously alluded to this election, albeit in a nutshell. The 1988 election was an important variable in the emergence of President Bush for two key reasons: first, it was the constitutional act that gave Bush the mandate to lead America. Second, the 1988 campaign presented political analysts with the opportunity to assess the Bush vision, his plan for America, and his overall character.

The 1988 presidential election campaign was lengthy, costly, and largely based on negative attributes of the contestants' characters. The 1988 campaign began and ended on the television screen. The two candidates spent over $30 million apiece on commercials. There was no doubt that the Bush campaign apparatus had first-class talent.

Americans were treated to an eighteen-month period of nonstop electioneering, characterized by a lack of serious issues such as the problems of the underclass, the Japanese economic challenge, or the budget deficit with a national debt of over $2.5 billion. Instead, Americans saw video attacks on the personalities of candidates, the Willie Horton saga, and issues on the importance of the U.S. flag and patriotism. The Horton affair became a big issue in that it stirred the emotions of Americans on issues of race and crime.

Horton, a black man convicted of murder and rape in 1974 while on a weekend furlough from the Massachusetts prison where he had been sentenced for life without parole, was once again put behind prison bars for going on a rape spree. The Bush campaign seized this opportunity to point to Governor Dukakis as a liberal, out of touch with mainstream values. As governor of Massachusetts, the Democratic Party nominee for president had stubbornly resisted attempts to rescind furloughs for first-degree murderers until forced to do so by a state referendum.

Although the furlough policy was inaugurated by Dukakis' Republican predecessor, it became a campaign issue that tapped into the rich lode of white fear and resentment of blacks. It was a strategy that had been used before by Nixon and Reagan, and it worked well for the Bush handlers.

The campaign also delved into issues such as patriotism, especially after the Bush campaign seized on Dukakis's veto of a 1977 Massachusetts bill that required teachers to lead their classes in the Pledge of Allegiance. This was done to paint the Democratic nominee as a dangerous liberal unconcerned about American patriotism. At the RNC, Bush emphatically argued that he supported the policy of pledging allegiance. He led the crowd in reciting this pledge at the convention and in a number of subsequent political rallies held across the country. Bush aimed at telling America that he was more patriotic than his rival.

Although the Pledge of Allegiance issue succeeded in winning the Republicans some votes, in reality, it was not an issue. In the first instance, the bill that required teachers to lead their classes in the pledge each day had been found unconstitutional. But it served to keep the Democrats on the defensive. It helped project the Democrats as soft on defense and inheritors of intellectual doubt. Invariably, the Republicans were cast as vigilant and patriotic. The Republican campaigners reinforced this ploy by depicting Governor Dukakis's wife, Kitty, as being unpatriotic, as she had once been photographed burning an American flag while demonstrating against U.S. involvement in the Vietnam War in the 1960s. The allegation was never substantiated.

In the end, Dukakis, then fifty-five and a son of Greek immigrants, together with his running mate, Texan Bentsen, lost to Bush and Quayle. Bush won forty states and 426 votes for Dukakis's ten states and the District of Columbia. Reagan had won forty-nine states in the 1984 election. In the popular vote, Bush amassed over 47,154,349—54 percent—of the vote as opposed to 40,407,271 (46 percent) for Dukakis.

Analysts argued that the 1988 presidential election was won by Bush for several reasons. First, the Dukakis campaign appeared to fumble.

Bush continued to pin his opponent to the wrong side of largely emotional issues such as crime, gun control, and patriotism. Second, Dukakis lost in part because his arguments lacked an ideological framework. He based his campaign on proving competence rather than energizing the Democratic Party's constituents with ideological issues. The Democratic Party has traditionally received tremendous support from African Americans, trade unionists, and other liberal-oriented groups. These were not well charged, at least in an ideological sense, to vote unanimously for the Democratic candidate. Third, the prevailing "Republican mood" continued to take its toll. Democrats had lost four of the previous five elections. That the polls clearly favored Bush was reflective of the upsurge in Republican values. Whereas these mattered, it was also true that Americans had begun to perfect an emerging political culture that favored divided government. The trend clearly was that a Republican president would be checked by a Democratic Congress and vice versa.

On another level, fate has it that incumbent vice presidents would not easily emerge as winners in presidential elections. Bush became the first sitting U.S. vice president to be elected president since Van Buren in 1839. In 152 years, no sitting vice president had assumed leadership of the White House. This was jokingly referred to as the Van Buren curse. Whereas Bush ended this curse, like Van Buren, he was never to be re-elected. What emerged from an analysis of the 1988 campaign was that Bush had been largely underestimated. Bush was basically a beneficiary of an inept Democratic Party campaign and a defective Republican Party nomination process.

Bush, as Toner argued, did not really arrive in Washington, DC with a new agenda—as did Reagan in his bid to establish a government hands-off approach.[75] Bush was, like Reagan, suspicious of big government, but he did not fully imbue the Reagan solution to use markets and special interests as final arbiters in national affairs. On the contrary, Bush's vision, according to Jonathan Alter, was to solve American problems by rekindling the spirit of "duty, sacrifice, commitment, and patriotism."[76]

In his presidential inaugural address, Bush did not give enough policy direction to his administration.[77] He may have been playing politics or simply indicating that although he would shape things his way, some of

The Making of President George H. W. Bush

Reagan's policies would still apply. After all, he had been Reagan's vice president for eight years. Bush was eager to work with Congress to solve the budget problem and other issues inherited from the Reagan years. He borrowed a lot from the Kissinger school of foreign affairs but remained in charge, having mastered the rudiments of international relations during his stint at the UN and as envoy to China.[78]

Regarding the controversial civil rights agenda, Bush remarked, "I have always felt the need to stand for fair play and against bigotry, I certainly would like to have an administration that projects that."[79] According to Bush, his aim was to do better than Reagan in appointing more minorities to executive positions in federal jobs. In his first budget, Bush sounded more Democratic than Republican by proposing increased spending on some social programs while rolling back taxes on capital gains.[80] But his vision was Republican to the core—emphasizing smaller government, reliance on individual responsibility, and an increased role for the private sector in the provision of government services.[81]

In his first address to the Congress, Bush outlined his methods for solving America's myriad of problems. He pledged new funds for biomedical research and development, housing for the homeless, cleaner air, and elimination of illegal narcotics, as well as space flight for the National Aeronautics and Space Administration (NASA). Bush was considered to be more an admirer of President Kennedy than a Republican when he proposed the creation of Youth Entering Service to America Foundation (YES), similar to the Peace Corps program.

In conclusion, the making of President Bush could be initially traced to his patrician birth and upbringing. No doubt his résumé confirms his exploits as an achiever. It would be inconceivable to judge Bush as an accidental president if we trace his rise to the highest office from his days in Hanover to his days as vice president. A second dimension favoring his rise to the presidency has more to do with the Republican mood that engulfed America from the Nixon days. This mood gained more currency in the Reagan revolution of which he was part as a vice president of Reagan between 1980 and 1988. Bush built his vision, partly basing his priorities on his innermost convictions and, to a considerable extent, on pragmatic Republican principles during his time.

Notes

* Margaret G. Warner, "Bush Battles the 'Wimp Factor,' A Searching Look at the Vice President's Most Persistent Political Liability," *Newsweek*, October 19, 1987, 30.
1. Ibid., 29–30.
2. Ibid., 32.
3. John W. Gardner, *On Leadership* (New York: The Free Press, 1990), 16.
4. Ibid.
5. Gardner, *On Leadership*, 17.
6. Warner, "Bush Battles the 'Wimp Factor,'" 29.
7. Ibid., 32.
8. Ibid.
9. Ibid., 35.
10. C. B. Wortman, E. F. Loftus, and M. E. Marshall, *Psychology* (New York: Alfred A. Knopf, 1985), 327 and Michael Barone, "The Presidency: Mamas' Boys and Papas' Pride," *The Washington Post*, August 8–14, 1988, 26–27, National Weekly Edition.
11. Warner, "Bush Battles the 'Wimp Factor,'" 32.
12. Ibid.
13. Dean K. Simonton, *Why Presidents Succeed: A Political Psychology of Leadership* (New Haven, CT: Yale University Press, 1987), 131.
14. Warner, "Bush Battles the 'Wimp Factor,'" 35.
15. Edward S. Greenberg, *The American Political System, A Radical Approach* (New York: Scott Foresman and Co. 1989), 179.
16. Warner, "Bush Battles the 'Wimp Factor,'" 29.
17. Ibid., 36. In fact, former President Carter had warned that Bush was becoming very familiar with the press. Familiarity with the press, he argued, has a way of breeding contempt. See, Jonathan Alter, "Bush Reaches Out," *Newsweek*, January 30, 1989, 16.
18. Ibid., 32–35.
19. Ibid.
20. Jules Witcover, *From Adams and Jefferson to Truman and Quayle: Crapshoot, Rolling the Dice on the Vice Presidency* (New York: Crown Publishers, 1992), 307.
21. See George H. W. Bush, *All the Best, George Bush: My Life in Letters and Other Writings* (New York: Scribner, 2000). Nancy Bush Ellis, cited in Margaret G. Warner, "Bush Battles the 'Wimp Factor,'" 30.

22. Maureen Dowd, "Biography of a Candidate: Man in the News; Making and Remaking a Political Identity: George Herbert Walker Bush," *New York Times*, August 20, 1992, A1.
23. President Reagan was fondly known as the "Great Communicator," in part because he had worked in the movie industry and was able to charm his audiences. Bush lacked similar skills. See, for example, "Ronald Reagan: The 'Great Communicator,' Former Actor Launched a Modern-Day Republican Revolution," CNN, June 8, 2004, http://www.cnn.com/2004/ALLPOLITICS/06/05/reagan.obit/index.html
24. Joel K. Goldstein, *The Modern American Vice Presidency: The Transformation of a Political Institution* (Princeton, NJ: Princeton University Press, 1982), 249.
25. Simonton, *Why Presidents Succeed: A Political Psychology of Leadership*, 20.
26. Witcover, *From Adams and Jefferson to Truman and Quayle: Crapshoot, Rolling the Dice on the Vice Presidency*, 307.
27. Ibid., 308.
28. Ibid.
29. Ibid. As early as 1975, President Ford had already recognized Bush as the first choice among his Republican colleagues. Bush was then chairman of the party. See, Richard Reeves, *A Ford, Not a Lincoln: The Decline of American Political Leadership* (London: Hutchinson Publishers, 1976), 133.
30. "Poor George," *The Economist*, August 13, 1988, 11–12.
31. Witcover, *From Adams and Jefferson to Truman and Quayle: Crapshoot, Rolling the Dice on the Vice Presidency*, 310.
32. Ibid., 314.
33. Alter, "Bush Reaches Out," 22. See Ronald E. Pynn, *American Politics: Changing Expectations* (Dubuque, IA: Brown & Benchmark, 1993), 321.
34. "Poor George," *The Economist*, 12.
35. Witcover, *From Adams and Jefferson to Truman and Quayle: Crapshoot, Rolling the Dice on the Vice Presidency*, 315.
36. Simonton, *Why Presidents Succeed: A Political Psychology of Leadership*, 23. Also see Nelson W. Polsby and Aaron Wildavsky, *Presidential Elections: Strategies and Structures of American Politics*, 12th edition (Lanham, MD: Rowman & Littlefield, 2007), 88.
37. Clinton Rossiter, *The American Presidency* (New York: A Mentor Book, 1962), 132.
38. Ibid., 132–133.
39. Ibid.
40. Ibid., 134–135.

41. Ibid., 135. Also see Cabell Phillips, *The Truman Presidency, The History of a Triumphant Succession* (New York: Macmillan, 1966), 52.
42. Charles Sellers et al. *A Synopsis of American History* (Chicago: Rand McNally, 1977), 439.
43. Ibid., 437.
44. Everett Carll Ladd, "On Mandates, Realignment and the 1984 Presidential Election," in *Taking Sides II*, ed. Eugene Kuzirian and Larry Madaras (Guilford, CT: Dushkin Publishing Group, 1987), 357.
45. Gary Sick, "The Election Story," *New York Times*, April 15, 1991, A17. Also see George F. Will, *The New Season: A Spectator's Guide to the 1988 Election* (New York: Simon & Schuster, 1987), 39.
46. Earl Black and Merle Black, *The Rise of Southern Republicans* (Cambridge, MA: Harvard University Press, 2002) and Robert A. Rutland, *The Republicans: From Lincoln to Bush* (Columbia: University of Missouri Press, 1996).
47. "American Survey," *The Economist*, August 20, 1988, 24.
48. Ibid.
49. Witcover, *From Adams and Jefferson to Truman and Quayle: Crapshoot, Rolling the Dice on the Vice Presidency*, 307.
50. George F. Will, "How Reagan Has Changed America," *Newsweek*, January 9, 1989, 14–15.
51. Lucius J. Barker, *New Perspectives in American Politics: The National Political Science Review* (New Brunswick, NJ: Transaction Publishers, 1989), 385.
52. Lucius J. Barker, "Limits of Political Strategy: A Systematic View of the African American Experience," *American Political Science Review* 88, no. 1 (March 1994): 5.
53. Ibid.
54. Holcomb B. Noble, Louis Uchitelle, and Edmund L. Andrews, "Milton Friedman, the Champion of Free Markets, Is Dead at 94," *New York Times*, November 17, 2006, 1. Also see James E. Anderson, "Economic Policy: Comparative Advisory Arrangements," in *Presidential Policy Making: An End-of-Century Assessment*, ed. Steven A. Shull (Armonk, NY: M.E. Sharpe, 1999), 234.
55. Lucius J. Barker, "Limits of Political Strategy: A Systematic View of the African American Experience," 50.
56. Will, "How Reagan Has Changed America," 20.
57. Ibid., 17.
58. Ibid., 14.

59. Will, *The New Season: A Spectator's Guide to the 1988 Election*, 88.
60. Ibid.
61. Ibid.
62. Irving S. Shapiro, *America's Third Revolution: Public Interest and the Private Role* (New York: Harper & Row Publishers, 1984).
63. "American Survey," *The Economist*, 34.
64. Will, *The New Season: A Spectator's Guide to the 1988 Election*, 52.
65. Alter, "Bush Reaches Out," 22–29.
66. Ibid.
67. John Barry and Tom Morganthau, "The Defense Dilemma," *Newsweek*, January 23, 1989, 13 and Eleanor Clift and Thomas DeFrank, "The Inauguration," *Newsweek*, January 23, 1989, 23–26.
68. Ibid.
69. Ibid.
70. Warner, "Bush Battles the 'Wimp Factor,'" 36.
71. Ibid., 30.
72. Will, *The New Season: A Spectator's Guide to the 1988 Election*, 41.
73. Kevin P. Phillips, "Once Reagan Goes, the Party May Be Over for the GOP," *The Washington Post*, July 6, 1986. Reprinted in Eugene Kuzirian and Larry Madaras, *Taking Sides*, 364.
74. Robin Toner, "Tactical Governance," *Democratic Governance: America in the 21st Century* (Syracuse, NY: Syracuse University, 1990), 171.
75. Ibid., 173.
76. Alter, "Bush Reaches Out," 14.
77. Ibid., 16.
78. Ibid., 19.
79. Ibid.
80. Fred I. Greenstein, *Presidential Difference: Leadership from FDR to George W. Bush* (Princeton, NJ: Princeton University Press, 2004), 168.
81. For details on the Republican agenda, see Newt Gingrich, *To Renew America* (New York: Harper Collins Publishers, 1995).

CHAPTER 4

BUSH AND THE GULF WAR OF 1991

> *From the outset, then, this would be George Bush's challenge—in the end, his war. Yet the adventure in the Gulf was also to demonstrate America's intent to deal with threats to his new idea of world order and to prove the nation's military ability to overcome the Vietnam syndrome.*
>
> —Jon Roper*

Bush's presidency came in the wake of the progressive demise of the Soviet Union and the cold war era. Bush brought an incredible amount of foreign service experience to the White House, having served as ambassador to the UN and China. Bush was expected to grapple with America's global strategic goals, including defense issues.[1] Bush was more of a foreign policy president than a domestic policy president. Walter Williams even assessed Bush as an incompetent president insofar as domestic policy-making processes were concerned.[2] Nevertheless, Bush's performance in the foreign affairs arena seems to have been impressive, although there are contrasting opinions. However, there seems to be some belief that the Bush administration lost its chance of serving for two terms by its overemphasis on foreign policy objectives in the 1992 election. The Bush administration, like its predecessor, put a high premium on internationalism. But Reagan, unlike Bush, had one extra point; Reagan had become an effective president as a result of the immense public affection he enjoyed.[3] Bush forgot one key point—although foreign policy is important, its importance is secondary when it comes to gaining votes.[4] Will contended that "elections are rarely decided" by international successes.[5] But it is apparent that the Reagan-Bush years reinforced the common belief that the presidency was about foreign policy. Prior to his election as president in September 1991, Clinton was quoted as saying, "People now believed the presidency is about foreign policy."[6] Bush's actions in the international arena could, thus, be rationalized.

Before detailing Bush's internationalist record, it is prudent to note that his conduct as president of the world's primary superpower had wider ramifications globally. Bush's tenure has been historically set at a time when globalization of world issues was the norm. Therefore, if he "failed" in America, this must be seen as only a small part of the global project. Americans may judge Bush as a failure in the domestic field, but this judgment may not necessarily apply to the international arena.

This chapter examines Bush's presidency in the international arena. It employs two major theoretical approaches to the study of the presidency: first, the role approach and second, aspects of game theory combined with the coalition approach. A role approach in this context implies that Bush's behavior was with reference and deference to the expectations that others had about how he should behave. Against this background, it is possible to raise questions of whether or not Bush conformed to the normative expectations of the American public.

Game theory is helpful in disclosing why President Bush made certain choices in foreign policy initiatives. Bush planned to reap maximum payoffs in terms of pleasing key stakeholders and enhancing his ratings. For coalitions, it is a formula for realizing common objectives among a number of actors. Bush acted prudently by creating incentives for other nations to work with him in creating a "new world order." In coalitions, political units work together and agree to coordinate their actions to achieve goals they cannot attain independently. In all cases, it is an outcome of protracted bargaining over the end results by rational groups. In American politics, the foreign and domestic policy arenas are often the work of intense lobbying and coalition building strategies among different interest groups.

These approaches will be useful in discussing the Bush era in terms of the causes and consequences of the Gulf War of 1991, the Strategic Arms Treaty initiatives signed with Gorbachev, Bush's uneasiness in accepting Boris Yeltsin's leadership in Russia, the "death" of doctrinaire apartheid in South Africa, and the UN's operation to save starving, war-ravaged Somalia, as well as democratization of the global agenda. This chapter addresses Bush's new world order rhetoric, as well as the country's European worries over the future of NATO and Europe.

We examine these issues in light of the insinuation that Bush lacked a clear vision. Ignatius questioned Bush's behavior during the Gulf War and his deals with post–cold war Russia, doubting the administration's adherence to any clear plan.[7] This is in contrast to Bush's words constituting his vision of "a kinder, gentler America as part of a more peaceful, democratic world…I am getting this vision thing down pretty good."[8]

The United States and Iraq in the Reagan-Bush Era

The story of the relations between the United States and Iraq in the 1980s and 1990s was as exciting as it was depressing. The story was exciting because Iraq, at one time, had been an ally and depressing because the honeymoon was short lived. The Persian Gulf region was classified by most authorities on foreign affairs as an area in which the United States had vital interests. Indeed, even before Bush settled into the Oval Office in January 1989, there were predictions that he would have to watch out for trouble in the gulf area.[9]

Reagan already had trouble with the aftermath of the Iran Contragate scandal. The Iran-Iraq War was an unexciting affair. The West may have preferred a win-win situation, but the prolonged war indicated vulnerability in the area. But Iraq, during the Gulf War with its neighbor, was clearly favored by Reagan.[10] Iran was seen as the bigger troublemaker in the wake of the fall of the pro-American Shah Pahlavi. The United States maintained a "close watch" on gulf region activities throughout the Reagan era. The situation appeared antagonistic when U.S. intelligence detected, in September 1989, an Iranian navy ship attempting to locate dangerous mines about fifty miles northeast of Bahrain. Secretary of Defense Casper Weinberger, Secretary of State George Shultz, and President Reagan agreed that the Iranian ship, *Iran Ajr*, should be sunk with its load of mines. The Reagan administration's move was an immediate success. The Iranians cried foul and blamed the "great Satan," the United States.[11]

The whole idea of U.S. policy in the gulf was linked with trade. The United States had to maintain marines to protect its shipping interests. In the cold war era, the strategy entailed checking Soviet influence and protecting Arab allies from aggression by Islamic fundamentalists. U.S. policy interests in the region included the sensitive issue of Israeli security.

As a member of the Reagan administration, Bush was an influential adviser to the president on policymaking for the Persian Gulf region.[12] Bush had a good grasp of U.S. foreign policy and diplomacy. As a patrician, upper-class citizen, diplomat, Ivy League alumnus, and CIA boss, Bush was theoretically better placed than Reagan to tackle some of the volatile international crises.[13]

This did not mean President Reagan was inactive. Indeed, it was quite the contrary. For example, Shultz, his secretary of state, acknowledged that although individuals such as Bush and Jesse Helms—congressman, Republican–North Carolina—had significant voices in the Reagan foreign policy machinery, Reagan remained a leader with "clear objectives and at the end of the day he truly did look for the right thing to do."[14] There was a general confusion of roles in the Reagan administration, as

Shultz acknowledged, citing the outspokenness of Helms and Democratic Speaker of the House Jim Wright of Texas.[15]

When Bush assumed office, he did not want to depart heavily from the principles of his predecessor. Powerful voices in the Reagan era, including Baker, joined the Bush administration.[16] These advisers were dealing with a changing Persian Gulf, an area that had just suffered a major war between Iran and Iraq (1980–1988) and an area that the CIA had recognized as "dangerous," as it was possibly joining the ranks of nuclear bomb holders. The main suspect was Hussein. It would be recalled that in 1982 Israel bombed a French-built nuclear reactor east of Baghdad. This scenario meant that the Bush administration had to set a policy on Iraq, for Iraq had acquired extensive military hardware and was rich in terms of resources.[17] Iraq had the second largest oil reserves in the region after Saudi Arabia—a fact that could tilt the balance of power in the region. Hussein's army was reputed to be the fourth largest in the world and was seen in Western eyes as disproportionate to the country's security needs. But Bush wanted Iraq rehabilitated, as he saw Iraq as an important player in normalizing the gulf and Middle East region.[18] Nevertheless, the record of U.S.-Iraqi relations, just as with modern Iran, was not the best.

Between 1967 and 1983, there were no diplomatic links in the traditional sense. It was only after 1984 that the Reagan administration opened serious diplomatic relations with Iraq. Newspapers reported that the United States had advanced Iraq half a billion dollars in credits and was pleased that Hussein had recognized Israel's rights. It turned out that Hussein was merely interacting with the United States in return for support in his war against Iran. Hussein contended that the war could have ended if the United States and Soviet Union desired to end it. The United States sold over $10 billion worth of weapons to Iraq and also to Iran through third-party arrangements. It was argued that the United States had an ulterior motive for letting the two Islamic nations fight it out as a means of weakening them and enhancing Israel's domination in the region. The contention, therefore, was that while Hussein had accepted American military and financial support, he resisted the notion that Iraq be turned into a U.S. satellite state.

Additionally, suspicions still existed. As late as February 24, 1990, Hussein publicly castigated U.S. policymakers for maintaining a naval presence in the Persian Gulf area. The tragedy of the U.S.-Iraqi hostilities was that unlike the preemptive strikes ordered by Reagan in 1987, the U.S. intelligence network did not do a good job in preventing Iraq's invasion of Kuwait. There was a report that CIA Director William Webster informed Bush on July 28, 1990, of an imminent invasion, but Assistant Secretary of State John Kelly told Congress that such a possibility was a "matter pertaining to internal OPEC deliberations."[19] Rich Stuchiner argued that the Bush administration could have protested to Hussein immediately and possibly averted war.[20] This incident was added to the list of CIA failures. The CIA's earlier "estimate" in 1989 was that "Saddam Hussein would not make trouble for the next three years."[21] Senator David Boren, chairman of the Senate Select Committee on Intelligence, acknowledged this failure. Nevertheless, the mistake was made. The crisis that placed Bush on the international scene for the longest time during his presidency was triggered by Iraqi strongman Hussein al-Tikriti. On August 2, 1990, Iraqi troops began taking over Kuwait. Hussein was ruling a bankrupt or near-bankrupt state as a result of having fought the neighboring Islamic state of Iran in an eight-year war. It was believed that the invasion of Kuwait would ensure that Iraq controlled important oil fields and would hike oil prices to help Iraq foot the bills of its war debts. The second version of this thesis was that Hussein wanted the Emir in Kuwait to reduce oil supplies and usher in an oil crisis to reduce supplies and push up prices, thereby boosting the Iraq treasury.

A more controversial explanation was the historical explanation provided by Roderick McDonald.[22] According to this version of the problem, Iraq invaded Kuwait to (re)claim its legitimate territory, its nineteenth province. Kuwait, for most of the eighteenth century, was occupied by nomadic peoples of several clans. By the turn of the eighteenth century, it was obvious that the Al-Sabah dynasty was in control of the geographical entity in question. The area had been under British protection but became fully independent in 1961. Iraq did not recognize the independence of

Kuwait, and the ruling family sought military protection from Britain. The British and its allies in the Arab League agreed to protect Kuwait from imminent Iraqi aggression. In 1963 a new Iraqi government recognized Kuwait, thereby ending the Arab League intervention.[23] The subsequent Iraqi regime never stopped to claim territorial control over the lands at the Shatt Al-Arab Estuary.

Western electronic media, print media, documentaries, and films depicted Hussein as an ambitious imperialist. In framing the war against him, Western powers called him a murderous leader. The Western media portrayed Hussein as a leader wishing to control the gulf area. Hussein scored an intellectual victory in the eyes of many Arab scholars when he attributed his invasion of Kuwait to the Western world's inaction on the Palestine issue. The Iraqi leader wanted to occupy Kuwait so that the Israeli occupation of the Arab Palestine lands would cease. Secondly, Syria under Haffez Assad was not friendly with Kuwait and occupied Lebanon. In 1983 Reagan ordered the occupation of Grenada. Israel also invaded Lebanon in 1982. Turkey, a Western ally, occupied Cyprus in 1974; several UN resolutions had been passed to urge Turkey's withdrawal but to no avail. There was little international pressure for withdrawal as was the case of the Iraq-Kuwait situation. Hussein's linkage strategy, where he proposed that Israel and Syria withdraw from the territories they occupied before Iraq would pull out from Kuwait, appeared to be a logical trade-off.[24] A critic of the linkage plan, Alter argued that "Israel's occupation of the West Bank and Gaza Strip...[was] as a result of Arab aggression."[25] In other words, Israel had the sovereign right to take whatever measures necessary to protect its territorial integrity and ensure national security. The occupation by Israel had been for defensive purposes because its Arab neighbors, other than Egypt, refused to adhere to UN Resolution 242 to recognize Israel's existence.

The invasion of Kuwait challenged American leadership and their allies. It also upset the indigenous Kuwaiti leadership. The immediate reaction by the U.S. president was to "kick his [Hussein's] ass out of Kuwait." Bush backed his rhetoric by committing troops to the gulf region and mobilized Americans for war. The American public also became electric, and a national debate on the issue began. It evoked bad memories of Vietnam. From the outset, the Bush administration was preparing for war as soon as Iraq had invaded Kuwait. The massive troop buildup was a reflection of this claim. The troop buildup was designed to "persuade Saddam Hussein to withdraw from Kuwait without hostilities."[26] However, Bush reiterated that the United States was deadly serious about pushing Iraq out by whatever means necessary. The United States mobilized the international community to condemn the invasion. Bush held several briefs for coalition purposes with other world leaders including Gorbachev, King Fahd of Saudi Arabia, Egyptian leader Hosni Mubarak, British Prime Minister Margaret Thatcher, and French President François Mitterrand. Bush also consulted with congressional leaders.

Through U.S. initiatives, the UN General Assembly and Security Council condemned the Iraqi invasion and called for Iraq's immediate withdrawal from occupied Kuwait. The UN quickly imposed sanctions on Iraq. Individual Western governments punished Iraq in their own ways. Thatcher ordered a freeze on Iraqi assets in the United Kingdom. Bush, convinced that Hussein would not withdraw from Kuwait on the terms offered by the UN, decided to impose a deadline for withdrawal. The withdrawal date was set for January 15, 1991, after which time the United States and its allies would use force to end the occupation.[27] The UN deadline was basically a Bush deadline. Bush's military strategists had advised him that it was the preferred time to attack Iraq, as it would be a period before the holy month of Rajab. It would be unsuitable for war to be fought in March when the holy Ramadan fasting season began in the Islamic world. The weather in March would be severe for the high-tech smart weapons and the marines.[28]

By December 1990 President Bush had been able to create an allied force of at least twenty-eight nations. His leadership epitomized America's global cop status. Critics argued that the Bush administration bribed these nations to join in the ensuing war by forgiving loans amounting to $7 billion owed by Egypt and promising arms to Syria and Saudi Arabia.

Bush placed around four hundred and thirty thousand men and women in the gulf area, making it the largest deployment of U.S. forces outside the country since the Vietnam War. Although the United States was backed by its Western allies, the entire operation was under General Colin Powell as chairman of the U.S. Joint Chiefs of Staff. The key field commander of all the Desert Shield and Desert Storm operations was General Norman Schwarzkopf Jr. of the United States.

In the debates on the reasons for U.S. intervention, the main reason for use of U.S. forces was to secure cheap oil. "We are there because of oil…we import more than 50 percent of our oil" was common rhetoric.[29] Carole Resnick explained that the war was about corporate power.[30] Resnick's thesis was that the presence of U.S. troops in the gulf area was for securing profits and protecting the merchant ships and oil fields. The idea of protecting Israel was basically a secondary issue because the United States ultimately protects "its economic and political interests first."[31] Baker summed it as a war to protect American jobs.[32] President Bush downplayed the role of oil in the war. Other commentators sought to provide moral justification for the war. For example, Rick Coughlin put it bluntly that the war was not about oil but a struggle of good versus evil. Coughlin doubted, however, that Bush was the quintessence of American goodness.[33] The *Daily Orange* pointed out that Americans were not serious people and "never fail to place image above substance…we fought the Gulf War largely for pride."[34]

A third version of the U.S.-Iraqi War was that the United States was meeting its obligation as a protector of democracy. America, under Bush, attacked Iraq because Bush could not defend democracy while "restoring a feudal order in Kuwait."[35]

Moral issues aside, the military buildup and subsequent skirmishes in the gulf were part of the usual strategy by corporate America's military-industrial complex to sell arms, to create jobs, and to help push the United States out of the recession.[36]

Although efforts were made to reconcile Bush and Hussein, the decision had already been made. All over the world there were war protests. The pleas for peace within America thought the Bush rhetoric was unmerited because what Hussein did was not unprecedented. Other critics argued there were cases where the American government killed its innocent people and that Hussein was not the only bloodthirsty leader. For example, the *Alternative Orange* cited the case of Philadelphia, where, in 1985, the mayor of the city ordered a bombing that led to eleven deaths among African Americans.[37] Other critics regarded the military option as too expensive. For example, Governor Dukakis of Massachusetts commented that the United States had been a partner with Hussein for ten years and it was not making sense to fight him even though his action was unacceptable. Others, like journalist Charles Peters of the *Washington Monthly*, thought President Bush was anxious to avoid being called a wimp. Bishop H. H. Brookins of the African Methodist Episcopal (AME) Church in Washington, DC condemned Hussein but wanted Bush to take time before making a declaration of war.[38]

As the deadline approached, voices were raised that more time was needed for the sanctions to work. Secretary of State Baker made efforts to meet with Iraqi Foreign Minister Tariq Aziz. World leaders like Mitterrand and Shevardnadze called for peaceful solutions. UN Secretary General Javier Perez De Cuellar met the concerned parties, but Hussein refused to budge. The UN ultimatum remained a theoretical threat to Hussein. Regardless, President Bush and his U.S.-led coalition could not hold back from war any longer, as they had gone the extra diplomatic mile to have Iraq move out of Kuwait. At the end of the January 15 deadline, President Bush went on the air to explain to the American public why the United States was in the gulf.

In his message to America on why the United States was in the gulf, President Bush observed that Hussein had, in August 1990, ordered Iraqi tanks into a defenseless Kuwait. The well-armed Iraqi troops, numbering over one hundred thousand, violently attacked innocent children and tortured women and men. The soldiers violated diplomatic conventions and harassed envoys attached to Kuwait. Bush explained that America had to move into the gulf for three main reasons. First, American troops were needed to punish aggression. Second, American troops were needed to protect national security. The gulf area was the world's economic lifeline that could not be tangled by Hussein. Besides, Hussein was armed with chemical, biological, and possibly nuclear weapons that he could use to dominate the gulf and bulk of the world's petroleum reserves.[39] The aggression would lead to oil prices doubling and prove risky for fledgling democracies, as well as poor countries of the world. Bush stated, "Energy security is national security."[40] Third, American troops were needed to free innocent civilians held hostage by the Iraqi leader.

Bush's address extended United States resolve that Iraq must withdraw from Kuwait and that the Al-Sabahs be returned to the throne in Kuwait. President Bush reiterated the need for stability in the gulf region, a policy traced to Truman's vision, especially as that which concerned the security of Israel and the "puzzle of Palestine."[41]

THE GULF WAR AND THE VIETNAM SYNDROME

Throughout the period between August 1990 and January 1991, the American public was concerned with the possibility of another outbreak of the Vietnam syndrome. As was widely reported, in the wake of the war, Bush had remarked that it was his hope "that when this is over we will have kicked for once and for all the so-called Vietnam syndrome."[42]

American soldiers had been humiliated in the decade-long war against the communist guerrillas in Vietnam. In the name of containment of the Soviet Union, Americans gave their lives beginning with the Eisenhower administration through to his successor J. F. Kennedy to Johnson and all the way to Nixon. Nixon's "Vietnamization" of the war was an attempt to reduce direct U.S. military action to save American lives. Nixon blamed former Presidents Eisenhower to Johnson for applying the containment policy incorrectly.[43] Nixon made his most difficult foreign policy decision amidst frustration by the American public. His decision to gradually withdraw almost five hundred and forty-three thousand U.S. troops from Vietnam reflected the reality that the country had to be flexible in its foreign policy.⁴⁴ The United States was being drained by the war in Vietnam and the immediate benefits to the U.S. citizens were difficult to quantify, articulate, or even discern. The Vietnam lesson had turned into a nightmare. About fifty-eight thousand Americans had been killed in combat, two hundred and seventy thousand wounded, and over $150 million lost in costs by the time the last U.S. soldier withdrew in March 1973 from Vietnam. The war in Vietnam divided Americans in a manner that was almost as contentious as the Civil War of 1861–1865. In terms of costs, Vietnam was second only to the Civil War.

The Vietnam War affected all Americans. It was the longest war in modern U.S. history, a factor that made its psychological effects most disturbing. George C. Herring suggested that Nixon's phrase, "Vietnam syndrome," was a reality in everyday U.S. foreign policy conduct and engagements.⁴⁵ Herring argued that Reagan was determined to cure America from the hangover of Vietnam. The Reagan administration wanted to wipe out the bad memories of U.S. failure in Vietnam to restore the United States' position that had been undermined by that war.⁴⁶ Reagan believed that Vietnam was a noble war in which the United States played a part in stopping aggression from a totalitarian regime. Reagan's main message was that the U.S. loss in Vietnam was because its military had been "denied the permission to win by the successive administrations."⁴⁷ When Reagan attacked El Salvador, he was not going to allow it to be another Vietnam. President Reagan's policy was to avoid the mistakes made in Vietnam; he therefore gave the army permission to use its full might to complete its mission.

Reagan put to rest the psychological stigma of the Vietnam years when he ordered the invasion of Grenada on the pretext that the troops were to save American lives. At stake in the El Salvador, Grenada, and Nicaragua incidents was a post–Vietnam American assertiveness. The United States wanted to strengthen its imperial policy in the Caribbean and Central American region.⁴⁸ America's enemies threatened U.S. citizens and troops overseas, even those serving in international peacekeeping missions. For example, in Iran, Ali Akbar Velayati warned that the "region had reached the threshold of another Vietnam" when U.S.

Marines were ordered by the Reagan administration to attack Iranian gunboats in September 1987.[49]

In Somalia, the tribal warlords invoked Vietnam and threatened to destroy U.S. troops within the UN peacekeeping mission. Therefore, it was not surprising that Hussein, in his psychological attacks on the United States before the outbreak of the war, spoke of a repeat of Vietnam. Hussein pointed out that Americans would swim in their blood if they attacked Iraq. Hussein thought the war over Kuwait would be the Armageddon and the "mother of all battles."[50]

Bush, in ordering U.S. troops into the gulf in the wake of the Iraqi invasion of Kuwait, was not spared the Vietnam metaphor, but he planned to defeat Iraq without creating another Vietnam. Bush declared, "In our country, I know that there are fears of another Vietnam, …let me assure you, should military action be required, this will not be another Vietnam. This will not be a protracted, drawn-out war."[51]

Bush explained to the American nation that he would not repeat Johnson's strategy of backing the war efforts in incremental terms. He remarked, "I will never, ever agree to a half way effort."[52] According to President Bush, he was to move quickly, using massive force to cause an Iraqi withdrawal. For Bush, waiting for sanctions to cripple the Iraqi government would be an exercise in futility, as it would lead to a dangerous standoff with negative economic consequences the world over.

Regardless of Bush's public statements, there was widespread fear that the Iraqi problem could well be another Vietnam. Bush explained that the massive U.S. troop buildup in Iraq was to protect the sovereignty of Kuwait and to stop Iraq's aggression. In strikingly similar terms, on April 7, 1965, Johnson stated that the United States was in Vietnam to defend South Vietnam's independence and to uphold its sovereignty.[53] Second, the fight against Iraq was basically a result of a war between Iraq and Kuwait that had become an international war.

In the concomitant struggle in Iraq, more than twenty-five countries rallied behind the United States to fight Iraqi aggressors. The Vietnam affair was basically sparked off by a war between two Vietnams; however, the United States, under Johnson, Americanized the war on behalf of South Vietnam to battle the Vietcong and North Vietnam. The United States was backed by Australia, New Zealand, the Philippines, Thailand, and South Korea, who was the only ally that gave more than token aid.[54] The Vietcong and North Vietnam received massive military aid from China and the Soviet Union.

Although Bush assembled several countries to back him on the war path against Hussein, he did not succeed in "Arab-izing" or de-Americanizing the Gulf War of 1991. Americans had the biggest share of the troops. Even the Japanese and European allies did not match the United States' financial commitment. This fact resembled Johnson's failed model of Americanizing the war in Vietnam.[55] To assert that the Gulf War was fully Americanized would be false, as all the allies, including the noncombatant Israel and the passive Arab allies, like Syria and African Muslim Senegal, all played an important part in ensuring the psychological and physical victory over Iraq. The Saudis, for example, with Kuwait, paid substantial amounts of oil revenues to America for defending them.[56]

The Bush Plan Receives Congressional Backing

Historically, the United States had always kept troops within the vicinity of the gulf region. With the invasion of Kuwait in August 1990, Bush quickly began a troop buildup. He followed, albeit carefully, his predecessor's strategy in Grenada, Libya, and Panama without holding discussions with Congress. The rule of the game was that since enactment of the War Powers Act of 1973, American presidents could initially engage in wars almost arbitrarily. The War Powers Act limited a president's ability to declare war against sovereign states but only after the initial commitment of troops. The president was required to withdraw troops after sixty days of deployment in a war theater unless Congress granted an extension or ordered otherwise.

President Bush's military buildup in the gulf area in the aftermath of the Kuwait takeover by Iraq was subjected to the usual checks and balances of power in the U.S. political system. More than fifty congressmen were against Bush's unilateral decision to commit troops in the hot desert under the military jargon code, Operation Desert Storm. A number of congressmen filed suit in the U.S. Supreme Court to stop the president from further troop deployment until congressional authorization had been received. This event certainly pleased Hussein's men who thought Bush would not go ahead with his threat to use force as he would be stopped by a democratic-controlled Congress.

An emotional debate ensued in the U.S. Congress, as it appeared that Hussein would not withdraw his troops from Kuwait and that a military option was desired by the Bush administration. In the House of Representatives, there were sixty-seven more "aye" votes for Bush to attack Iraq than those against. In the Senate, five "yes" votes for the Bush plan made the difference.[57] Congress was in agreement with President Bush that, come K Day—K for Kuwait—if Iraq did not pull out of Kuwait, the president was free to use the U.S. military to remove the Iraqis from Kuwait. The battle in Congress was not an easy one, and the Bush administration had to engage in intensive lobbying. The Democrats' main bone of contention was that the UN embargo against the aggressor had not been given ample time to yield fruit. A key factor in ensuring that Bush got congressional support was recognition that the U.S.-led coalition would collapse with humiliation if Bush had been refused authority. Besides, there was the issue of American superiority, and in any case, the troops were already in Saudi Arabia and parts of the Middle East.

Although there were calls for peace on American university campuses and elsewhere, Bush and his defense staff were eager to go to war. Protests in several towns denounced this "Bush War" and demanded no "blood for oil." Protesters argued that the war was oil and therefore not justified, but the president had decided the time was ripe to send a clear and unequivocal message to Hussein that Americans would not accept Iraqi occupation of Kuwait. Americans would use force to achieve the objective to free Kuwait. Congressional solidarity reinforced this conviction and Bush, after consultation with the Pentagon, shelved his wimp image to declare war on Iraq.

Hussein's miscalculation was that his battle-tested troops would defeat the American infidels. Hussein theorized that the war would take longer than the United States imagined. Worse still, Hussein fought the allies with a divided mind, hoping, on the one hand, that he would inflict pain into the ranks of the U.S. and allied troops and, at the same time, evoke anti-Israeli sentiments to split the Arab coalition.

Hussein's strategy involved expanding the conflict by attacking Israel. The military command in Iraq attacked Israel using a well-developed, long-range gun named after Hussein—the Al-Hussein Scud Missile launchers. It took the Bush administration considerable persuasion, tact, and skill to restrain Israel from joining the fighting party. Indeed, one could credit the Bush administration for ensuring the gulf coalition was retained during the crisis period. It was a difficult endeavor. Traditionally, Muslim republics in the Middle East would not fight side by side with Israel, but they morally did so.

Most of the Arab nations had sad memories of the Suez War of 1956 and the Yom Kippur War of 1973 when the Israelis defeated Egypt, an Arab state. However, thanks to Carter and his Camp David initiatives, Egypt was one of the few Arab nations that abided by UN Resolution 242, which recognized the right of Israel to exist. Most other Arab states never accepted Israeli nationhood, and it would have been inconceivable for them to join Israel in a war against an Islamic state.

Saudi Arabia and Egypt surprised many commentators on Middle East affairs by taking the side of the United States. The two countries argued that Israel had a right to retaliate if attacked by Iraq.[58] Syria, on the other hand, took strong exception to any Israeli response.

Bush also used diplomatic skills in ensuring Soviet neutrality. The Soviet Union had long been sympathetic to Iraq, but Gorbachev's peace plan was merely "noted and appreciated" by Bush, although it gave the green light to the American-led counterattack on Iraq. This symbolized Bush's ability to assert American forcefulness where its vital interests necessitated a hard-line stand. Bush insisted to the Soviets and Arabs that the United States was not ready at that time to accommodate talks that would entail settling the issue of Palestine.

WORLD PROTESTS: BUSH AND IRAQGATE

Bush and his generals began bombing Baghdad on January 16, 1991, at the end of K Day. The UN and the U.S. Congress had given the green light for U.S. and allied forces to remove Iraq by force from occupied Kuwait. The U.S. strategy involved first launching aerial bombardment schemes before using ground forces toward mid-February 1991. It was the biggest ground attack since World War II. Bush had given Iraq another deadline before the ground attack but to no avail. He consulted with former presidents and key congressmen before opening fire from the ground.

The air raid against Iraqi forces had devastated Hussein's men in record time. Hussein's war-making machine was considerably weakened. A few scud missiles were fired at Israeli posts, but Israel restrained itself. The horror of war was at hand in every American and Arab nation. The United States used massive bombing, including the B-52 carpet bombing. Back at home, Bush and his supporters began sloganeering about support of the U.S. Marines. "Support the troops" became a national battle cry during Desert Storm. As the war progressed, there was an outcry that the war should be put on hold and ended.

Protests in Washington, DC were organized on January 26, 1991, where speakers included Jesse Jackson, Daniel Ellsberg, Molly Yard, and others.[59] Many newspapers, other media editorials, and letters from readers protested that the Gulf War of 1991 was unnecessary. Other commentators called for the impeachment of Bush. McDonald argued that Bush should be impeached for several reasons. First, the Senate should have impeached Bush for "high crimes and misdemeanors," as he failed to preserve and protect the U.S. Constitution by sending troops to the Middle East that were overwhelmingly from poor white, black, and Latino communities. The president should have upheld the Constitution by protecting the rights of minorities.[60] Second, Bush, as president, violated his constitutional oath by "bribing, intimidating, and threatening others," including members of the UN Security Council, to support his attack on Iraq. Third, McDonald saw his "killing of innocent civilians" as a violation of the Hague Conventions of 1907 and 1923 and the 1949 Geneva protocols, arguing that Bush violated human rights by declaring war.[61] Fourth, when Bush approached Congress for a declaration of war, he had already dispatched troops into the war theatre, thereby rendering useless any substantive debate by the U.S. Congress. Bush had already declared war and put American soldiers' lives in danger. This warranted an impeachment and trial of the president. Finally, Bush simply "acted in a manner contrary to his trust as president," and therefore, he should have been impeached.[62] The arguments were not taken seriously by the U.S. House or Senate, and President Bush was spared of what Johnson went through in the mid-nineteenth century (1867)—impeachment for high crimes.

Outside America the war was met with protests of equal or greater veracity. In Africa, peace demonstrations were held in Algeria, Egypt, Libya, Nigeria, South Africa, Sudan, and Tunisia. In Egypt, the government of Hosni Mubarak imposed visa restrictions for citizens of Algeria, Morocco, and Tunisia because these governments were appalled by Egypt's role in the war. In Nigeria, Shiite Muslims were dispersed by riot police in Lagos. Significantly, Sudan and Tunisia outright supported Hussein.

In Asia, protests were recorded in Bangladesh where Muslims backed Hussein. At Tehran University, about two thousand students demonstrated in support of Hussein, even though Iraq and Iran had just fought an eight-year battle. The Japanese cities of Okinawa, Osaka, and Tokyo also experienced limited antiwar demonstrations. Still, large pro-Iraq demonstrations were held in Pakistan on January 18, 1991; in Lebanon; and in India at the New Delhi Embassy. Demonstrations occurred on January 25 at the U.S. Embassy in Manila, Philippines.

Thousands of people demonstrated in European cities against the Bush war. In Amsterdam, antiwar protestors were stopped by police on January 18, 1991, and in Oslo at the U.S. Embassy. Demonstrations in

Rome, Italy, on January 19, 1991, attracted over one hundred thousand people. In Berlin, over ten thousand children with candles protested, as did adults, in Bonn on January 26, 1991. In the United Kingdom, there were rallies across the isles to protest the war and rallies in the Russian towns of Leningrad and Moscow.

In the Americas, protests were recorded in Canada at Montreal, Ottawa, and Vancouver. Others were in São Paulo, Brazil and Argentina. There was no nation in the world that was "happy with the war," and antiwar protests in Australia, Ireland, and the former Yugoslavia all emphasized the unpopularity of the American-led battle against Iraq.[63]

The Gulf War of 1991 cost over one hundred thousand Iraqi lives and thousands of civilian casualties. There were environmental damages, as over nine hundred and fifty Iraqi oil-producing wells were set aflame. Oil spills as a result of attacks on tankers cost over $1 billion. The Tigris River was badly polluted by allied attacks on nuclear reactors. The war cost Americans' lives and money. The Gulf War of 1991 was a very important war for the Bush presidency.[64] Some commentators argued that it "kicked the Vietnam Syndrome."[65] The war raised President Bush's Gallup opinion poll approval rankings and gave him immediate political capital.

The war had been executed. Hussein's men withdrew from Kuwait. In his withdrawal speech, President Hussein maintained his position that Kuwait was Iraqi territory:

> O valiant Iraq men, O glorious Iraq women. Kuwait is part of your country and was carved from it in the past... The harvest in the mother of battles has succeeded. After we have harvested what we have harvested, the greater harvest and its yield will be in the time to come, and it will be much greater than what we have at present, in spite of what we have to present in terms of the victory, dignity and glory that was based on the sacrifices of a deep faith which is generous without and hesitation of fear.[66]

According to Hussein, Iraq withdrew "as a result of the ramifications which included aggression by thirty countries...whose repugnant siege was led in evil and aggression by the machine and the criminal entity of America and its major allies."[67] In Iraq, the war was generally conceived as a third-world war given the magnitude of the damage it caused and the large number of players involved.

President Bush released a diplomatic message to celebrate his victory. His speech observed that

> no one country can claim this victory as its own. It was not only a victory for Kuwait but a victory for all the coalition partners. This is a victory for the United Nations, for all mankind, for the rule of law and for what is right.[68]

The story of the U.S.-Iraqi war did not end with the defeat of Hussein in the mother of all battles or defeat of all battles. The American press published a damaging report on the Bush administration's conduct of foreign policy. The press unearthed a scandal that came close to the Casey-Reagan-Oliver North "Iran-contra gate" saga. The story goes that the Bush administration helped Iraq acquire arms and even abetted the invasion of Kuwait. In short, Bush was not "Mr. Clean." Nixon went down with Watergate, Reagan retired with Iran-contra gate, and Bush would be remembered for "Iraqgate," the term coined by the media.[69]

The U.S. press reported that throughout the Reagan-Bush and Bush-Quayle administrations, Hussein received arms from the United States government. The United States secretly armed Iraq and Iran in their war of 1980–1988 to weaken the two states and check the influence of the Islamic revolution. Iraq, according to Murray Waas of the *Village Voice*, wanted back into the Western alliance.[70] The United States was said to have been more sympathetic to Iraq in its war against Iran. Arms shipments to Iraq were distributed through Egypt, Jordan, and Kuwait. Among the weapons that Hussein later used against the United States were the HAWK anti-aircraft missiles. This sale was a violation of U.S. law. The United States sold material for making chemical weapons, particularly nerve gas, to Iraq.[71] A Pennsylvania firm also sold material for making huge gun barrels to Iraq.

Additionally, the U.S. Department of State appeared to have continuously supported Hussein despite his repeated threats to annex Kuwait. Through their actions, the Bush administration did nothing to stop Hussein from going ahead with his plan to invade Kuwait.[72] Bush and his staff gave signals that the United States would not interfere with Iraq if it attacked Kuwait. According to the *Alternative Orange*, the state department was unhappy when Secretary of Defense Cheney told the press that the United States would defend Kuwait if attacked by Iraq on July 19, 1991.[73] The state department's spokesperson, Margaret Tutwiler, asserted, "We do not have any defense treaties with Kuwait and there are no special defense or security commitments to Kuwait."[74] The U.S. ambassador to Iraq, April Glaspie, in a meeting with Hussein on July 25, 1991, was reported to have told Hussein that the United States had no opinion on the issue. Waas also argued that Bush rejected a congressional decision of July 27, 1991, to impose limited sanctions on Iraq. The report accused Bush of doing nothing when advised by CIA Director Webster that Iraqi invasion of Kuwait was imminent. Nonetheless, the Bush administration reiterated its "no opinion" stance. The verdict by several commentators was that "the Bush administration could have prevented the Iraqi situation" and checked Hussein's invasion of Kuwait.[75] In fact, a cynical view of the Iraqgate scandal was that the scud missile that Hussein employed to attack the United States, its allies, and Israel was partly built by Soviet, German, and Iraqi technicians—but was financed by the United States! Commentators argued that money to Iraqi arms agents was siphoned through the Atlanta Branch of the Banca Nazionale del Lavoro (BNL), whose manager was later prosecuted.[76]

Intellectual arguments against the Iraqgate scandal rejected the aforementioned claims. For example, Kenneth Juster challenged the framers of Iraqgate and suggested that it was a myth rather than a reality.[77] Juster argued that Iraqgate was an act of misinformation by the news media to criminalize foreign policy differences. According to Juster, there was no evidence that the Bush administration deliberately armed Hussein. Juster defended loans to Hussein's government, arguing that they were for agricultural support and not nuclear, biological, or chemical weapon manufacture. The loans were disbursed until the day of the Iraq-Kuwait war. The problem with that position was that it was not clear if the money released from U.S. taxpayers was diverted to military endeavors. Juster took the position that all that Bush wanted was an Iraq with which he could work.[78] Americans needed Iraq to be integrated into its scheme of gulf politics, and agricultural credits were one way of building a rapport. At any rate, Iraq did not have diplomatic relations with Iran between 1967 and 1983. Thus, the only mistake the Bush administration committed was its failure to keep the affair public. The downside to the issue was that no serious debate on U.S. policy toward Iraq before the Gulf War had been entertained by the Bush administration.[79]

Besides Iraqgate, President Bush was in the public limelight at the conclusion of the war with Hussein. This time the issue was different. Bush did not please some U.S. officials because Hussein remained in power despite the chaos that he unleashed on the international community. President Bush realized the dangers of that concern and called for an uprising against Hussein. He incited Iraqis to oust Hussein from Baghdad and promised American development assistance. Bush also pledged moral support for the Kurds of Iraq. The Kurds, who by 1991 numbered about 4 million, constituted a fourth of the Iraqi population and were at war with Hussein's regime and had continuously sought autonomy. However, the dream for Kurdistan was never realized.

The Kurds' issue was not resolved because it would spark off another conflict in the region. Kurds traced their origin to the biblical Medes who had occupied Babylon. The Kurds traversed sections of Turkey—over 10 million—and another 6 million migrated into Iran, the former Soviet Union, and Syria. A large number of Kurds known as the "Mountain Turks" living in Turkey supported pro-Western interests, which complicated the picture. President Bush did not provide the Kurds with any meaningful support. Nixon, at the behest of Shah Pahlavi of Iran, denied the Kurds military backing and, instead, ordered the CIA in 1973 to instigate a Kurdish uprising against Iraq. The Shah had preferred the unrest to weaken Iraq with whom he had border disputes.

In 1988 President Reagan backed Hussein when he was at war with the Ayatollah's Iran. Hussein received American dollars that were then utilized for purchasing chemical weapons that poisoned over twelve thousand Kurds in Halabja. The bottom line was that even though Bush silenced Hussein, his policy was not to replace him. Bush was more comfortable maintaining the status quo than moving into an unpredictable situation.

In some circles, particularly among American-Arab allies, there was a strong feeling that ousting Hussein was a precondition to the establishment of peace and tranquility in the gulf region. For example, during a visit to Kuwait by Secretary of State Baker, the temporarily exiled Emir Sheik Jaber al-Ahmed al-Sabah's Prime Minister Sheikh Saad made it clear that there would be no peace if Hussein remained in power.[80] The United States was encouraged by the uprisings in a number of Iraqi towns, but these were insufficient to bring down the Baghdad government after the humiliating defeat by U.S.-led allied forces. To replace Hussein was not the Bush administration's immediate goal; in any case, to use U.S. forces for this purpose went against the UN mandate. Senator Lugar of Indiana was one of the strong voices in support of more action to drive Hussein out of power. But the Bush administration, despite rhetoric from the president urging the Iraqi people and military to "take matters in their own hands to force Saddam Hussein, the dictator, to step aside,"[81] were clearly uncomfortable with Iraq being ruled by a possibly pro-Shiite Iran leader. The Bush administration was cognizant of the fact that Hussein's Sunni were a minority in Iraq. The leader of the militant Shiite Iraq, Mohammed Bakr al-Hakim, was a known sympathizer with the Iran-backed Muslim fundamentalists who were dreaded by American authorities since the Iran hostage saga of the Carter era. The overriding factor was that the U.S. could not punish Hussein further without causing cracks in the international system. French President Mitterrand and Soviet leaders could not support American troops heading for Baghdad.

Moreover, the tendency to treat wars as personal feuds between two leaders was evident in the Gulf War. The Gulf War of 1991 was, in large measure, a conflict of inflated egos. Evan Thomas argued that Bush was "being criticized for personalizing his feud with the Iraqi strongman."[82] If that were so, then Hussein may have had the last laugh. Bush left the White House in January 1993 with Hussein still regarding himself as sultan.

Mark Lance, writing on Bush's priorities, put it succinctly by stating that the United States was "unlikely to get anyone better than Saddam Hussein," and therefore, to have him assassinated would only exacerbate regional instability.[83] The latter argument explained President Bush's decision not to please the hawkish U.S. Congress and pursue Hussein to the end. In doing this, Bush demonstrated a sense of moderate pragmatic statesmanship. The Iraqi case illustrated the tendency of President Bush to emphasize rationality in foreign policymaking and the attainment of specific objectives.[84] Bush went on record to state that his quarrel was not with the Iraqi people. Of course, some critics saw the president's rhetoric as contradictory.

In a nutshell, Bush's foreign policy retained some elements of the Reagan doctrine, such as using force when necessary while promoting international capitalism within an American framework. More profoundly, it was a period of change in style, with President Bush exhibiting a more hands-on approach than hitherto practiced. It was an era of flexibility in managing a fast-changing international environment.

NOTES

* Jon Roper, *The American Presidents: Heroic Leadership From Kennedy to Clinton* (Edinburgh, U.K.: Edinburgh University Press, 2000), 166.
1. John Barry and Tom Morganthau, "The Defense Dilemma," *Newsweek*, January 23, 1989, 12.
2. Walter Williams, "George Bush and Executive Branch Domestic Policy Making Competence," *Policy Studies Journal* 21, no. 4 (1993): 170–171.
3. George F. Will, *The New Season: A Spectator's Guide to the 1988 Election* (New York: Simon & Schuster, 1987), 40.
4. Ibid., 51.
5. Ibid., 52.
6. Barry Schweid, "Dateline Washington: Warren's World," *Foreign Policy* no. 94 (spring 1994): 137.
7. Ignatius cited in Walter Williams, "George Bush and Executive Branch Domestic Policy Making Competence," 711.
8. Richard M. Smith, Thomas M. DeFrank, and Ann McDaniel, "An Interview with Bush: The Deficit Is the Top Priority for the New President," *Newsweek*, January 30, 1989, 19. Also see Carol Bell, *The Reagan Paradox: U.S. Foreign Policy in the 1980s* (New Brunswick, NJ: Rutgers University Press, 1989), 172.
9. Bell, *The Reagan Paradox: U.S. Foreign Policy in the 1980s*, 167.
10. Warner, "Bush Battles the 'Wimp Factor,'" *Newsweek*, October 19, 1987, 45.
11. Ibid., 44.
12. Bell, *The Reagan Paradox: U.S. Foreign Policy in the 1980s*, 157.
13. Ibid.
14. George P. Shultz, *Endless Turmoil for How Much Triumph?* (New York: Charles Scribner's Sons, 1994), 153–154.
15. Ibid.
16. Bob Woodward, "The Secret Wars of the CIA; Covering Up for a Sick President," *Newsweek*, October 5, 1987, 56 and Russell Watson and John Barry, "A U.S. Ambush in the Gulf: New Tactics Produce Small but Satisfying Victory as Iran Is Trapped in the Act of Laying Mines," *Newsweek*, October 5, 1987, 24–25.
17. Kenneth Juster, "The Myth of Iraqgate," *Foreign Policy* no. 94 (spring 1994): 118. Also see Tom Mathews, "The Road to War: A Behind-the-Scenes

Account of Gross Errors and Deft Maneuvers," *Newsweek*, January 28, 1991, 54–65.
18. *Miami Herald*, March 12, 1986, 12A and *Miami Herald*, March 13, 1986, 22A.
19. *The Alternative Orange*, February 13–27, 1991, 9.
20. Ibid.
21. Joseph S. Nye Jr., "Peering Into the Future," *Foreign Affairs* 73, no. 4 (July/August 1994): 84. Also see Ken Adelman, "Was Our Intelligence Astray in the Gulf," *The Washington Times*, March 25, 1991, D4.
22. Roderick McDonald, "The Gulf Crisis: An Historical Perspective," *The Alternative Orange*, October 25–November 3, 1990, 3.
23. Elana Levy, "A Plea for Peace in the Middle East, Local Activist Calls for Examination of U.S. Policy," *The Alternative Orange*, October 25–November 3, 1990, 1. The offer was presented by Hussein on August 8, 1990, but was rejected by the United States and its allies.
24. Ibid.
25. Jonathan Alter, "Why 'Linkage' Doesn't Connect," *Newsweek*, January 21, 1991, 24.
26. Levy, "A Plea for Peace in the Middle East, Local Activist Calls for Examination of U.S. Policy," and Tom Post, "Will Saddam Try To Duck the Punch?" *Newsweek*, December 31, 1990, 42.
27. Tom Morganthau et al. "Should We Fight?" "By Committing More Troops to the Gulf, Bush Fueled the Wrenching Policy Debate," and "Congress and the Country Are Waiting To Be Persuaded," *Newsweek*, November 26, 1990, 26.
28. Ibid.
29. T. Boone Pickens, "Oilman and Investment," *Newsweek*, November 26, 1990, 31, and "Americans Take Sides," *Newsweek*, November 26, 1990, 31–34.
30. Syracuse Peace Council, *Peace Newsletter*, February 1991, PNL 580, 22.
31. Ibid.
32. Peter McGrath, "Must Our Wars Be Moral?" *Newsweek*, November 26, 1990, 38.
33. Rick Coughlin, "Dehumanizing the Enemy and the Persian Gulf War," *The Alternative Orange*, March 14–28, 1991, 9.
34. *The Daily Orange*, April 12, 1991, 5.
35. McGrath, "Must Our Wars Be Moral?" 38.
36. *The Alternative Orange*, February 13–17, 1991, III, no. 6, 1.
37. *The Alternative Orange*, October 25–November 31, 1990, III, 1, 1. Also see Rich Stuchiner, *The Alternative Orange*, October 25–November 3, 1990, 4.

38. Tom Morganthau et al., "Should We Fight?" and "Americans Take Sides," *Newsweek*, November 26, 1990, 31–35.
39. George Bush, "Why Are We in the Gulf," *Newsweek*, November 26, 1990, 28–29, 42.
40. Ibid.
41. John Aloysius Farrell, "George Bush, War, and the Spirit of American Exceptionalism," *The Boston Globe*, March 31, 1991, 12, and Marianne Means, "Bush Should Capitalize on Momentum War Has Given Him," *Seattle Post—Intelligencer*, March 6, 1991, A14.
42. See Michael T. Benson, *Truman and The Founding of Israel* (Westport, CT: Praeger, 1997), and John S. Snetsinger, *Truman, the Jewish Vote, and the Creation of Israel* (Stanford: Hoover Institution Press, 1974).
43. Richard Nixon, *The Real War* (New York: Warner Books, 1980).
44. Rowland Evans Jr., and Robert D. Novak, eds., *Nixon in the White House: The Frustration of Power* (New York: Vintage Books, 1971), 83.
45. George Herring, "The Vietnam Syndrome and American Foreign Policy," in ed. Eugene Kuzirian and Larry Madaras, *Taking Sides*, 317.
46. Ibid.
47. Edward S. Greenberg, *The American Political System: A Radical Approach* (New York: Scott Foresman and Company, 1989), 242.
48. Russell Watson and John Barry, "A U.S. Ambush in the Gulf: New Tactics Produce Small but Satisfying Victory as Iran Is Trapped in the Act of Laying Mines," *Newsweek*, October 5, 1987, 24–44.
49. Ibid.
50. Alan Cowell, "Confrontation in the Gulf: Leaders Bluntly Prime Iraq for Mother of All Battles," *New York Times*, September 22, 1990, Section 1, 4.
51. Evan Thomas, John Barry, and Ann McDonald, "No Vietnam Lessons of Southeast Asia Shape the President's Strategy in the Gulf," *Newsweek*, December 10, 1990, 24–25.
52. Ibid., 27.
53. Alexander De Conde, *A History of American Foreign Policy, Volume II: Global Power, 1900 to the Present* (New York: Charles Scribner's Sons, 1978), 363.
54. Ibid., 362.
55. George Brown Tindall, *America: A Narrative History* (New York: W. W. Norton and Company, 1988), 1377.
56. Stephen E. Ambrose, *Rise to Globalism, American Foreign Policy Since 1938* (New York: Penguin Books, 1991), 388.
57. Tom Morganthau with Eleanor Cliff, "Bracing for War: After an Emotional Debate, Congress Votes to Support the Use of Force. But Americans Are

Divided and Anxious About Conflict in the Gulf," *Newsweek*, January 21, 1991, 19. There were ten democratic votes for war in the Senate.
58. Ibid.
59. *The Alternative Orange*, February 13–27, 1991, 5.
60. *The Alternative Orange*, March 14–28, 1991, 3.
61. Ibid.
62. Ibid. Also see Morganthau with Cliff, "Bracing for War," 16, and Jerry Adler et al., "Prayers and Protest: the Peace Movement Comes to Sudden Life With Some New Faces Singing Old Songs," *Newsweek*, January 28, 1991, 36–39.
63. *The Alternative Orange*, March 14–28, 1991, 6.
64. Gabriel Kolko, *Main Currents in Modern American History* (New York: Harper and Row, 1976), 349.
65. Rich Stuchiner, "Where the Truth Lies, The Media Goes to War," *The Alternative Orange*, March 14–28, 1991, 10.
66. Saddam Hussein's speech on February 26, 1991, *Historical Documents of 1991*, Cumulative Index 1987–1191, ed. Hoyt Gimlin (Washington, DC: Congressional Quarterly, Inc., 1992), 103.
67. Ibid., 103.
68. President Bush's speech, February, 27, 1991. Ibid., 104.
69. The *US News and World Report* coined this word. See *U.S. News and World Report*, October 26, 1992.
70. Murray Waas, cited in *The Alternative Orange*, February 13–27, 1991, III, no. 6, 1, III, 6.
71. Ibid., 9.
72. Ibid.
73. In a letter to the African Association of Political Science Newsletter of September, no. 4, Tom Griffith of Seattle, Washington, observed that the whole world was cheated by the Bush administration in the sense that the administration actually wanted Iraq to invade Kuwait. AAPS, newsletter, September 1991, 2.
74. *The Alternative Orange* III, no. 6 (February 13–27, 1991): 6.
75. Ibid.
76. Alan Friedman, *Spider's Web: The Secret History of How the White House Illegally Armed Iraq* (New York: Bantam Books, 1993).
77. Juster, "The Myth of Iraqgate," 107.
78. Ibid., 114.
79. Ibid.
80. Thomas L. Friedman, "After the War: Diplomacy; Kuwaiti Leaders Tell Baker Democratization Is Coming," *New York Times*, March 10, 1991, 15.

81. Ibid., 16.
82. Evan Thomas, "The One True Hawk in the Administration Bush Is Set for War, Even if His Generals Aren't," *Newsweek*, January 7, 1991, 19.
83. Mark Lance, "On Specks and Logs," *Alternative Orange*, February 13–27, 1991, 12.
84. Daniel P. Franklin and Robert Shepard, "Is Prudence a Policy?" in *Leadership and the Bush Presidency: Prudence or Drift in an Era of Change?*, ed. Ryan Barilleaux and Mary Stuckey (Westport, CT: Praeger, 1992), 166.

CHAPTER 5

SECURITY, TRADE, AND DEMOCRACY IN LATIN AMERICA AND ASIA

> *Great nations of the world are moving toward democracy through the door to freedom. Men and women of the world move toward free markets through the door to prosperity. The people of the world agitate for free expression and free thought through the door to the moral and intellectual satisfactions that only liberty allows.*
>
> —President George H. W. Bush*

How presidents conduct foreign policy can have tremendous impact on the success or failure of their presidency. Observers of U.S. relationships with Latin America and Asia recognize that presidential peacemaking has been attained through various instruments, including promoting trade and democracy.

This chapter describes and analyzes President Bush's internationalist efforts to promote peace and security. Asia and Latin America are viewed by U.S. presidents as more vital to U.S. peace and security interests than many other nations. This chapter describes key concerns between the U.S. president and regional leaders in securing peace and argues that while the Bush administration retained key tenets of American diplomacy in much of Latin America and Asia, trends in globalization resulted in increased bilateral trade and security partnerships.

Due to the vastness of the Latin American and Asian regions, the chapter, by necessity, is a broad-brush analysis of the president's foreign policy initiatives and actions analyzing broad commitments and obligations.

Latin America and Monroe's Ghost

Since 1823, the Monroe Doctrine acted as the context for U.S.-Latin American relations. Historically, the United States regarded South America as its backyard, discouraging involvement of European powers. Great Britain supported deferring on hemispheric issues in South America while the United States reciprocated by deferring to Britain in Africa and elsewhere. In a December 1823 presidential address to Congress, President James Monroe articulated U.S. policy toward Western Europe in hemispheric issues and established the parameters through which the superpowers would engage South America. Subsequent U.S. presidents implemented policy toward the Latin Americas with the Monroe Doctrine in mind. Historians recorded various instances in which presidential actions in Latin America were evaluated in the context of Monroe's vision. By 1867 U.S. politicians condemned French interference in Mexico by invoking the Monroe Doctrine. In the 1940s President F. D. Roosevelt rephrased the approach in his Good Neighbor Policy. By the 1960s President J. F. Kennedy proclaimed the Alliance for Progress, reiterating a commitment to hemispheric cooperation. J. F. Kennedy explained,

> The Monroe Doctrine means what it has meant since President Monroe and John Quincy Adams enunciated it, and that is that we

Security, Trade, and Democracy in Latin America and Asia   93

would oppose a foreign power extending its power to the Western Hemisphere, and that is why we oppose what is happening in Cuba today. That is why we have cut off our trade. That is why we worked in the OAS and in other ways to isolate the Communist menace in Cuba. That is why we will continue to give a good deal of our effort and attention to it.[1]

This region, more than any other region, is within reach of the United States. This means the U.S. capacity to influence events in Mexico and other Latin American neighbors is profound. The Bush presidency, 1988–1993, was transfixed on this problem. In addition, immigration to the United States and the promotion of democracy were important issues underlying relations between the United States and Latin America.[2]

Friends or Foes?

U.S. policy varies with different Asian nations, but in all cases, trade and security are priorities.[3] For example, U.S.-Chinese, -Indian, -Indonesian, -Japanese, and -Philippine relations are governed on different criteria than those of smaller nations. In nations like South Korea and Taiwan, important strategic security and trade interests shape interactions. For example, the 1991 Gulf War convinced Japan to participate in a non-combat UN role. In coping with conflicts in India and Pakistan, Bush moved to a neutral position, emphasizing "restraint" rather than strategic support for Pakistan. The Bush administration adopted a more pragmatic approach, discouraging the emerging arms race. Regionally, the United States continued to closely monitor security concerns around North Korea and the Taiwan Strait. These and other issues are briefly discussed in the pages that follow.

Trade Worries

The 1990s witnessed the promotion of democracy and trade interests as they shaped U.S. relations with its southern neighbors. Lowenthal summarized U.S. core interests in Latin America in the 1990s as premised on strengthening Latin America's prospects for democracy.[4] U.S. bias toward the promotion of democracy was premised on the notion that democratic nations provided a better environment for business.

The New Republic doubted that Bush achieved high marks in attaining foreign policy objectives apart from a free trade agreement with Mexico and Canada.[5] President Bush, along with Canada's Prime Minister Martin Brian Mulroney, negotiated the enactment of the North American Free Trade Agreement (NAFTA) treaty, signed in October 1992. President Carlos Salinas de Gortari of Mexico signed the treaty on October 7 in San Antonio, Texas. It is noteworthy that Salinas is the only president to have visited with President Bush during each year of Bush's presidency.[6] The two men enjoyed cordial relations, making it easy for Bush to accomplish negotiations in a timeframe that was more conducive to U.S. manufacturers than Mexican workers. President Clinton obtained senatorial ratification for NAFTA in 1993.

Whether NAFTA should be considered a success depends upon one's interpretations of NAFTA's mission and goals. The dominant view was that its goal was to provide easy access and transfer of goods and services within the region by reducing tariffs. The official interpretation encompassed a variety of objectives that included facilitation of cross-border movement of goods and services and increases in investment opportunities in the region. Although these were noble goals, events after NAFTA questioned the treaty's efficacy. For example, the 1994 economic recession led to civil strife in poor southeastern Mexican regions, especially in Chiapas where the Zapatista National Liberation Front, a guerrilla movement, conducted insurgent acts of violence and protested against the marginalization of native Indian Maya. The violence and sense of disempowerment of many Mexican workers following NAFTA's implementation demonstrated the skewed nature of the benefits of increased trade and painted a gloomy picture of the economic model touted by American and Mexican leaders. By 1994, some economists linked the massive immigration across the U.S.-Mexican border as a spillover of the failure of NAFTA to promote equitable economic growth in Mexico. NAFTA favored big business and industrial concerns and provided limited benefits to the average worker.

President Bush, who had good personal relations with Argentine President Carlos Saul Menem, secured U.S. corporate interests in Argentina.[7] Menem, a right-wing politician who succeeded Raul Alfonsin, is credited with ending military rule in Argentina and initiating a private sector-led industrialization program that included the development of a *gasoducto*—natural gas transmission pipeline—to connect Argentinean gas fields to U.S. markets. Bush's son, Neil, pursued business interests in Argentina. Earlier, Neil had supported a plan to drill oil in Argentina financed by loans acquired through his association with the failed Silverado Savings and Loan Bank.[8] His other son, George W., then governor of Texas, hosted Argentinean leaders. President Bush made eight visits to that country, becoming the first U.S. president since Eisenhower to do so. These visits benefited U.S. companies such as the Texas-based Enron whose subsidiaries invested in gas pipelines.[9]

In return for Bush's support of Argentina, Menem supported President Bush during the U.S. war with Iraq. Menem hoped that NAFTA would be expanded to include countries such as Chile and Argentina in the future.

President Bush reviewed former Secretary of the Treasury Baker's third world debt strategy and agreed to work toward a debt reduction plan. Lowenthal noted the difference between the Bush administration and other administrations:

> The administration also seemed to abandon the previously complacent U.S. stance toward the debt problem—and to indicate that Latin American, Japanese, and other international views were being heeded by conceding that some debt reduction should be sought. Secretary of the Treasury Nicholas Brady outlined general proposals toward this end in March 1989 and the incipient Brady Plan was followed by concrete steps to alleviate the debt burdens of Mexico, Venezuela, and Costa Rica.[10]

In 1989 the debt stood at around $400 billion and had become unsustainable. Without solving this debt crisis, economic growth was not possible. The review was not a radical departure from the Reagan administration's cautious approach but was out of concern for reversing the trend in which the United States lost billions of dollars and many jobs as a result of delinquency. Bush saw the debt crisis as a threat to the United States, fueling resentment from the Latin American masses. Latin American leaders, including President Carlos Andrés Pérez and Mexican President Salinas de Gortari, proposed debt restructuring or suspension of principal payments. Bush set up a framework for dialogue aimed at easing the debt crisis and promoting economic development in Latin America.[11]

NATIONAL SECURITY REFORM DIRECTIVES

Presidential studies often evaluate a leader's managerial effectiveness. President Bush made improvements in the management of the nation's security policy by incorporating several institutional changes in the security and intelligence apparatus. For example, on the National Security Council (NSC), Bush conferred widely with National Security Advisor Frank Carlucci and Secretary of State Powell. On the date of his inauguration, Bush issued a national security directive providing the charter for NSC administration.

NARCO-POLITICS AND PROMOTION OF DEMOCRACY

In appointments to key security positions, President Bush appointed General Brent Scowcroft as national security advisor. Scowcroft was instrumental in shaping U.S. policy toward Nicaragua and other Latin American regions with large cocaine trafficking problems. Scowcroft's leadership refined the policy on managing drug trafficking embedded in the International Counternarcotics Strategy. The strategy covered several Latin American countries, including Colombia and Manuel Noriega's Panama. As director of the CIA, Bush had been friendly to Noriega, but as president, he considered him an adversary.[12] Perhaps the Panamanian dictator was among the first victims of Bush's global agenda of promoting democracy.

Although controlling the supply of illegal drugs was important, Bush recognized the need to attack demand in the United States as well. Bush demonstrated skillful diplomacy by acknowledging this to Latin American leaders. The National Drug Control Strategy initiated by the administration recognized the weakness of previous approaches that placed almost sole blame on Latin American producers of narcotics. Earlier, Bush directed the United States in Operation Just Cause to invade Panama and depose and arrest General Noriega on drug charges. Noriega was charged in Miami, Florida, for "conspiracy to transport cocaine into the United States. Mexico and Venezuela criticized this action. The invasion of Panama was a secondary function, to guarantee the continued neutrality and open access of the Panama canal."[13] Evidence showed that Noriega threatened the security of the canal and Americans living in the region.

President Bush met with César Gaviria Trujillo, president of the Republic of Colombia, to impress upon him the need to double efforts against drug trafficking. Bush had previously attended a conference on drug trafficking held in Cartagena, Colombia, in February 1990, where he met with Colombian and Bolivian leaders. The administration saw these meetings as consultative and continued them throughout the Bush presidency.

The Bush administration carefully distanced itself from Reagan's Nicaraguan policies.[14] Bush abandoned military use of the Contra army and accepted the framework for a Central American peace plan designed by Costa Rica's president, Óscar Arias. Bush accepted the results of the democratic elections in Nicaragua in February 1990.

Under the Bush presidency, democratic reforms in Latin America were encouraged. More specifically, U.S. diplomats played an active role in supporting the opposition party in Mexico. Mexico's former ruling party, the Institutional Revolutionary Party, eventually ceded power to the opposition, who supported political reforms. Similarly, the Bush administration created conditions for the eventual suspension of U.S. aid to Peru in 1992 to protest President Alberto K. Fujimori's authoritarian rule.

Although Bush reluctantly recognized Fujimori's self-coup in the spring of 1992, Fujimori had not always been a supporter of U.S. interests. In particular, Fujimori's *autogolpe*, that is, self-coup, had dampened the United States' and Organization of American States' (OAS) desire to enlarge achievement of economic reforms endorsed by the International Monetary Fund (IMF). A cursory examination of U.S.-Peruvian relations suggests there was much mistrust between the two leaders. Prior to the political crisis in May 1991, Fujimori's administration had reluctantly signed an accord to increase logistical support for the war on coca fields. The United States supported Fujimori's war against the terrorist Maoist guerilla organization, the Shining Path, or *Sendero Luminoso*. Bush enthusiastically provided funding to Peru's military, thereby helping the Peruvian government to deal a sizeable blow to guerilla activities, particularly terrorist acts and gross abuse of human rights. Bush's support received much praise from the international community, especially civil society in Latin America. In every instance, the support was consistent with Bush's larger vision of democratic enlargement.

Through his leadership, President Bush provided U.S. support to the UN and the OAS in promoting democracy in other hemispheric regions. The administration impressed upon the OAS the necessity of establishing and adopting rules to institutionalize democratic governance throughout Latin America. The OAS would provide a framework for cooperative action to ensure that democratic rule was not just a seasonal enterprise but a permanent feature of the region's political landscape. The dividends were immediate. For example, in Paraguay, the efforts led to democratic elections in July 1993. President Nicanor Duarte Frutos assumed leadership in August 2003 as head of state and head of government. The consultative approach was a dramatic departure from the more unilateral style of the Reagan administration. Bush's personal rapport with many world leaders helped him approach hemispheric regions in a less threatening manner than his predecessor.

When reviewing President Bush's initiatives in Latin America, there is a temptation to argue that he had the discretion to make the region the center of his international policy. However, events in the gulf region

Security, Trade, and Democracy in Latin America and Asia 99

presented a challenge in the context of any perceived nonrevitalization of interest in the region. Yet the policy was consistent and executed along the lines established in the previous administrations. The relationship between the United States and Latin America from 1989 to 1993 did not suffer much, and trade and democracy took a more profound center stage than the ferocious ideological battles of the past. Hemispheric diplomatic relations turned toward the larger picture of neoliberal democratic reforms.

CONCERNS IN THE PACIFIC RIM AND ASIA

Japan continued to be the most important U.S. ally in the Asia Pacific region. U.S. officials regarded Japan as the keystone to all trade and security policies in the Pacific. Japan had overtaken the United States in several areas of technological development and was a leading exporter of a variety of motor vehicles to the United States. Recognizing the growing unease in the U.S. auto industry, Bush urged the Japanese to make concessions and allow American automakers access to Japanese domestic dealerships. The Bush administration hoped Japan would ease trade restrictions and not just engage in "conceptual agreements," which were often targets of Japan bashing U.S. politicians. Since 1989, Japan overtook the United States as the largest provider of official development assistance (ODA) and became the major economic powerhouse in the Asia-Pacific region.

President Bush maintained security and economic cooperation between the United States and Japan. His administration maintained the close consultative style dealing with security and economic issues affecting the two countries. As an indicator, Japanese heads of state visited with President Bush each year during his presidency. For instance, Prime Minister Noboru Takeshita visited in February 1989, Prime Minister Toshiki Kaifu in March 1990, and Prime Minister Kiichi Miyazawa in March 1991 and January 1992. Bush and Japanese authorities maintained a common position on many matters such as the Iraq war, international security, and WTO issues.

China

Bush condemned Chinese authorities for using force on Tiananmen Square demonstrations, a series of student-led protests between April and June 1989 in Beijing. Protests were triggered by the death, due to illness, of Hu Yaobang, an individual widely perceived as a liberal by Chinese intellectuals. Hu had been forced to resign his position as general secretary of the Communist Party by the country's leader, Deng Xiaoping. The Tiananmen demonstrations led to the death of more than four hundred people, mainly workers and students, brutalized by members of the Chinese People's Liberation Army. The government of China continued to suppress freedoms of association and allowed only limited access for international press cadres, thus worsening its human rights credentials. The Chinese authorities ordered Cable News Network (CNN) to end its coverage of the demonstrations.

President Bush joined the EU in imposing an arms embargo on the People's Republic of China (PRC). Despite China's poor human rights record, President Bush maintained an engagement strategy with China. He continued to extend the most-favored-nation (MFN) status to China, arguing that it was wrong to isolate China if the United States hoped to exert influence, known as "normal trade relations." Bush repeatedly contended that trade with China was in the best interests of both countries. The 1990 trade figures show that China bought U.S. goods worth over $6 billion a year. Among purchased goods were American aircraft, wheat, chemicals, and lumber. Losing this market would cost America jobs and negatively impact the domestic economy. Bush further argued that China's neighbors, including Korea, Singapore, Thailand, and even Taiwan, encouraged him to continue trade engagements with China. Therefore, in extending MFN status in 1990, Bush argued that MFN

> is not a special favor. It's not a concession. It's the basis of everyday trade. And taking MFN away is one thing I said I would not do, that is, in doing that takes steps that would hurt the Chinese people themselves. I do not want to do that.[15]

Due to intense criticism over China's continued human rights abuses, Bush struck a more reconciliatory tone in his consultations with Congress. Critics felt that Bush's decision to maintain normal relations with China was based upon blind faith in the contacts he had established during his experience as an envoy there. In 1990 Bush appeared to be uncomfortable with repeated calls from lawmakers to end China's MFN status. In March 1992 Bush rejected the China bill that sought to put conditions on China's MFN status. Bush remarked,

> The sponsors of H.R. 2212 believe they can promote broad economic and foreign policy objectives in China by placing conditions on the renewal of China's MFN status. They expect that the Chinese will improve respect for human rights, cooperate in arms control, and drop barriers to trade, get a choice between losing MNF and addressing these concerns. Let me state at the outset that my administration shares the goals and objectives of H.R. 2212. Upholding the sanctity of human rights, controlling the spread of weapons of mass destruction, and free and fair trade are issues of vital concern. My objection lies strictly with the methods proposed to achieve the aims.[16]

President Bush did not want to go down in history as the president who isolated China but, instead, wished to be the president who facilitated change for human rights.[17] Bush's strategy entailed quiet diplomacy to avoid pushing China back toward Russia. Bush encouraged Chinese leaders to continue to work toward openness and stability.

President Bush encouraged emigration from China. In addition, the administration encouraged dialogue with China, who reciprocated by adhering to the Nonproliferation Treaty. In November 1992 the Bush administration waived satellite technology transfer curbs for China. Bush argued that the waiver would help reduce the U.S. trade deficit with China and provide jobs for American workers.

Concerns for human rights were high on President Bush's China agenda. President Bush had provided Tibetan refugees living in India and Nepal with immigrant visas to enter the United States.[18] In addition, Bush authorized a $1 million humanitarian aid package for Tibetan refugees as part of the Foreign Aid Bill.[19] Moreover, President Bush took the initiative to persuade Congress to pass a bill declaring Tibet an illegally occupied country whose genuine representatives were the Tibetan government in exile. As such, the bill recognized the Dalai Lama's authority. Bush gave rhetorical support to the Dalai Lama by urging China to end human rights violations in Tibet. In April 1991 the Senate passed a resolution stating that all Americans were united in the goals of freedom and human rights for Tibet.[20] Bush signed the bill into law on October 28, 1991.[21]

CAMBODIA

Although regionally important, Cambodia has not been a major concern of U.S. foreign policy. Former presidents Carter and Reagan were not cohesive in their approach toward managing the unending regional civil war and "killing fields" in Cambodia.[22]

As part of managing post–cold war global politics, President Bush called for a review of U.S.-Cambodian relations. Although much of Bush's policy toward Cambodia remained ambiguous, the president remained committed to supporting democratic reforms in the larger region. In May 1990 Bush told a news conference that the United States would welcome certifiably free and fair elections in Cambodia. The administration maintained support for anticommunist forces even though anticommunist members also backed the brutal Khmer Rouge regime. The administration contended it was not backing the notorious dictatorship.[23] Bush would support the promotion of democracy in Cambodia by denying Cambodia's seat on the UN if Cambodia included representatives from the Khmer Rouge Maoists and Phnom Penh Leninists. The *New York Times* reported,

> Although the Baker announcement represents a timely adjustment in some aspects of our policy, Washington is still pursuing the basic course it set nine months ago. It is trying to broker a U.N.-managed comprehensive political settlement that would end the fighting, introduce a U.N. peacekeeping force, verify the withdrawal of all Vietnamese forces, halt the external supply of arms

to the Cambodian factions and disarm their forces, and facilitate an internationally supervised free and fair election.[24]

Secretary of State Baker clarified that it was the administration's southeast Asian policy to provide humanitarian assistance to Vietnam and to open a dialogue with Cambodia. The administration's call for dialogue with Vietnam was intended to encourage Hanoi to understand that the United States would not maintain a permanent hostility toward that country. The Bush administration set the stage for the normalization of relations with Hanoi.

In pursuing his southeast Asian policy, Bush relied on diplomatic resources to impress upon Britain, China, France, and Russia the need to reduce violence and regional instability. Bush pursued diplomacy instead of supporting the Vietnamese-installed Phnom Penh regime because he believed that a comprehensive settlement involving all factions was the only way to prevent the Khmer Rouge communist takeover.

TAIWAN

Bush confronted several issues with Taiwan. These issues included Taiwan's application for membership in the General Agreement on Trades and Tariffs (GATT), arms sales, and security issues. The United States in continuing a "one China policy" transferred official recognition from Taiwan to the People's Republic of China in 1979, abrogating a treaty with Taiwan, a position maintained by Bush. The vague position recognized "One China" but encouraged Taiwan to acquire weapons for its defense. The United States pledged to defend Taiwan from China if the latter used force to assert its authority over the island.

Sino-American relations had been complicated by differing views on Vietnam. Previous U.S. presidential administrations listed Vietnam as a nation of concern, along with Cuba and North Korea. Nations of concern were identified as countries likely to gain nuclear weapons. Although China kept diplomatic relations with Hanoi, the United States did not. When Bush protested the 1989 Tiananmen massacre, China feared that the United States' warming up to Vietnam was an encirclement strategy.

The Bush administration can be credited with beginning a dialogue with Hanoi and normalizing relations with Vietnam, a country that conjured negative images for generations of Americans.[25] President Clinton followed Bush's opening to the country and visited Vietnam during his term.

Korea

The Bush administration did not denounce dictatorships in South Korea but conducted a major review of policy in consultation with the Pentagon and National Security Council. The administration continued to state that Bush was committed to human rights and democratic reforms in South Korea. Among the most visible authoritarian laws in South Korea was the national security law, often used to detain opponents of the regime. Notably, President Bush missed several opportunities to criticize the region. For example, the administration issued no comments on human rights abuses when Korean leader Roh Tae Woo visited President Bush in Washington on June 6, 1990. President Bush never used strong language to condemn human rights abuse in Korea, preferring, instead, to use quiet diplomacy.

An important achievement for President Bush was his facilitation of the peace talks between the two Koreas. Bush's initiative was one among the many that must be considered a huge step toward integration of North Korea into the mainstream of international politics. Bush should be credited for bringing North Korea to the table to discuss, among other things, its alleged development of nuclear weapons. The Bush administration's efforts also resulted in exchange visits among family members divided by the cold war. As Kenneth Quinones stated, most Koreans viewed the division of Korea at the 38th parallel as a "superpower betrayal of their desire for independence."[26] Many Koreans also blame the United States for the Korean War, whose awful legacy haunts millions of Koreans even today.[27]

Bush continued to favor dialogue with North Korea and encouraged the country to open its nuclear facilities to the UN's International Atomic Energy Agency inspectors. In July 1991 Bush informed visiting South

Korean President Roh Tae Woo that North Korea's nuclear weapons program was the most serious security concern facing east Asia.[28] However, the United States did not adjust its nuclear weapons deployment in South Korea to place in check North Korea's ambitions. Instead, the Bush administration resorted to increased diplomacy and negotiations as a more effective way to deal with North Korea's Stalinist leaders. The Bush administration developed a strategy in which North Korea would be presented with the choice of facing international isolation if it continued to assemble nuclear weapons. North Korea insisted on using its nuclear arsenals as a bargaining chip against its neighbors. Official sources suggested that North Korea would maintain nuclear weapons programs to check the threat of U.S. weapons deployed in the south.

Overall, the Bush record on human rights in Asia was mixed. The administration was inconsistent in its public condemnation of human rights abuses in Burma, Cambodia, East Timor, and Indonesia. At the same time, diplomatic rewards for democratic reforms in Singapore and Nepal were less than profound. The change of guard in Singapore was remarkable as its leader, long-serving Lee Kuan Yew, turned over his prime minister's post to Goh Chok Tong in November 1990. The Bush administration gave lukewarm support to minimal democratic changes in the Philippines, which had experienced a long period of human rights abuses under Marcos. According to the Human Rights Watch, in the Philippines, "the Bush administration continued its predecessor's policy of praising President Corazon Aquino's human rights achievements while downplaying ongoing serious human rights problems and permitting U.S. economic and security interests to take priority over human rights concerns."[29] Bush renewed agreements to control air and naval bases in the Philippines and provided over $10 billion in military aid to the Philippines.

INDIA AND PAKISTAN TURN NUCLEAR ON BUSH'S WATCH

One of President Bush's tacit failures was his lack of concentration on the growing tension between India and Pakistan and, especially, the two nations' nuclear arms race. Bush was unable to certify that Pakistan possessed nuclear weapons.[30] The Indo-Pakistan hostility exacerbated during 1990 and created anxiety for Bush. Robert M. Gates, Bush's deputy national security adviser, reportedly brought this issue to the attention of the president.[31] Gates visited the region and advised both parties that the benefits of a war over Kashmir would exceed its costs. He conveyed the message that the escalation of hostilities and the ensuing arms race were not in the long-term interests of the two Asian countries.

Under President Bush's watch, Pakistan and India advanced their nuclear arms capabilities. Pakistan broke its pledge to the United States not to enrich uranium over permissible limits. By 1990 Pakistani Abdul Qadeer Khan launched an "Islamic Bomb" to the cheer of Muslims all over the world. In October President Bush announced he could no longer provide Congress with Pressler Amendment certification that Pakistan lacked nuclear bomb capabilities. Bush terminated military assistance to Pakistan but permitted a limited number of commercial military sales to the country. Bush imposed sanctions on India and Pakistan for building nuclear bombs.

During the cold war, India tilted toward the Soviet bloc while Pakistan embraced the American-led Western alliance. After the Soviet invasion of Afghanistan in 1979, the ties between Pakistan and the United States became stronger. The United States needed Pakistan's support to defeat the Soviets in the region. Pakistan allowed the United States to use its territory as a base for weapons delivery to Afghan rebels, the Mujahideen, and for training them in combat techniques and war logistics. Pakistan sheltered more than 3 million refugees from Afghanistan. The rosy relations came to a standstill after Pakistan supported Islamic fundamentalists following the withdrawal of the Soviet Union from Afghanistan in 1989. On the other hand, Bush warmed up to India, thereby considerably improving relations between the United States and India. The momentum resulted in greater technological transfers to India, especially after 1993. Nonetheless, the United States still maintained an open-door policy toward Pakistan.

In conclusion, U.S.-Latin American and U.S.-Asian relations were guided by the broad triad of interests—trade, security, and the promotion of human rights and democracy. As President Bush pointed out in his inaugural address, the three broad objectives were not mutually exclusive.[32] Under Bush's leadership, there were marginal changes in emphasis from previous president's positions. The key difference occurred after the invasion of Iraq when all administrative energies were concentrated on the ejection of Hussein from Kuwait. In 1992 President Bush struggled with his re-election bid and limited his previously ambitious foreign policy agenda. The results of Bush's foreign policy initiatives were limited; the integration of Mexico into NAFTA, for example, did not lead to economic growth. Elsewhere it was business as usual as the post–cold war agenda gave impetus to neoliberal economic policies that included greater privatization of economies all over Asia and Latin America.

In terms of security, the administration failed to closely monitor nuclear proliferation in Asia. From most presidential observers, President Bush's most notable foreign policy engagements would be his strong condemnation of the events in Tiananmen Square in China, the fall of the Berlin Wall, the invasion of Panama, the Gulf War, the collapse of the Soviet empire, and the signing of NAFTA.

Notes

* George H. W. Bush, inaugural speech, January 20, 1989.
1. President J. F. Kennedy at an August 29, 1962, news conference, http://en.wikipedia.org/wiki/Monroe_Doctrine#Legacy
2. Robert A. Pastor, "The Bush Administration and Latin America: The Pragmatic Style and the Regionalist Option," *Journal of Interamerican Studies and World Affairs* 33, no. 3 (autumn 1991): 1–34. Also see Russell Crandall, *Driven by Drugs: U.S. Policy Toward Columbia* (Boulder, CO: Lynne Rienner, 2002).
3. Robert A. Cossa, "U.S. Foreign Policy in Asia: Churchill Was Right!" *Strategic Review* 23, no. 1 (winter 1995): 74–77 and James A. Baker III, "America in Asia: Emerging Architecture for a Pacific Community," *Foreign Affairs* 70, no. 1 (winter 1991–1992): 1–18.
4. Abraham F. Lowenthal, *The United States and Latin American Democracy: Learning From History* (Boston: World Peace Foundation, 1991), 383–405.
5. "What Foreign Policy? President George H. W. Bush's Leadership: The U.S. Foreign Policy Trajectory on Latin America and Asia," *New Republic* 205, no. 14 (September 30, 1991), 5–6. Also see Michael Cox, *U.S. Foreign Policy After the Cold War: Superpower Without a Mission?* (London: Pinter Press, 1995).
6. U.S. State Department, http://www.state.gov/r/pa/ho/c1792.htm, January 21, 2005.
7. Andres Oppenheimer, "Bush Badly Needs Latin American Ally," *The Oppenheimer Report*, http://www.miami.com/mld/miamiherald/news/columnists/andres_oppenheimer/1294749
8. Ana Simo, "Bush Friend Arrested for Illegal Arms Trafficking," http://www.thegully.com/essays/argentina/010607bush_menem.html (June 7, 2001).
9. Louis Dubose and Carmen Coiro, "Don't Cry for Bush, Argentina," http://www.motherjones.com/news/feature/2000/03/argentina.html
10. Abraham F. Lowenthal, "Rediscovering Latin America," *Foreign Affairs* 69, 4 (fall 1990): 27–41.
11. Editorial. "Go Easier on Latin Debtors Editorial," *Business Week* no. 3087, 112 (1992), http://www.businessweek.com/index.htm
12. Robert D. Schulzinger, *U.S. Diplomacy Since 1900* (New York: Oxford University Press, 1998), 361.

13. Wesley A. Fryer, "Defining and Refocusing U.S. Policy Toward Latin America" (1993), http://www.wtvi.com/wesley/uslapolicy.html
14. Lowenthal, "The United States and Latin American Democracy: Learning From History," 383.
15. President's Speech, News Conference News Session on China's Trade Status With U.S., *New York Times*, May 25, 1990, 12.
16. George Herbert Walker Bush Presidential Papers, CD-ROM and Bush Rejects China MFN Bill 03/02/92 USIA report, no. 217836 title ID TX-106, 1992.
17. "Bush Rejects China MFN Bill," March 2, 1992. USIA report, no. 217836 title ID TX-106 and Keith Richburg, "Back to Vietnam," *Foreign Affairs* 70, no. 1 (fall 1991): 111–131.
18. U.S. Public Law 101–649, signed October 28, 1990.
19. U.S. Public Law 101–513, signed October 27, 1990.
20. U.S. Senate Resolution 107.
21. U.S. Public Law 102–138.
22. Christopher Brady, *United States Foreign Policy Toward Cambodia, 1977–1992: A Question of Realities* (New York: St. Martin's Press, 1999).
23. White House news conference, speech, May 24, 1990. Widely circulated speech, http://www.whitehouse.gov
24. Stephen J. Solarz, "What New Policy Toward Cambodia?" *New York Times*, July 26, 1990.
25. Richburg, "Back to Vietnam," 111–131.
26. C. Kenneth Quinones, "Korean Reconciliation—Half Way There," in *Korean Security Dynamics in Transition*, ed. Kyung-Ae Park and Dalchoong Kim (New York: St. Martin's Press, 2001), http://www.vuw.ac.nz/~caplabtb/dprk/half_way.html. Also see Republic of Korea, http://www.hrw.org/reports/1990/WR90/ASIA.BOU-10.htm
27. Quinones, "Korean Reconciliation—Half Way There."
28. Don Oberdorfer, "U.S. Refuses to Shift Nuclear Arms in South Korea: Plan Had Been Proposed as Part of Deal To Bring North Korean Program Under Control," *Washington Post*, July 3, 1991, A23.
29. Human Rights Watch, *Report* (1991), http://www.hrw.org/reports/1989/WR89/Philippi.htm
30. Armando F. Mastrapa III, "India and Pakistan: An Asian Nuclear Peace?" (paper presented at the 49th Annual Meeting of the New York State Political Science Association, Jamaica, NY, April 28–29, 1995), http://mastrapa.home.mindspring.com/asian_nuclear_peace.html

31. Devin T. Hagerty, "Nuclear Deterrence in South Asia: The 1990 Indo-Pakistani Crisis," *International Security* 20, no. 3 (winter 1995), http://www.mtholyoke.edu/acad/intrel/sasianuk.htm
32. Carothers emphasized this point in Thomas Carothers, *Aiding Democracy Abroad: The Learning Curve* (Washington, DC: Carnegie Endowment for International Peace, 1999), 56.

Chapter 6

Standing Up for the Voiceless in Africa

I salute former President Bush for launching Operation Restore Hope—a military mobilization for a mission of mercy in Somalia. What a proud moment it was to see American soldiers help to feed starving children in a place far from our shores but clearly close to our hearts.

—Warren Christopher*

The contributions of President Bush to the political stability and humanitarian revitalization of Somalia is one of his most important legacies. Those writing African history will remember the Bush administration as apostles of democracy and will draw parallels with President J. F. Kennedy's moral support during the decolonization effort in the early 1960s. However, Bush's success in Operation Hope is preceded by more difficult periods in American relationships with Africa.

The goal of this chapter is to trace the evolution of Bush's role in Africa's history through his administrative positions—the U.S. ambassador to the UN, the director of the CIA, and vice president, as well as president. The first section situates Bush's approach to Africa within the lingering cold war environment inherited from Reagan. Several key influences on Bush's actions—or inactions—and constraints on his options are presented. The second section focuses on his presidency and his role in Somalia's stabilization through Operation Hope. The third section discusses neo-isolationism as another policy orientation in areas of vital interest, such as Nigeria and South Africa. The fourth section responds to the key policy issue of promoting democracy in Africa. The section describes one of the hallmarks of President Bush's promotion of democratic policy in Africa.

BUSH'S HISTORY WITH AFRICA AND THE COLD WAR LEGACY

While campaigning for the Republican Party presidential nomination in 1980, Bush stated that he would make human rights the hallmark of his foreign relations with Africa but that "strategic interests would also count."[1] During the same occasion, he posited that if the United States ignored Africa, it was at its own peril. As president, Bush made no trips to sub-Saharan Africa, but before assuming the presidency, Bush was involved in issues concerning Africa's development. In November 1982, as vice president, he visited seven African countries. In his speech in Nairobi, Bush remarked,

> My visit to Africa has shown me encouraging examples of African nations that are building their own institutions to broaden political participation and advance their frontier of freedom...We realize however, that nations cannot reap the benefits of individual freedom in an environment of insecurity. We attach high importance to strengthening Africa's security and are partners in building the necessary conditions for security.[2]

His most visible contacts with Africa are traced back to his days in the UN where Bush's vision included Africa. Bush conformed to the established norm of supporting dictators sympathetic to American interests, especially dictators combating communism. This point became

Standing Up for the Voiceless in Africa

a campaign issue when the Democratic challenger accused Bush of promoting an unprincipled foreign policy that embraced established despots around the world. Clinton challenged President Bush's commitment to human rights by reiterating "President Bush's ambivalence about supporting democracy and his eagerness to befriend potentates and dictators."[3]

The reality was that for most of independent sub-Saharan Africa's history, the United States shaped its relations with African states within the cold war framework. In many cases, U.S. presidents supported murderous regimes that were not left leaning. While the two polar views had some merit, the conduct of the Bush administration in its new relations with Africa was a watershed in the history of these nations. Bush understood Wilson's idealism of spreading democracy overseas. Yet Bush found that his predecessors could not apply its tenets to most of the third world during the cold war era.

In Africa, Bush inherited a messy cold war–related environment. There was the Angolan civil war in which the United States backed União Nacional para a Independência Total de Angola (National Union for Total Independence of Angola [UNITA]) under Jonas Savimbi against Augustino Neto and his successor, Jose Eduardo dos Santos, of the Soviet-backed Movimento Popular de Libertação de Angola (Popular Movement for the Liberation of Angola [MPLA]). The Angolan game plan was part of the Reagan Doctrine, an initiative meant to support any third-world guerrillas proclaiming a laissez-faire philosophy and denouncing communism.[4] The Reagan-Bush administration supplied the UNITA guerrillas with sophisticated weapons using its Congolese connections. Bush continued this strategy even though the USSR expansionism in Africa had been greatly weakened.[5] The cold war in this part of Africa during Reagan's administration was never cold; it was hot. The victims were Africans.

Bush inherited the burden of dealing with apartheid South Africa. Since 1948, the Nationalist Party under the minority whites saw racism as a workable panacea to their continued control over a predominantly black African nation. The National Party's ability to sustain power depended upon subordinating native populations and framing its domination in terms of racial superiority. The Group Areas Act and other laws in South Africa allowed for segregation, not along the familiar separate but equal divides but by providing Bantustans, translated into "homelands," for Africans. South Africans lived separate and unequal lives with black Africans suffering unspeakable injustices.

U.S.-African relations were tainted with racist suspicions and inclinations. Roger Morris, who worked for the Republican administration under Nixon, implied that Nixon and Kissinger, Nixon's key foreign policy player, were insensitive to the race issue.[6] Nixon critics argued that it was more than insensitivity to the race issue; they argued that it was racial prejudice that informed the manner by which Africa was marginalized. These critics considered Nixon's plan to be hostile to African Americans[7] and, by extension, to all blacks.

The position on the Nixon administration downplays initiatives by the Reagan administration, including its promulgation of the Anti-Apartheid Act of 1986, an act that prohibited loans to and investments within South Africa. The Reagan administration implemented measures to assist victims of apartheid and undermine some of its inhumane policies. The 1986 Act empowered the U.S. president to work with "other industrial democracies to help end apartheid and establish democracy in South Africa."[8] Although some media pundits saw this as a public relations ploy on Reagan's part, the act stopped the United States from importing strategic minerals vital to U.S. war-making machinery. The act was an important element in the political matrix that eventually ended apartheid and initiated the desegregation process in South Africa.

Although Bush did not depart radically from the previous strategies, he could be credited for taking a fresh look at South Africa and working through Congress to speed up political reforms in this troubled land. During President Bush's tenure, theoretical doctrinaire apartheid collapsed. President de Klerk, the last Nationalist Party chief, released Mandela from jail in 1990.

No other American president in the post–World War II era had a chance to witness the release of the world-famous prisoner who had served twenty-six years. While Bush may not be credited for pressurizing de Klerk to release Mandela, he takes credit for persuading key leaders in Congress to accept the reality of South Africa ending apartheid. In July 1991 the Bush administration called on Congress to lift the sanctions against South Africa.[9] Bush provided logistic leadership to ensure that the new South Africa was integrated into the community of civilized nations. As Larry Berman and Bruce Jentleson observed, in the apartheid question, Bush did not tow the line of former President Reagan but, instead, demonstrated pragmatism.[10] Berman and Jentleson suggested that even though there was pressure from Reagan Republicans to lift sanctions, the Bush administration pledged not to lift these sanctions completely. Bush believed that sanctions were an important psychological blow to the racist regime in South Africa.

Besides the contentious apartheid problem, the United States found itself involved in other conflict areas of Africa. For example, there was the unending civil war in Liberia, a state founded for freed American slaves. Additionally, there was a war in Eritrea that sought to separate Eritrea from Ethiopia. The Eritreans eventually succeeded. Then there were wars between RENAMO—which stood for Resistência Nacional Moçcambicana (Mozambican National Resistance)—and FRELIMO—Frente de Libertaçao de Moçambique (Mozambique Liberation Front)—in Mozambique, an extension of the cold war. Last, there was the violent disintegration of the Somali state. These conflicts are important because they were proxy wars in the global cold war rivalries. The Bush administration established mechanisms that prepared for postwar settlements to usher in a new era of negotiations.

OPERATION RESTORE HOPE: THE LAST BUSH ACT

The last major foreign policy act of Bush was in the name of Somalia, an African state in the Horn of Africa engaged in a clan-based civil war. The Somali nation is basically pastoral and is one of the poorest nations on earth. Its main income-generating activity was the sale of animal products to Saudi Arabia and other parts of the Middle East. Since 1969, it had experienced misrule by the late dictator, Barre. As resources dwindled, various elite factions struggled to control meager resources such as foreign aid. Barre, whose army had killed former President Abdirashid Ali Sharmarke in the coup d'état of October 1969, ruled with an iron fist, rewarding his friends and relatives with state funds and resources and denying any dissenting voices access to the meager resources. Under Barre, Somalia lost the Ogaden War against Ethiopia in 1977 to 1978. In the 1980s Somalia, like the rest of sub-Saharan Africa, experienced deteriorating economic conditions, and by the end of the decade, clan-based militiamen organized to control whatever resources they could amass from the collapsing Barre regime.

It was clanship rather than tribalism that shaped the wars in Somalia.[11] A few clans benefited while other clans complained. Among these clans, the Issaq, Majeerteen, and Hawiye, (Abgal and Murasade subclans) backed the various "warlords" at different times and for entirely selfish reasons. For example, the Abgal clan backed United Somali Congress (USC) of Mohammed Kanyare Afrah—part of Ali Mahdi Mohammed's faction. The most visible warlord was General Mohamed Farah Aideed, leader of the Somali National Alliance (SNA), who gave the international community the greatest challenge in his attempt to end the escalating war.

The international community found itself involved in the war in Somalia when signals were received that the famine was devastating hundreds of children, men, and women and that Somali warlords were preventing relief agencies from delivering food and medicine to the victims. Operation Restore Hope was a purely humanitarian initiative led by a U.S.-backed international force. Its mandate was to provide security to relief agencies as they delivered resources to starving and dying Somali citizens.

Bush, acting on the advice of his ambassador to Kenya, decided to militarily intervene to ensure that the warring parties in Somalia did not continue looting food meant for the starving Somalians.[12] More than three hundred and fifty thousand people had been killed by war and famine. Bush ordered U.S. troops into Somalia beginning December 9, 1992. Initially, the U.S. force was to assist in peacekeeping efforts and airlift food to the victims—to restore hope. On May 1, 1992, the U.S.-led Unified Task Force (UNITAF) handed over its job to a UN team, the UN Operation for Somalia (UNOSOM II), whose broad mandate was to "create a secure environment for the delivery of humanitarian relief"[13] and to disarm the warring factions with the objective of strengthening civil structures and promoting efforts for reconstruction.

Initially, the airlift of famine relief food in 1992 was quite successful. Kenneth Allard, in *Somalia Operations: Lessons Learned*,[14] argued that problems arose when U.S. Marines began to pursue warlord Mohamed Farah Aideed on October 3, 1993, at the instigation of some Bush administration officials.[15] The Aideed forces killed eighteen Americans and wounded seventy-eight. Many Somali citizens and residents were killed as well.

Allard attributed the failures of Operation Restore Hope in Somalia to a lack of clear U.S. objectives.[16] Clark, on the other hand, saw weak congressional oversight as a major factor in the Somalia debacle.[17] In the end, the UN troops lost 121 lives and the U.S. troops lost 36 lives at the time of UN withdrawal from Somalia in March 1995. Clinton, upon assuming the U.S. presidency, ordered a quick pullout by U.S. troops from Somalia. This was done by March 1994. A few American soldiers had been captured by Aideed's men and were dragged through Mogadishu streets, a spectacle shown on Western media. Americans quickly abandoned the idea of giving hope to Somalia. It would appear that Bush started a fire that he never put out; he never had the chance to put it out. Bush could not use the strategy of massive force to overpower the Aideed faction.

The Somalia debacle was an anticlimax to the Bush administration's foreign policy successes. The U.S. role as a global policeman was questioned by Somalia warlords whose continued mischief denied thousands of people their food supplies. Even though the United States operated within the framework of the UN in its intervention in Somalia, its fifteen months in the hot desert was basically an acknowledgement of the geopolitical importance of the Somali-Horn of Africa region. The event was not reminiscing the cold war strategy of aiding friendly states.[18] The issue was more about Somalia being strategically placed. In the cold war era, control over Somalia meant "control of access ports, airfields, and access to Cape Route."[19] The Bush administration could not ignore the Somalia war and, as in the rest of Africa, "it kept its options open in its dealings."[20] The U.S. leadership was not impressed by the aftermath of the Somalia war. Even the UN was dismayed at its failure to restore peace and security in Somalia. The UN pulled out without achieving its core objectives. For the United States, the lives lost in Somalia led to increased interest within Congress on the U.S. role in peacekeeping missions. The Republican hawks were furious over the lack of clear policy guidelines of the U.S. presidency on its commitment of troops to UN peacekeeping operations. The Somalia lesson was a bitter pill that Bush swallowed, but it had no direct bearing on his rating. The Somalia saga was a wasted project in the sense that the U.S. role turned out to have been symbolically misconstrued.[21] Aideed and his cohorts saw the Bush plan in the Horn of Africa as imperialist.

On the official level, aid to Somalia was humanitarian. African heads of state acknowledged this gesture as such. When Sam Nujoma, president of Namibia, visited the White House at the invitation of President Clinton in June 1993, his succinct statement was representative. In his address, he noted,

> I'm grateful that your government and your people have decided when the people of Somalia were faced with the tragedy of starvation and death, it was during the Bush administration when President Bush decided to send U.S. troops before UN troops went to put an end to the civil war and the starvation of the people of Somalia."[22]

In American politics, the role of interest groups provides explanations for the other side of the coin. The decision by Bush to send troops was essentially a by-product of "the business as usual" lobbyists of corporate America—in this case, the petroleum giants.[23]

"The oil factor in Somalia" was an argument well articulated by a *Los Angeles Times* journalist, Mark Fineman.[24] Evidently, four American petroleum giants—Conoco, Phillips, Amoco, and Chevron—supported the move to station U.S. troops in Somalia. Before Barre was overthrown and the nation disintegrated into civil strife in January 1991, these companies struck deals with the Somali government to explore and drill oil and natural gas resources in nearly two-thirds of the country. The companies had already invested billions of dollars in the desert region by the time the clan wars began. President Bush was moved to act in the way he did by the oil interests—to secure their safety while promoting national security aspirations.

The same oil corporations had done their groundwork on the congressional level and the Bush initiative of sending in troops was not resisted at all. That the twenty thousand American troops were not detailed to ensure that relief supplies reached the poor was further evidenced in the fact that Conoco temporarily housed the U.S Embassy staff in the wake of continued insecurity. According to the *Los Angeles Times*, the oil interests wanted to ensure that the deals made by Barre were guaranteed when peace returned. The newspaper quoted a petroleum engineer with the World Bank confirming the existence of rich supplies of oil in Somalia.[25] This claim was verified by independent geological surveys conducted offshore by Marathon Oil Group of London and the Texas-based Hunt Oil Company.[26] In 1986 Vice President Bush officially dedicated Hunt's refinery near the Yemeni town of Marib when he was informed of the existence of oil reserves in the same area. An underground rift, or valley with huge oil reserves, juts into Northern Somalia. Thus, there is a powerful argument to explain that corporate power with its allies in Congress found a supportive presidency able to articulate a humanitarian policy while protecting economic interests. The Bush policy was not a zero-sum affair but a complex set of calculations.

NEO-ISOLATIONISM AS ANOTHER POLICY ORIENTATION

The Bush administration showed a tendency for embracing neo-isolationism as its other policy orientation toward Africa. Moving away from cold war dynamics, the Bush administration sustained the realist posture of past foreign policy by responding to African economic issues only when the results offered huge payoffs. Nonpolitical American interests outside the humanitarian encounters in Africa are rather limited. Only Nigeria and South Africa have economies in which American businesses hold significant stakes. During the Bush era, African states generally experienced a decline in real growth to the extent that they were dismissed as fragile or suffocating economies not worth of serious investments. Sub-Saharan Africa was politically unstable. Because the 1980s and early 1990s were periods of poor performance, financial aid was the chosen path for recovery. The Bush administration's support averaged $2.7 billion per year. This figure is quite minimal compared to the aid given to Asia, Eastern Europe, or Israel.[27] With this kind of performance, U.S. authorities did not see much contribution from Africa to the expanding markets, and consequently, U.S. engagement was marginal.

To a lesser extent, the support Asia, eastern Europe, or Israel receives from the United States is a result of intense lobbying by ethnic interest groups in foreign policymaking. No one doubts the overriding influence of the American Israeli Public Affairs Committee (AIPAC) in winning resources for Israel. It has successfully managed to petition the American power structures, as well as the public, to treat Israel favorably. AIPAC has been able to develop skills that have enabled it to sway public opinion to its side. Yossi Shain, quoting Nathan Glazer and Daniel Moynihan, posited that as early as 1975, ethnic influences became the most important determinant of American foreign policy.[28] The Diaspora, a people with common national origins who reside outside of their original land, had considerable leverage to influence financial aid to Israel.

In a similar vein, Youngnok Koo wrote that there were about three hundred registered East Asian lobbies in Washington, DC, representing the interests of Japan, South Korea, and Taiwan. Japan spent about $50 million a year to maintain a Washington presence, including embassy staffers for business concerns alone.[29] Several Japanese firms hired expatriate lobbyists to make their case to government agencies.

Among the important ethnic lobby groups with a voice in foreign policymaking are the Cuban American National Foundation, the Greek Americans Hellenic Institute of Public Affairs Committee, and a number of informal groups representing the Czech Republic, other former Soviet Union bloc countries, and Ukraine. Political science professor Uslaner argued that in recent years, decision making on foreign policy resembles the discord typical of domestic policy making.[30] With regard to Africa, Representative George W. Crocket Jr. observed, "I wish blacks were organized like that" (AIPAC).[31] The African American lobby groups such as Transafrica and the Congressional Black Caucus have been less influential.

However, some success was achieved in the release of Mandela in the sense that his release was attributed to the Comprehensive Anti-Apartheid Act, enforced vigilantly by the Bush administration. Milton D. Morris, vice president of research at the Joint Center for Political and Economic Studies in Washington, DC, in an essay on "African Americans and the New World Order," reiterated the crucial role played by African Americans in eliminating apartheid from the South African constitution.[32] Morris drew out the similarity between the civil rights movement and the struggle by Africans and other people fighting for freedom from dictatorships. He observed,

> It is particularly noteworthy that, as this powerful freedom movement spread across Eastern Europe, Asia, and Africa, it was accompanied by the strains of Black America's great anthem of freedom, "We Shall Overcome," testifying to the connection with and inspiration from the civil rights movement in America.[33]

Africa was seen as having a smaller population and a smaller income base with which to attract significant American investments. Africa lacked the relevant infrastructure, savings environment, and other ingredients necessary for greater involvement compared to Japan, NAFTA, ASEAN, or the EU. Africa was not attractive to the powerful concerns in the world's premier capitalist polity.

Most scholars and observers of African international relations can also deduce the ensuing marginalization of Africa in terms of three other variables. First, America during the Bush era was growing increasingly conservative. Bush had been elected on the hope that he would continue the conservative agenda of the Reagan years. Conservatism for foreign policy meant cutting back the government or, for some, reinventing it. This entailed reducing foreign aid to Africa and other "marginal" areas.

Second, the domestic conditions in the immediate post–Reagan era were depressing to the ordinary citizen. The gaps between the rich and the poor were widening, and American youth were increasingly less optimistic about their future as costs of living surpassed their means.

Third, it was necessary for Bush to deal with the wider question of charting the course for post–cold war capitalism. For fifty years, Africa was a playground in the war against "the evil empire" but harvested nothing from the spoils. Africa witnessed the sustenance of dictatorships in the name of containment. Surely, this was not a Bush policy. How was Bush to undo this imbroglio short of unleashing a new wave of chaos?

Bush's policy in this direction was two sided, as it included applying bilateral and multilateral efforts to reorder the very essence of African government and statehood. In tandem with this policy was the use of psychological means to preach to African governments the need to stop their trademarks of corruption, ethnic conflicts, and environmental degradation. African nations were to embrace accountability and democracy as the new virtues if they desired foreign relations with the United States.

Of the different U.S. involvement strategies on the continent, the one that strikes most as a legacy of the Bush administration is the democratization process. Stated differently, the Bush administration was the first one in Africa's independent history to put an end to the notorious use of the cold war card by African dictators. This card alone was inevitably translated into U.S. support, and the dictatorships once more were rejuvenated; the United States, on several occasions, saved the late Congo strongman, Mobutu Sese Seko, even when the Bush administration knew that he represented forces of oppression.[34] Mobutu, a dictator since 1965, established one-man rule without any checks and balances. Mobutu had enormous "power to deploy troops, stop traffic—trap the people's leaders in a hopelessly corrupt negotiation scheme"[35] and aimed at "blood, blood and blood again."[36] The United States also backed the illegitimate regime of Barre in Somalia. Barre had initially been a darling of the Soviet Union but switched gears to embrace U.S. politicians when the Soviets backed the Marxist-Leninist Ethiopian leader, Mengistu Haile Mariam, during the 1977–1978 war over Ogaden territory between Ethiopia and Somalia.

OF DEMOCRACY: "WE KNOW WHAT WORKS, FREEDOM WORKS. WE KNOW WHAT'S RIGHT: FREEDOM IS RIGHT" (BUSH)

The Bush era was an exciting time for Africans who yearned for the second liberation. Historically, America had supported Africa's struggle for independence. Unfortunately for Africa, this was in the wake of cold war hostilities. Realism in U.S. foreign policymaking often made it difficult for America to back the struggle for democracy. The Bush administration had no cold war to fight. It gave this liberation battle a chance on the African continent. What, then, was this democratization process about in the Bush era?

During his inaugural speech, President Bush was unmistakably clear about his commitment to the democratization of the world. He declared that the "totalitarian era is passing…Great nations of the world are moving toward democracy—through the door of freedom."[37] He asserted that

> I come before you and assume the presidency at the moment rich with promise. We live in a peaceful time, but we can make it better…For a new breeze is blowing; and a world refreshed by freedom seems reborn; for in man's heart, if not in fact, the day of the dictator is over. The totalitarian era, its old ideas blown away like leaves from an ancient lifeless tree.[38]

At the heart of U.S. policy in Africa was the belief that Africans must liberate themselves from authoritarianism and embrace democracy, that is, liberal democratic values, if they wanted to remain a customer of U.S. aid and friendship. The Bush administration's assistant secretary of state for African affairs, Herman J. Cohen, set the record straight by appreciating the efforts that Africans were making toward eliminating dictatorships.[39] His message reiterated the administration's rededication to Africa's search for development but insisted that the Republicans would only assist regimes that practiced democracy. Countries that denied their citizens the rights to associate, to speak out, and to free press would not fit into the Bush vision.

The U.S. administration rejected the position taken by many African leaders against multiparty systems, arguing that "the U.S. believes that multi-party democracy has proven to be the most resilient and productive form of democratic pluralism."[40] The one-party state that characterized most of Africa was basically anachronistic. The Bush administration had promised to remain "engaged in Africa's progress toward democracy and not to abandon Africa when democracy was achieved."[41] This promise put the United States on a war path with several of its former client and pseudoclient states.

The first casualty was Francophone Africa's Brigadier General Mathieu Kérékou, who had ruled Benin for over eighteen years. He was defeated in elections by a former World Bank official, Nicéphore Soglo. The democratic hurricane of change wiped out old governments in Cape Verde, and São Tomé and Principe, after multiparty elections during early 1991. In Mali, General Traore lost office after twenty-four years. In Togo, even though strongman Eyadema retained power, he was forced to accept political reforms. In Gabon and Cameroon, the incumbent dictators made several concessions. The same applied to the Ivory Coast, which, since its independence, was under the personal rule of the late President Félix Houphouët-Boigny. He was challenged by an aspirant but won the ensuing election. The point is that he was challenged for the first time in a decade. Omar Bongo of Gabon also had to endure strong competition from prodemocratic elements in the fall of 1990. The democratization epidemic became too strong for other countries in Africa and resulted in civil strife as the cases of Somalia and Liberia demonstrated. The democratic forces in these two countries resorted to violence. Samuel Doe was eventually killed as Barre was expelled from Somalia. What Africans were saying was that despots must go. Africans wanted a voice in their governance, and Bush's government provided the environment for this wind of change to sweep across the continent.

A classical example of the implementation of this Bush diplomatic whirl was the case of Kenya. Ambassador Hempstone served in Kenya for thirty-six months and wrote his memoir, *Rogue Ambassador*, where he recorded his battles with Kenyan authorities in his efforts to implement President Bush's policies.[42] He argued that he was not always supported by the state department, but he was still seen as one of the key figures behind the implementation of political reforms in Kenya that culminated in the return to multiparty politics.[43] Hempstone questioned the murder of a prominent Kenyan politician, a foreign minister whose last mission, ironically, was a visit to Washington, DC and the arrest of opposition leaders Kenneth Matiba and Charles Rubia, who had opposed the regime of President Moi and protested the government's pursuit for the human rights lawyer, Gibson Kamau Kuria. Hempstone's style of diplomacy was a little bit too frank for the Kenyan strongman Moi. For example, Ambassador Hempstone observed the following:

> I told Moi and Kiplagat (the country's Permanent Secretary to the Ministry of Foreign Affairs during Smith Hempstone's tenure) that there is change coming. It is happening all over the world and the question is not whether change is going to come or not; the question is whether you are going to come or not.[44]

The bottom line is that Hempstone was relaying the basic foreign policy gospel according to Bush.

Hempstone's speech before the House Committee on International Relations, after his tour of duty, summarizes this eventuality. The speech read, in part,

> President Bush and Secretary of State James Baker had, on several occasions in 1989, made it clear publicly that the U.S. would reserve its strongest political support and most of its foreign economic assistance for those African nations that stood

up for human rights, lived by the rule of law and supported the expansion of democracy.[45]

Hempstone continued,

> The scales had begun to fall from my eyes within my first visit, three months in Kenya. When I conducted a review of the 1988 Kenyan presidential elections, I found they had been conducted with a degree of chicanery, blatant even by African standards. Obvious winners had been declared losers—the balloting was not secret and candidates clearly enjoying only minimal support had been certified as victors.[46]

With regard to the first multiparty elections in Kenya since 1966, Hempstone added that Moi and KANU used every trick in the book—and some not there—to skew the vote in their favor. At least 1 million young Kenyans and possibly many more—out of an electorate of about 10 million—were prevented from going to the polls because the government said there were no cards to register them. Police, soldiers, teachers, health workers, and other civil servants were warned to vote for Moi and KANU or lose their jobs. Dissident politicians found their in-country travel curtailed and were denied access to state-owned television and radio stations. The three major opposition parties were denied permits to hold rallies and were prevented from opening branch offices. Opposition parliamentary candidates were abducted or beaten to prevent them from filing their papers. Independent journalists were harassed. More than one thousand opposition tribesmen lost their lives when two hundred and fifty thousand of them were forced out of their homes in western Kenya—where their votes might have made a difference—back to their tribal homelands. The printing presses worked overtime—the money supply increased by more than a third within a few weeks—to fund KANU candidates who already had the active support of the police and the provincial administration.[47]

The scenario that the former ambassador described is what the Bush administration set out to undo. Indeed, Hempstone acknowledged that it was desirable to do so. Hempstone also noted that in the spring of 1990,

President Bush and Secretary of State Baker had made it clear that it was policy to work for the promotion of democracy in Africa, including multiparty rule in authoritarian states.[48]

When Moi and other African strongmen retained their offices, even after creating little space for the opposition in an unprecedented fashion, it was with a sense of regret that his envoy bemoaned the Clinton victory over Bush in 1992. It is widely believed in Africa that had Bush been re-elected, the "democratization projects" would have been successful. In the words of Hempstone,

> President Bush had been defeated for re-election eight weeks before Kenyans went to the polls. My personal sadness at his failure to win a deserved second term, which meant my leaving my job in Kenya half-done, was somewhat lessened by the not unreasonable assumption that a Democratic president would, if anything, take a harder line on African policy.[49]

In the case of the Democratic Republic of Congo (DRC), formerly Zaire, the personal rule of Mobutu had, for the first time since 1965, received disapproval from the United States in 1990. Mobutu had consolidated his rule using some of the worst methods of authoritarianism in human experience to retain power. Due to cold war dynamics, Mobutu received tremendous amounts of creditor patience and support despite his dictatorial and human rights abuses. Mobutu's government received support from Western lending institutions, such as the IMF, without regard to what the money did for the ordinary Congolese masses. What Mobutu did was use these and other resources from the state to reward his cronies. Most of his clients had no managerial expertise, with the result being economic disaster.

By 1990 Mobutu's privatization of state resources proved unpalatable even to the IMF. Coupled with pressure for economic and political reform from the U.S. ambassador to the Democratic Republic of Congo, Melissa Wells, one-man rule was, no doubt, on its last leg. It was no longer in the interest of the United States to keep this near-bankrupt government afloat. Consequently, U.S. undersecretary of state for Africa,

Herman Cohen, told Congress in 1991 that it was time to usher in democracy for Congo. The break with the United States in 1991 was exacerbated by the fact that America was no longer interested in backing Savimbi's rebel UNITA in Angola aligned with Mobutu and the South African racist regime that was on its way out. During the cold war, Savimbi was on the CIA payroll.[50] Under the Bush administration, he was no longer an ally.

The withdrawal of American support boosted the morale of the widespread insurgency building to the east of Congo and in the capital city of Kinshasa. Savimbi budged and allowed a conference to be held in August 1991 under Catholic Archbishop Laurent Monsengwo Pasinya where a council was established to organize for the handing over of power from Mobutu to his rival, Étienne Tshisekedi wa Mulumba, a native of mineral-rich eastern Kasai. Mobutu withered the opposition challenge by buying off his rivals and using the divide-and-rule strategy, combined with instigating tribal clashes. Savimbi organized attacks against Congolese Tutsi living around North Kivu (Banyamulenge) and, with crony Kyungu wa Kumwanza, governor in the copper-rich Shaba province, attacked immigrants from Tshisekedi's Luba-Kasai region.

While Savimbi prevented Tshisekedi from taking full charge, he miscalculated the resolve of the armed Alliance des Forces Democratique pour la Liberation (AFDL) led by Laurent Désiré Kabila. It is this movement that eventually pushed Savimbi out of Kinshasa in May 1997, forcing him into exile in Morocco. Although Mobutu survived the official opposition challenge to him, there is no doubt that the role played by the Bush administration was a catalyst in his eventual ouster.

Those writing African history will remember the Bush bureaucrats as apostles of democracy and will possibly draw parallels with President J. F. Kennedy's moral support during the decolonization effort in the early 1960s.

NOTES

* Warren Christopher, address to African-American Institute Conference (Reston, VA: U.S. Department of State, May 21, 1993).
1. *Africa Report* 25, no. 3 (May/June 1980): 39–41.
2. *Africa Report* 28, no. 1 (January/February 1983): 40.
3. Mitchell Locin, "Clinton Calls Bush Unprincipled, Dictator Friendly," *Chicago Tribune*, October 2, 1992, C4.
4. Naomi Chazan et al. *Politics and Society in Contemporary Africa* (Boulder, CO: Lynne Rienner, 1992), 409.
5. Ibid.
6. Roger Morris, *Uncertain Greatness: Henry Kissinger and American Foreign Policy* (New York: Harper and Row, 1977), 131–132.
7. Lucius J. Baker, "Limits of Political Strategy: A Systematic view of the African American Experience," *American Political Science Review* 88, no. 1 (March 1994): 6.
8. Committee on Ways and Means, U.S. House of Representatives Overview and Compilation of U.S. Trade Statutes, January 6, 1987, Chairman Joseph K. Dowley, 100th Congress, Session, Washington, DC, 555.
9. Chazan, et al. *Politics and Society in Contemporary Africa*, 439.
10. Larry Berman and Bruce Jentleson, "Bush and the Post-Cold War World: New Challenges for American Leadership," in *The Bush Presidency: First Appraisals*, ed. Colin Campbell and Bert Rockman (Chatham, NJ: Chatham, 1991), 105.
11. Abdi Ismail Samatar, unpublished seminar paper, undated.
12. Jeffrey Clark, "Debacle in Somalia," *Foreign Affairs* 72, no. 1 (1993): 19.
13. *African Association of Political Science (AAPS) Newsletter* (June 1993), 14, and Hugh Neville in *Daily Nation*, June 20, 1995, 11.
14. Kenneth Allard, *Somalia Operations: Lesson Learned, National Defense* (Washington, DC: National Defense University Press, 1995), cited in *Daily Nation*, April 24, 1995, 8.
15. Ibid.
16. Ibid.
17. Clark, "Debacle in Somalia," 10.
18. Richard M. Nixon, *U.S. Foreign Policy for the 1970s: Building for Peace, A Report to the Congress* (Washington, DC, February 25, 1971), 11.
19. Geoffrey Kemp, "U.S. Strategic Interests and Military Options in Sub-Saharan Africa," in *Africa and the U.S., Vital Interest*, ed. Jennifer Seymour Whitaker (New York: New York University Press, 1978), 123.

20. Claude Ake, "Rethinking African Democracy" in *Africa and the U.S., Vital Interest*, ed. Larry Diamond and Marc F. Plattner, *The Global Resurgence of Democracy* (Baltimore: John Hopkins, 1993), 81.
21. Carol Bell, *The Reagan Paradox: U.S. Foreign Policy in the 1980s* (New Brunswick, NJ: Rutgers University Press, 1989), 157.
22. Federal News Service (Nexis Wire), June 16, 1993.
23. *Los Angeles Times* (Nexis Wire), January 18, 1993.
24. Ibid.
25. Thomas E. O'Connor of the World Bank headed a three-year study of oil prospects in the Gulf of Aden off Somalia's coast in 1991. See *Los Angeles Times*, January 18, 1993, and Global Research, "America's Interests in Somalia: Four Major U.S. Oil Companies Are Sitting on a Prospective Fortune in Exclusive Concessions," Center for Research on Globalization, January 3, 2007, available at http://www.globalresearch.ca
26. *Los Angeles Times* (Nexis Wire), January 18, 1993.
27. U.S. Department of State Dispatch, 7, no. 33 (August 12, 1996): 415.
28. Yossi Shain, "Ethnic Diaspora and U.S. Foreign Policies," *Political Science Quarterly* 109 (winter 1994–1995): 811–841.
29. Youngnok Koo, "East Asian Lobbies in Washington: Comparative Strategies," Occasional Paper, Asia Program, Prepared for a colloquium at the Wilson Center, Washington, DC, May 14, 1985, 45.
30. Eric M. Uslaner, "All Politics Are Global: Interest Groups and the Making of Foreign Policy," in *Interest Group Politics*, ed. A. Cigler and B. A. Loomis (Washington, DC: Congressional Quarterly, 1995), 369.
31. Robert Pear and Richard Berke, "Pro-Israel Group Exerts Quiet Might as It Rallies Supporters in Congress," *New York Times*, July 1987, A8.
32. Milton Morris, "African Americans and the New World Order," *The Washington Quarterly* 15, no. 4 (autumn 1992): 52.
33. Ibid.
34. M. G. Schatzberg, "Military Intervention and the Myth of Collective Security: The Case of Zaire," *The Journal of Modern African Studies* 27, no. 2 (1989): 316.
35. *African Association of Political Science Newsletter*, new series, no. 4 (September 1991), 3.
36. Ibid., 4.
37. George H. Bush, presidential inaugural speech, press release, USIS, American Centre, Gemini Circle, Madras, India, (official text) GS 506:1/20/89 and GS 507:1/20/89.
38. Ibid., GS 506:1/20/89.

39. *African Association of Political Science Newsletter*, new series, no. 4 (September, 1991) op. cit., 1.
40. Ibid.
41. Ibid.
42. *Daily Nation*, June 30, 1995, 1, and Smith Hempstone, *Rogue Ambassador* (Sewanee, TN: University of the South Press, 1997).
43. *Daily Nation*, June 30, 1995, 1.
44. Pius Nyamora, *Daily Nation*, July 1, 1995, 22. Also see Claude Ake, "Rethinking African Democracy," in *The Global Resurgence of Democracy*, ed. Larry Diamond and Marc F. Plattner (Baltimore: John Hopkins University Press, 1993), 77.
45. Smith Hempstone, Federal News Service, September 26, 1996.
46. Ibid.
47. Smith Hempstone, letter to Eric Otenyo and telephone interviews, November 2004.
48. Smith Hempstone, Federal News Service, September 26, 1996.
49. Ibid.
50. Ken Fireman, *Miami Herald*, January 31, 1986, 1.

CHAPTER 7

A NEW WORLD ORDER?

Sounds like an old book with a new cover.
—Jesse Jackson*

This chapter is about overarching changes in world politics and the international order. Every student of foreign policy knows that prior to 1989, the dominant feature in international politics was the rivalry between the Soviet Union and the United States. For decades, global capitalism competed against global socialism. The world was divided between the poor south and rich north. While the United States continued to serve as a model for worldwide democratic governance, vast areas knew no human rights and no basic freedoms. Though observers have counseled that exporting democracy was not necessarily tenable in some cultures, the core values of respect for human dignity and rights to self-governance were universal principles. The idea that a new world order was possible gained currency in the wake of President Bush's presidential election. Bush was the first president in a world without cold war rivalries. His election coincided with a significant revolution in globalization and world politics. President Bush advocated changes in global trade, governance, and peace, as well as security. If there was anything like a new world order, Bush had a lot to do with it. This chapter explores the various interpretations of the doctrine of the new world order, particularly President Bush's leadership in articulating its vision and scope.

Bush spoke about the new world order on many occasions during his presidency, and there can be no comprehensive Bush Doctrine without a new world order component. A new world order means different things to different people. It might mean a transformation of the old order into a new state, it may connote new ways of life, or it may simply be an empty slogan. It implies a world devoid of the Eastern-Western divide, a world with U.S. leadership in place, and a world in which liberalism in the marketplace and democracy are encouraged to flourish. It is a world in which the efficacy of the state is tested by nationalist pressures globally.

A new world order has peculiar characteristics. An obvious distinction requires that some treatment be accorded to the international system minus cold war rivalries. This would entail the United States putting in place a mechanism to breakdown the nonalignment movement. This clearly was not the world order Bush envisioned.

A new world order of the type articulated by Bush pursued two broader foreign policy objectives. Besides creating markets and enhancing market interdependency, a new world order should consciously attempt to reduce the growing gaps in the world's major regions. Needless to say, there was clearly a problem of world poverty, dependency, and underdevelopment. There may not have been meaning to a new world order without the elimination of nomenclatures such as the third and fourth world. The second objective hinges upon the realization of a stable and peaceful democratic world. In this objective, the new system would theoretically be devoid of authoritarian regimes and would enhance global peace through guaranteeing good governance among world societies.

The largest volume of literature on this vision stems from the emergence of an international system devoid of the old U.S.-USSR rivalries. The realignment of global politics witnessed the demise of the bipolar system and acclimation of the West's political superiority over the Leninist dogma. The Soviet Union was wounded and broken by its subnationalistic and ethnic contradictions and lost the ideological campaign to spread communism around the world. The end of the Soviet empire meant only Ukraine and Russia had the military and economic might that could be felt outside the Soviet Union. Stated differently, the two retained some potential to affect the balance of power politics in Eastern Europe. This meant only the United States could flex its muscles without any serious challenges. Jowitt acknowledged that "thermonuclear Russia still exists—but the imperial construct called the Soviet bloc is gone."[1]

AMERICA INSPIRING THE WORLD

Former British Prime Minister Thatcher thought that the unfolding scenario was "awesome" in providing opportunities for the United States to accept the burden of world leadership.[2] She observed that the West was poised to become the major player in the international field of power politics. She admitted she was an "undiluted admirer of American values and the American dream" and believed the United States would "inspire not just the American people, but millions of people across the face of the globe."[3]

If the new world order had to do with Americans inspiring the world, the American president took responsibility. The changes occurred under President Bush's watch. Bush was to provide global leadership to establish new rules of international politics. In the Gulf War of 1991, Bush argued that it was fought in the spirit of establishing a new world order. It was a war about "more than one small country, it is a big idea, a New World Order with new ways of working with other nations, peaceful settlement of disputes, solidarity against aggression, reduced and controlled arsenals, and just treatment of all people."[4]

Even if one visualized the new world order as a common American phrase like "Pax Americana" or "American hegemony," the Bush initiative was a demonstration of the United States' ability to marshal a collective security system and stop aggression by a rogue nation. Bush was implementing a version of Wilson's idealism to make the world a safer place for democracy. He did so partly because he enjoyed personal rapport with several world leaders, thanks to his long experience in the diplomatic world, as well as in the CIA. There have not been many U.S. presidents with a similar track record. America's leadership under Bush could only last if the new world order was about using military might to act as a global police force. Bush was conjuring a new world order by his actions against Iraq. He believed the American people were not against this scheme, and he saw his high approval ratings after the war as political capital. He was confident enough to ignore any criticisms of American projection of power in weaker nations. Bush remarked that there was no antiwar movement in America and that "there were only a couple of voices, but we do not hear them."[5] Bush exhibited so much confidence that commentators began noting examples of courageous leadership. Here was a president who was ready to assume world leadership, even if it meant use of force. In the new world order, war would be unleashed on all nations opposing American domination. Hussein was the first victim. He tried to defy UN Security Council Resolution 678, which required he vacate Kuwait. Walt Shepperd saw the Bush agenda as a mere plot of making "the world safe for McDonald's franchises and guaranteeing tranquility until at least a billion burgers are sold."[6] All of the Bush rhetoric of "lodging his bet with a UN shroud" to attack Iraq was in the name of business as usual. However, Bush's new world order meant more than business as usual. It was a part of an imperialist instinct to use military might for investments. Bush's policy was evident in his early well-publicized remarks on markets and freedom: "We know how to secure a more just and prosperous life for man on earth through free markets, free speech, free elections, and the exercise of free will unhampered by the state."[7]

CRITICISMS OF THE NEW WORLD ORDER

After the situation in Iraq, some Brazilian newspapers sensationalized a story that Bush would attack Brazil. This followed reports in some U.S. media that Brazil abetted Iraqi crimes by assisting Hussein in the manufacture of the Scud-B missile. Some American circles believed the Brazilian government was sympathetic to Hussein. Administration officials were angered by the failure of Brazil to emulate its southern neighbor Argentina to send troops to support the U.S.-led allied forces. According to the Bush administration, Brazil's inaction was unacceptable since it was one of the major Ibero-American nations. It was noteworthy that tiny Honduras had sent a token force to back the United States. U.S. Ambassador to Brazil Richard Melton argued that if Brazil wanted to be treated as a member of the first world, it had to "assume the responsibilities of a first world nation—by, for example, supporting the U.S. in the Gulf."[8] Would this, then, imply that in the new world order, the United States would allow conformist regimes to be promoted into the ranks of the first world? Would the United States permit Carlos Menem's Argentina to join this old club while placing stumbling blocks on Fernando Collor de Mello's Brazil? Bush wrote to President Collor de Mello warning him that Brazil must not sit on the fence during the gulf crisis.[9] The warning opened a proverbial can of worms in Brazilian-U.S. relations. Many Brazilians saw Bush's new world order as a plot to extend genocide in the colored world. Skeptics thought that Bush's new world order was about racism. Coming under attack were the U.S. Agency for International Development (USAID) programs such as population control and programs in Brazil that were viewed as criminal. Arguments were presented to the effect that USAID sponsored illegal sterilization of about 7.5 million Brazilian women, many of whom were black.[10] Women never gave their consent or knew anything about this new world order plot or conspiracy. The U.S.-led environmentalism agenda for Brazil was criticized as part of the antipoor people nature of the emerging new world order. For Marxist critical thinkers, similar environmental triangulations were regarded in negative terms as a move by rich industrial nations to protect sources of mineral wealth. The environmental politics of the Amazon were seen in this context.[11]

While different interpretations of the unfolding international order abound, leftist scholars criticized the Bush Doctrine by arguing it was designed to establish America's new military-centered global order where market incomes and resources were shared through the use of political and military dominance. James Petras[12] saw the Gulf War as America's attempt to ascend to global supremacy and resubordinate Europe and Japan. Historically, the United States had assumed this role in 1945 at the end of World War II, but in the 1980s, a number of lesser powers had challenged U.S. economic prowess. Japan, in particular, made tremendous strides in global investments, surpassing the United States and sending signals that U.S. influence was on the decline. This possibility was evident in South America and Asia. Former President Reagan attempted to reverse this trend by using force to control Grenada, Nicaragua, and Panama. Bush was, perhaps, executing the Reagan plan in a most vicious form. Bush intended the United States to use force to gain markets and expand its productive capacity and rebuild itself economically.

The new world order was Bush's reaction to the deteriorating power of the United States. If the decline continued, the United States would be forced to make unpalatable internal structural reforms. An easy way out was to seize any external opportunity and make capital out of it. The gulf situation provided this opportunity. The world would be tricked by the United States' mass propaganda machinery into believing that Iraq was a dangerous country that must be tamed and that the United States was a champion for self-determination and global freedom. The Gulf War, according to this school of thought, was not about oil but about "creating the foundations for launching a new set of political, economic, and social relations to sustain the U.S. as the dominant power in the world."[13]

The war, Petras argued, was also a scheme for protecting client regimes "whose interests are linked to this U.S. global project."[14] After all, the Arab oil sheikhs and monarchies recycled their petrodollars in U.S. banks. In the final analysis, the new world order resembled the eighteenth century mercantilist world. The United States was using its military force to extract surplus value from satellite states and charging for its military service to states wishing to enjoy this protection. The Japanese and European oil merchants seemed to have fit this scheme in the aftermath of the Gulf War of 1991. In that context, the new world

A New World Order? 139

order would, therefore, entail use of military force to coerce possible challenges. Petras saw Bush as a product of extractive capital. Bush's world order, Petras predicted, would fail due to its ideological defects.

In retrospect, Bush saw the demise of communist Russia as a chance to start new alliances and to enhance so-called democratic institutions as a means of achieving justice for most of the world's people. In devastating Hussein's Iraq, Bush was implementing this new world order. Nye asserted that although there was a new world order, from a realistic point of view, it did not begin with the Bush-Hussein war. A new world order was not only an issue of balance of power among state actors but also incorporated the elevation of international institutions, such as the UN, into instruments of ensuring adherence to the rule of law, respecting international law, and upholding human rights among nation states. The new world order was not a recycled version of the traditional European concept of balance of power.

Bush wanted America to use its leverage and position as the only economic and military power to achieve the objective of restoring peace in key global spots. Clearly the rules of this scenario had to be solidified, and as some rules began to unfold, critics saw the world drifting toward anarchy. The world become less orderly, and many commentators believed the cold war may have been a more peaceful time.

The aforementioned comments were premised upon the occurrence of several remarkable events. First, several Central and Eastern European nation states disintegrated into chaotic war theaters. The rapid transformation of European boundaries in the new epoch was well exemplified by Yugoslavia. Warren Zimmerman, the last U.S. ambassador to Yugoslavia, suggested that the Bush administration, throughout the crisis period in Yugoslavia, desired unity and democracy for the area.[15] The core conflict in the Yugoslavian problem was between the Croats and the Serbs; it was ethnic at its core, and foreign intervention was unlikely to change decades of suspicions.

Historically, Yugoslavian republics were identified with distinct cultural and ethnic groupings held together by authoritarian political structures. The state had three tiers of political authorities with regional and local government jurisdictions sometimes exercising influence greater than those of the state in Belgrade. In the ensuing ethnic rivalries, Serbians wanted greater territorial and political control. The Serbians, about 40 percent of the population, had since the Tito days believed they received a raw deal from the federal government.

The conflicts and bloodletting began with Croats and Slovenes seceding in 1989 to 1991. Secretary of State Baker arrived in Belgrade in June 1991 to mediate the warring parties. Baker expressed President Bush's hope that Yugoslavia would hold together and remarked to Prime Minister Markovic that "if you force the U.S. to choose between unity and democracy, we will always choose democracy."[16] Perhaps Baker was underscoring the Bush vision of a democratic world as opposed to a consolidation of statehood in troubled lands. By the end of June 1991, hostilities between Slovenia and federal forces were causing grave concern. Croatia and Slovenia announced their independence. Serbs clashed with Croats, but the federal forces backed the Serbs and the war escalated. The Bush administration's preference for democracy had come under attack. Alexander M. Haig Jr., U.S. secretary of state under Reagan between 1981 and 1982, supreme allied commander of NATO from 1974 to 1979, and Nixon's former White House chief of staff from 1973 to 1974, criticized President Bush for not using the resources available to him to end the war in Yugoslavia.[17] According to Haig, after it had been realized that the Serbs in Belgrade, Bosnia, and Croatia were the aggressors, President Bush should have taken the lead to use a little force or threaten to use force under a NATO arrangement. This, he argued, may have set limits to the violence. Critics, thus, blame Bush for failing to lead the world to eradicate the Serbian threat. The Yugoslavian case is just one among many of the disorders of the new world.

Jowitt considered the border problems in the Soviet Union, including the case of Azerbaijan, Georgia, and Ukraine, as other areas of potential disorder in the emerging disorder.[18] Added to this list was the Central Asian Republic of Chechnya, which sought sovereignty from Moscow.

Former USSR President Gorbachev had also challenged the authority of those managing this new world order. According to Gorbachev, the

A New World Order?

world had continued to experience crisis after crisis, dashing the hopes of the international community in the unipolar system.[19] Gorbachev posed the question, "Why did the new world order that we envisioned dissolve so quickly and abjectly into the new world disorder?"[20] He offered some reasons as to why the Bush-Baker project collapsed in less than five years.

First, the West was not prepared for the disintegration of the Soviet Union's totalitarian regime. Subsequently, no mechanisms were developed to solve the ensuing problems. Moscow lacked a tradition of democracy and consultative diplomacy, and hence, it could not hold its rebellious states together.

Second, the West miscalculated its foreign policies by assuming that the world would be easily governable without the USSR-U.S. rivalry. As former leader of the Soviet Union, Mikhail Gorbachev stated, "It was an illusion, for now it is clear that America was never in a position to establish order and guarantee respect for human rights all over the planet."[21] Gorbachev argued that no Western powers could successfully ensure that role even if they coordinated international efforts. The old world order was, therefore, in a sense, more stable because the threat of communism provided a rallying point for the West. Gorbachev quoted American millionaire George Soros,

> If we were to be frank about it, we would have to admit that the Western democracies are going through a phrase of moral bankruptcy, that they no longer know what they are fighting for and which principles they are defending.[22]

Gorbachev's central thesis is that the present world disorder is a manifestation of the lack of shared concepts for behavior in a rapidly changing world.

The problems of sovereignty were not only confined to Central and Eastern Europe. Boundary transformations also took place in Africa. This transformation can be evidenced from the dissolution of Ethiopia by Eritrean secession and disintegration of Somalia into warlord-controlled enclaves. These changes came in contradiction to earlier resolutions to maintain colonially established boundaries. In 1963 African leaders had, through the Organization of African Unity, pledged to uphold all its boundaries established by the colonial powers in 1885. The breakaway of Eritrea was unprecedented and a cause of insecurity in the region. More importantly, ethnic nationalism in Africa had always been suppressed by an authoritarian one-party regime. With Bush proclaiming a new world order, democratic forces supported by U.S. foreign policy meant that the dictators would be challenged. Many of them did not accept the possibility of losing power, and instead, they sponsored ethnic clashes to maintain their power. In several cases, the ethnic clashes were followed by calls for regionalism and outright secession. Congo and Kenya fit this profile.

In the case of Asia, the death of North Korean strongman Kim Il Sung and the fear that his country was poised to join the nuclear-armed nations presented new challenges to security in the area. North Korea and Cuba remained doctrinaire communist states even though the Bush plan proclaimed the new world order as a triumph of liberal capitalism.

Was U.S. foreign policy capable of creating a true world order with communism still around? Skeptics argued that the spirit of the true world order had been defeated by the failures of Bush and his successor, President Clinton. Clinton was expected to articulate a vision of a post–cold war system. A Clinton critic thought in the 1992–1994 period that the new administration displayed no sense of urgency in checking the drift toward an international disorder.[23]

The greatest challenge to Bush's new world order was its unfortunate association with racism. In many circles, the new world order was tainted by racist fears. Mwangi Kagwanja, a researcher based in South Africa, argued that with the Bush plan, a new wave of racism and poverty began to affect mainly African, Asian, and South American countries.[24] This was the position taken by Abdul Alkalimat, professor of African American studies, who warned that the United States must not be allowed to lead the world but needed to be "defeated and transformed."[25] The position taken by Alkalimat was that in the unipolar world, it was necessary to understand the inner workings of the U.S. political system. The U.S.

system, he contended, was basically structured along racist lines, and it was this racist ideology that the new order espoused. The United States, it was argued, sought to incorporate China and Russia into its global scheme of liberal democracy. This scheme would eventually marginalize the poor Africans and other peasants in Asia and Latin America. The racist agenda in the new world order, according to Alkalimat, entailed launching a psychological war against African people to legitimize their underdevelopment. Such works as *The Bell Curve*, which concluded that blacks are inferior, were seen in that context.[26]

Additionally, African countries had been asked to restructure their economies to fit into the U.S. global scheme. Through the U.S.-led institutions such as the IMF and World Bank, African countries were required to encourage antiwelfare programs and support Western capitalist penetration programs. As Alkalimat noted, "The structural adjustment programs progressively pauperised African people including the vital middle class."[27] The net result of the U.S. penetration scheme was poverty. Alkalimat asserted, "There is no social order if more and more people are outside the social contract with no legitimate income and the society with no way to otherwise circulate goods and services to them."[28]

Alkalimat's contention that the Bush administration contributed to the upsurge in racism and negative economic growth in Africa was a flawed argument. The 1980s were considered lost decades for Africa and South America. Obviously, African poverty and racism had more to do with colonialism, and Bush was nowhere in this picture. The structural adjustment programs were necessary because several of the implementing countries had mismanaged their economies through tribalism and corruption.

AFRICAN AMERICANS RAISE QUESTIONS ABOUT THE NEW WORLD ORDER

On the U.S. home front, the new world order came under attack from a number of well-meaning African Americans. These included political activists Leonora Fulani, Jesse Jackson, and Reverend Al Sharpton, who thought that the United States should not really push for an ambiguous new world order when its backyard was problematic. Fulani and Sharpton declared a black world order to challenge the Bush plan. Fulani, the chairperson of the New Alliance Party (NAP), thought that the United States lacked real democracy, particularly for its African American and Latino peoples.[29] To Fulani, the new world order ought to require real democracy in the United States. Fulani argued that Bush intended to rule the world viciously and that in the case of the Gulf War, he was not really interested in protecting the people of Kuwait.[30] "It's bold to impose a New World Order on people who were never part of the old world order."[31]

The black world order, according to Sharpton, was essentially to combat racism. He was critical of the use of African Americans in disproportionate numbers in wars overseas, such as the Gulf War, when at home "in Harlem, New York, Detroit, Chicago, and Syracuse, they are not worth anything."[32] Jackson echoed these sentiments in a sermon entitled The Challenge of the True World Order.[33] Jackson once challenged Bush and ran for U.S. president in 1988. Jackson dismissed the Bush new world order rhetoric as an old book with a new cover. He preached, "If we can go to Vietnam and the Persian Gulf to free other peoples' communities, all these places around the world, we need to stand up and free our own communities."[34] Jackson denounced President Bush because Bush had called Los Angeles Police Chief Gates "America's Top Cop Hero" when he knew quite well that Gates' police force had beaten black motorist Rodney King in a racist attack. Jackson thought the new world order should begin at home. The administration, he felt, should have put more effort in providing jobs, security, and better health plans for minorities in addition to ridding the United States of racism, anti-Semitism, and other moral ills.

Milton D. Morris of the Joint Center for Political and Economic Studies in Washington, DC, in an essay on African Americans and the new world order, posited that while there was a definite new order, it was not as Bush envisioned.[35] He argued that the world order the president envisioned was a simpler one than what was transpiring. In Morris' opinion, black Americans were skeptical of the Gulf War for the simple reason that the domestic problems facing them were overwhelming. Their economic circumstances were worsening, and they were disproportionately represented in the armed forces. The use of force on people of color around the world as a foreign policy tool was in bad taste.

Morris argued further that African Americans input to foreign policymaking in the United States was minimal and none of their views were factored into the decision-making process. He called for reforms along the following lines: (a) to implement global policies that promise to improve U.S. competitiveness and expand domestic opportunities for all segments of society, (b) to broaden the U.S. foreign policy focus from a Eurocentric to a global one that more fully recognizes the third world, and (c) to strengthen the United Nations and other international institutions to manage conflicts and meet critical needs.[36] An important addition to what would be an acceptable new world order is one that tackled the poverty problems in Africa, the Caribbean Islands, and Haiti. This would be done through infusion of aid from the affluent nations to impoverished regions. The tendency of the United States to shift USAID funds to Eastern Europe rather than Africa was also questioned. A debt relief plan was essential for Africa's recovery. Without this, the new world order meant nothing to African Americans. In short, an overhaul was required in U.S. foreign policy.

BUCHANAN'S ATTACK

The new world order doctrine as first proclaimed in Bush's speech to the United Nations in 1991 was severely criticized by Pat Buchanan. Buchanan had sought and failed to earn a Republican Party nomination to run for president in 1996. His platform was, in part, premised on the doctrine of patriotism and America first. Buchanan believed that the path taken by President Bush to go to war in Iraq in 1991, as well as "compulsive internationalism" and free trade, were policies against America's greatest traditions. For Buchanan, the Republican Party's internationalism that Bush championed was a sure path to ruin much like the end of the British empire. He wrote in his criticism of the new world order,

> ...Republican internationalists were now joining with Wilsonian globalists to tie America down like Gulliver in some 'New World Order' where U.S. wealth and power would be put at the service of causes having nothing to do with the vital interests of the United States.[37]

Thus, the new world order continued to be without peace, as the proliferation of nuclear weapons was likely to increase. The chances of China, Germany, and Japan taking an increasingly important role in international affairs became real.[38] Bush's proclamation seemed to have been symptomatic of his great admiration of Nixon's foreign policy doctrine of retrenchment in world affairs, retention of existing treaty commitments, and provision of military support to American allies whenever threatened or attacked.[39] For the Bush administration, isolationism was not an option. After all, Bush was a part of the Nixon administration that had embraced a highly internationalist agenda. Much of the conduct of the Bush administration during the Gulf War can be seen in this light. The new world order retained these core values. As Nixon earlier remarked,

> This administration must lead the nation through a fundamental transition in foreign policy... We are at the end of an era. The postwar order of international relations—the configuration of power that emerged from the Second World War was gone. With it were gone the conditions which had determined the assumptions and practice of U.S. foreign policy since 1945.[40]

The bottom line was that Bush, like Nixon, served as U.S. president in a transitory era. However, Bush clearly saw his epoch as absolutely significant. He was to oversee the transition from the cold war to a new world order, and he set the agenda for new world balance of power configurations. Bush, like Nixon, wanted U.S. influence to be exerted as much as possible. He could not cede this influence but sought to build on it. While the new world order began to unfold, its future and shape was unknown. Bush was credited with signing the Strategic Arms Reduction Treaty (START) with Gorbachev in 1991, making a significant contribution to world peace and ending the cold war.[41] Bush was reputed to have cajoled Gorbachev into accepting Germany's recruitment to NATO. Bush also continued disarmament talks with Boris Yeltsin and, in the June 1992 talks, attained a win-win situation with Russia, thereby retaining America's leadership in key weapon systems capability.

Additionally, a weakened Russia in the new world order did not mean a power vacuum in Europe. America had to confront the challenge from "Project Europe."[42] The Maastricht Treaty, reducing the old French-German rivalries, sought to strengthen Europe's bargaining power in world politics. As Americans argued about returning to isolationist policies, Project Europe directly consolidated the old "spheres of influence" in Africa, Asia, and South America. However, this was within the framework of isolationism in the United States, thereby confirming the emergence of the disorder discussed by Gorbachev and others.[43]

In conclusion, although the debate on an emerging new world order is contentious, President Bush gave it a basis of comparison with past forms of political management.[44] The new world order may have been a myth, depending on one's analytical framework. For Africa, Bangladesh, India, and South America, problems of poverty remained intractable; no new world order existed for people struggling for basic needs. It was neither new nor an order; it was simply a changing world. Its main characteristic was the continuation of unbridled global capitalism and poverty. It was a world replaced by uncertainties. The groups of people who ruled the world in the old order continued to rule the world in the new world order. The disorders of capitalist markets and corruption marginalized the weaker actors even further. The triumph of new Wilsonianism, increased globalization, and trade were important attributes associated with the Bush administration's management of this transition.

Notes

* Jesse Jackson, sermon delivered to the Brooklyn AME Community Church, April 7, 1991.
1. Ken Jowitt, "The New World Disorder," in *The Global Resurgence of Democracy*, ed. Larry Diamond and Marc F. Plattner (Baltimore: John Hopkins University Press, 1993), 247.
2. J. McKenna, "Thatcher Calls on U.S. to Dominate World," *Herald Sun*, June 19, 1991, 61.
3. *The Times*, London, August 6, 1990, 8. Also see, Michael White, "Thatcher Among Friends in Chicago," *The Guardian*, June 17, 1991.
4. Joseph S. Nye Jr., "What New World Order?" *Foreign Affairs* 71, no. 2 (spring 1992), 83.
5. Walt Shepperd, "A Billion Burgers Sold, Bush's New World Order Means More Business as Usual," *Syracuse New Times*, April 3–10, 1991, 6.
6. Ibid.
7. George Bush, *New York Times*, January 21, 1989, 10.
8. Carlos Wesley, "Bush Threatens Brazil: 'You Are the Next Target,'" February 11, 1991, EIRNS, 1. An interesting dimension to this war is that in Kenya, for example, primary school children in an art exhibition portrayed Hussein as "the tough man of the Gulf." The children depicted him as a hero of the third world. David Aduda, "Pupils Depict Saddam as Hero at Exhibition," *Daily Nation*, June 23, 1995, 6.
9. Attributed to Manoel Francisco Brito of *Jornal do Brasil*, February 9, 1991, cited in Wesley, "Bush Threatens Brazil: 'You Are the Next Target.'"
10. Ibid.
11. Ibid.
12. James Petras, "Gulf War and the New World Order," *Economic and Political Weekly* 46, no. 9/10 (March 2–9, 1991): 482–484.
13. Ibid.
14. Ibid., 483.
15. Warren Zimmerman, "A Memoir of the Collapse of Yugoslavia," *Foreign Affairs* 74, no. 2 (March/April, 1995): 6.
16. Ibid., 12.
17. Alexander M. Haig Jr., "Bosnia: The Hard Options Left to End the Stalemate," *Daily Nation*, July 5, 1995, 6.
18. Jowitt, "The New World Disorder," 248.
19. Mikhail Gorbachev, "Bringing Order to the New World Disorder," *Indian Express Hyderabad*, September 7, 1995, 1.

20. Ibid.
21. Ibid.
22. Ibid.
23. William E. Odom, "How To Create a True World Order," *Orbits, A Journal of World Affairs* 39, no.2 (spring 1995): 155–156.
24. Peter M. Kgwanja, "How New World Order Has Bred Racism, Poverty," *Daily Nation*, March 20, 1995, 6. These views are also shared by Okello Oculi, who wrote "New International Aggression Order," African Association of Political Science, *AAPS, Newsletter*, September, 1992, 1.
25. Abdul Akalimat, "Antiracist Education and Political Process" (paper presented at the Pan-African Colloquium on Educational Innovations in Post-Colonial Africa, Cape Town, South Africa, December, 1994). Cited in *Daily Nation*, March 20, 1995, 6.
26. Ibid.
27. Ibid.
28. Ibid.
29. *The Black Voice*, Syracuse University, February 22–28, 1991, 23, no. 17, 1–7.
30. Ibid.
31. Ibid.
32. Ibid.
33. Jesse Jackson, sermon delivered to the Brooklyn AME Community Church, April 7, 1991. The church pastor was Rev. Dr. Larry T. Kirkland Sr.
34. Ibid. Also see Herb Boyd, "What To Do About America's Ghettoes? Debate Is Revived in Age of New World Order," *The New York Amsterdam News*, March 30, 1991, 5.
35. Milton D. Morris, "African Americans and the New World Order," *The Washington Quarterly* 15, no.4 (autumn 1992): 5–51.
36. Ibid.
37. In May 1995 Helmut Kohl, German chancellor, hinted to this at a campaign rally at Wuppertal Town during the North Rhine-Westphalia State Elections, *Daily Nation*, July 3, 1995, vi.
38. Patrick J. Buchanan, *A Republic, Not an Empire: Reclaiming America's Destiny* (Washington, DC: Regnery, 1999), 327.
39. Marian D. Irish, "The President's Foreign Policy Machine," in *The Future of the American Presidency*, ed. Charles W. Dunn (Morristown, NJ: General Learning Press, 1975), 146.
40. Richard Nixon, *U.S. Foreign Policy for the 1970s: Building for Peace, A Report to Congress*, Washington, DC (February 25, 1971), 3.
41. Walter Williams, "George Bush and Executive Branch Domestic Policy Making Competence," *Policy Studies Journal* 21, no. 4 (1993): 700–717.

42. Noel Malcolm, "Project Europe a Rival to U.S.?," *Foreign Affairs* 74, no. 2 (March/April 1995): 54.
43. Also see Earl W. Foell, "Making Sense of the World New World Order and Disorder," *World Monitor* (March 1991): 36. Foell noted that there is an escalation in terms of conflicts and war. There have been over one hundred and thirty wars—civil wars, rebellions, and invasions—since 1945. This implies that no real change in world order is evident.
44. George H. W. Bush and Brent Scowcroft, *A World Transformed* (New York: Knopf, 1998).

Chapter 8

At Home

> *But at home in America the use of Presidential power was more complicated than it was abroad.*
>
> —Theodore White*

When Bush succeeded Reagan, "Poor George" was in trouble and appeared weakened when measured against a highly popular Republican colleague.[1] Conservative media pundit Wills thought Reagan had left behind a better-off America with considerable improvements in the GNP.[2] Other commentators thought the right-wing Republican statesman, with the magic of Reaganomics, left Bush "a daunting list of national problems."[3] The first and most pressing of these problems was the budget deficit, followed by unanswered tax problems and a deteriorating education system. Additionally, Bush inherited the unfinished "War on Drugs," that is, narcotics; an illiberal medical system worsened by costly service fees and charges; and a host of environmental headaches.

Various lobby and interest groups expected Bush to place their respective policies as priority items on his agenda. Former Presidents Ford and Carter, in a report to President Bush, advised that "Americans are ready to do what has been done; all they want is leadership..."[4] They continued,

> George Bush must provide a vision of a nation that is strong diplomatically, militarily and economically, and is, at the same time compassionate toward the poor, the undereducated, the homeless, and the hopeless. But the president-elect's task is different from that of those who have gone before him. He has to achieve these lofty goals in the face of a $148 billion budget deficit.[5]

From the onset of Bush's tenure, he was expected to tackle gargantuan tasks. Could he meet these challenges without raising taxes? Could he restore the fiscal balance and make America's economy grow and achieve more competitiveness in the wake of the Asian economic challenge? As Bush stated in his inaugural address,

> America is never wholly herself unless she is engaged in high moral principle. We as a people have such a purpose today. It is to make kinder the face of the Nation and gentler the face of the world.[6]

The president's agenda[7] was designed to make America kinder and gentler through reforms in social security, housing, and the environment, as well as child care. It advocated better management of the federal government, including providing the right signals for efficiency to flourish and giving Americans assured defense protection within a more peaceful world. Bush knew these were difficult tasks, but as a politician in the highest office in the land, he had to provide leadership to make America respond to this agenda.

The Bush administration was to solve these problems within a legislature framework shaped partly by the opposition Democratic Party. The administration coexisted with a Congress that, in many cases, tilted decisions to support expensive government programs.

On a more specific level, Bush grappled with uncertain defense needs, especially in terms of policy choices on types of weapon systems to be developed or discarded in support of America's global strategic requirements and responsibilities. The United States had to set the record straight on sensitive strategic arms control, particularly the large stockpile of nuclear warheads and arsenals. In the international field, problems of third-world debt(s) and international terrorism, including "new communism" by religious fundamentalists, were pertinent.

Some media commentators thought Bush faced more military and geopolitical problems than all previous occupants of the Oval Office since Truman's presidency. On the domestic front, Bush was confronted by a growing recession, erosion of the middle class, and a mounting budget deficit. This fact became popular public discourse. For example, Peter Drucker asserted that no administration in American history ran a larger deficit than that of President Bush.[8] During Bush's first three years in office, the United States experienced the deepest and longest recession since 1945. Even though Reagan was part of the budget deficit problem, he did not provide coherent answers on how to solve it. Reagan had authorized huge defense expenditures to win the cold war through economic means. However, the subsequent end of the cold war meant that Bush had to manage unstructured change. Part of this change process was the culmination of a new world order. Bush recorded relative success in articulating his post–cold war international order. At least at the rudimentary level, the Bush administration began demanding democratic governance all over the world. The United States assumed the role of global policeman and Hussein was among the first victims of the Bush strategy.

At the end of his initial successes in the international arena, several interest groups expected Bush to use his gains to advance a new American order at home.[9] Comparisons were made between Bush and his predecessors in light of Bush's limited domestic agenda. For example, Johnson's former lawyer, Harry McPherson, thought that if Johnson served in the 1990s, he could have, at the end of the 1991 Gulf War, doubled the War on Poverty.[10] In McPherson's view, the Great Society agenda would have been realized. Nixon, with his new American Revolution, could have continued the broad conservative agenda of Eisenhower. Reagan "would have cut back the role of government more"[11] and pursued the new federalism as part of the Reagan Revolution. Bush was not a domestic policy-oriented president, and his record on the home front appeared less illustrious compared to the scores of his policies on the international scene.

Before discussing the Bush record at home, it is important to note that domestic issues are not mutually exclusive from those on the international level. Indeed, basic international relations theory teaches that it is domestic actors who play an important role in shaping the conduct of actors in the international arena. Thus, when the Bush presidency is placed under scrutiny, the separation of the home and international components must remain essentially academic.

Bush's home policies and politics need to be visualized in terms of his basic conservative orientation on a variety of domestic issues, including but not limited to minority rights, health, education, housing, and aging, as well as management of the budget, to mention just a few of the key domestic concerns of his administration. Conservatism is about attitudes, ideologically constructed as defending the status quo. While accepting change, conservatives create change in a gradualist manner. The main characteristics of conservatives include belief in traditional religious values, greater identification with state and local governments, patriotism, free markets, and less belief in the power of centralized government, as well as promotion of social stability through gradual "changes within existing institutions."[12] This is in sharp contrast to the liberals, who emphasize utopian equality, government reform, strong central government, public regulation, and individualism. Dunn and Woodward argued that the United States has experienced a number of conservative cycles evident in the Eisenhower, Nixon, and Ford administrations.[13]

The 1980s marked the emergence of a new kind of conservatism symbolized by Reagan's patriotic rhetoric. This ideology sought to return America to a nostalgic past when values of family and work were part of growing up in America. Liberalism was blamed for the declining health, education, and general standards of living in America. Reagan aggressively pushed the conservative agenda, and Bush faithfully followed the lead started by Reagan to continue pushing this agenda.[14]

While Republicans were the major proponents of conservatism, America's ailing economy provided an impetus for the upsurge in a conservative mood in the country. This was because conservatism entailed being duty consciousness and promoting patriotism.[15] Rossiter concluded, "It is subtle thesis of reverence, traditionalism, distaste for materialism, high morality, moderation, peacefulness and the aristocratic spirit."[16]

The conservative mood of the 1980s was evident in the swing-to-the-right voting pattern within the U.S. Congress.[17] Witness, for example, the strong support that the House and Senate Democrats gave the Gramm-Rudman balanced budget amendment. This fiscal reform amendment was enacted to eliminate the budget deficit through "cutting domestic programs bequeathed by the New Deal and Great Society."[18] The message was that many Democrats had been somewhat converted to the conservative agenda in a pragmatic sense.

As for the Republican pundits, many were convinced that the Bush presidency would provide fresh unity in the conservative movement. Bush had a firm grip on the Republican Party's machine and was considered an ideological conservative.[19] Some leading conservatives, such as Mitchell E. Daniels Jr., a former Reagan White House political director, voiced the belief that Bush was elected primarily because of his ideology of small government, strong defense, education vouchers, and stabilization of social security, as well as tax cuts. According to Daniels, Democrats were on the verge of becoming a permanent opposition on Capitol Hill, and therefore, he advised the president against giving in to congressional demands that did not serve the conservative agenda.[20]

Several influential conservative think tanks, including members of the Hudson Institute and the Heritage Foundation, regarded Bush's victory in the 1988 election as one more step in the shift toward conservatism that began in the 1950s. America's "right turn," especially the role of the media and conservative leaders, is well documented and need not be repeated here.[21]

For instance, John Mashek observed that the election of Bush was evidence that "the Republican Party and America was relatively comfortable with a moderate conservative and not the television evangelist, far-right conservative Pat Robertson."[22] While the claim that the country had shifted to conservatism gained currency, particularly after Reagan's eight years in the White House, the congressional victory in 1994 seemed to give liberals pause for a moment of self-reflection.[23] While the election of Clinton in 1992 raised doubts about the saliency of conservatism as the governing philosophy for the majority of Americans, the 1988 election did not resolve the question of leadership in the conservative movement. There was much debate on who would be the nominal leader of the movement. Although a number of think-tank commentators were undecided on where the locus of American conservatism would fall, the matter was settled when representatives from several conservative groups pledged to support the Bush administration. For example, Amy Moritz, president of the National Centre for Public Research, regarded Bush as the political leader of the conservative movement.[24] In a letter congratulating Bush on his election as president, conservative leaders drawn from various interest groups, such as Citizens of America, American Freedom Coalition, and American Conservative Union, expressed hope that Bush would continue Reagan's policies and appoint conservative officials in his administration. The letter stated in part, "The 1988 Republican Party Platform, which you championed in your campaign, supports the cause of anti-communist freedom fighters worldwide, the deployment of SDI, the right to life, no new taxes, and the continuation of the Reagan/Bush economic recovery program."[25]

Bush assumed the presidency with a conservative hat on his head. His first one hundred days in office were boom days for the conservatives. The president's politics and thinking were essentially influenced by the conservative mood and culture prevailing in his day.

BUSH AND MINORITY POLITICS

When Bush became president, the civil rights agenda had not been exhausted. Minority rights of African Americans, Hispanics, Native

Americans, women's rights, and issues concerning gays and lesbians were all pertinent in America. Ethnic minorities during the Bush presidency evaluated his economic politics in terms of policy impacts on their well-being. For example, the recession in 1990, it is argued, worsened living conditions of blacks and other minorities more than it hurt whites. The minorities were concerned with Bush's Gulf War of 1991 and his other international schemes, including the new world order, as these minority groups seemed disproportionately affected. African Americans raised their voices against the Gulf War because they felt over-represented in the Armed Forces. The same position was taken by African American groups during the Vietnam War. SNICK, for example, issued a statement against the deployment of African Americans in combat against the communists. Moreover, civil rights activist Jackson argued that Bush's Middle East adventure was premised on frivolous reasons. Jackson posited that the president would have done better liberating America from its domestic problems such as homelessness, drugs, and crime than he did in liberating Kuwait. These were problems that disproportionately affected blacks and Hispanics.

African Americans in the Bush era came into public view when Bush nominated an African American, Clarence Thomas, as an associate justice of the Supreme Court. Further attention was focused on American health problems, particularly federal programs such as Medicaid, Medicare, and the AIDS epidemic. Minorities were anxious for the Bush administration to correct the anomalies in these sectors. The same interests focused on reforming education as it disproportionately marginalized these groups of minority citizens.

The list of minority concerns was neither exhaustive nor mutually exclusive. These areas of interest were to a large extent an American problem. The point was that Bush was evaluated in terms of whether his administration contributed significantly to the improvement of these disadvantaged minorities. Second, did the vulnerable African Americans improve on their civil rights gains during the 1988–1993 timeframe? To address these questions, examination of Bush policies and their impact on minorities is necessary.

The beginning point was that the Republican Party had traditionally been a friend of African Americans, at least in the sense that it was the party of Lincoln. *From the Deck to the Sea: Blacks and the Republican Party*[26] is a chronicle of historical relations between African Americans and Republicans that analyzed race-related policies from Lincoln to Bush (1861–1991).

Additionally, it was Republican Abraham Lincoln who issued the Emancipation Proclamation in 1863 to ban slavery. Republican radicals were responsible for the passage of the Thirteenth, Fourteenth, and Fifteenth Amendments to the U.S. Constitution that gave African Americans further rights. Yet, in the twentieth century, many African Americans judged Democratic presidents as being more civil rights friendly. For example, F. D. Roosevelt received about 70 percent of the African American vote in 1936. F. D. Roosevelt's era marked the beginning of migration of minorities to the Democratic Party. Johnson's era from 1964 marked the golden age for the civil rights movement in the United States.[27] In recent years, blacks have traditionally given Republican presidents little support—a mere 10 percent since 1964 through to the Bush election in 1988. The rationale cited was that Bush was not expected to advance the cause of minorities.

This position was articulated in the works of a number of authorities on race issues in the United States. For instance, Lucius Barker saw Bush as an extension of the Reagan era—one that he thought was insensitive to issues of interest to African Americans. Barker noted, "As expected, and given his constituency base, President Reagan gave little support to African Americans and pro-civil rights interests."[28] Still, the Reagan era, which Bush was a part of, brought a "total redefinition of racial equality."[29]

Barker thought the Reagan administration misconstrued the gains of the civil rights movement in the 1960s as being unfair to whites.[30] The Reagan administration dismantled many programs, such as those on affirmative action, through appointment of officials whose views were not supportive to the African American cause. For example, agencies like the Civil Rights Commission and the Civil Rights Division in the

Department of Justice in the Reagan era were headed by conservatives who overturned judicial policies favorable to pro-civil rights interests.[31] Ironically, the Reagan era was marked by an increase in the number of elected black officials. However, due to Reagan's budget cuts, these officials had few or no resources to push through programs favorable to African Americans.[32]

As Reagan's running mate in 1984, Bush promised to follow Reagan's policies.[33] Barker argued that Reagan slowed progress on civil rights and Bush did likewise.[34] Barker wrote, "Once in office, President Bush continued to take positions and actions that were not supportive of African American interests."[35] Augustus Jones, in an evaluation of the Bush administration's handling of civil rights policy, came to a different conclusion. While observing that, in some instances, Bush followed the footsteps of Reagan, in others, Bush set his own direction.

On a balance sheet, Bush attempted to walk on a tightrope between supporting minority rights and advancing the cause of conservatism. He certainly did better than Reagan.[36] Among Bush's appointees were supporters of the civil rights agenda such as Arthur Fletcher, chairman of the Civil Rights Commission; Louis Sullivan, secretary of the Department of Health and Human Services; and William Lucas as assistant attorney general for civil rights. The policies and actions that constituted a reversal in the gains of the 1960s seem to be rooted in domineering influences of the right-wing elements in the Bush administration. Among these were the appointments of attorneys David Souter and Thomas to the U.S. Supreme Court. Bush made a strong effort to reach out to minorities, and in his first year, this cost him support from his party.[37]

Bush's roots and inclinations were with the moderate elements in the conservative wing of the Republican Party.[38] Bush appeared to be following Reagan's civil rights policies only in as much as he yielded to the pressures of the Republican right. In his inner self, he favored civil rights matters being "handled by moral persuasion."[39] During his Yale days, Bush had run the United Negro College Fund (UNCF) and considered himself a friend of African Americans. The president, after a few days in office, told Richard M. Smith of *Newsweek* that

> I have always felt the need to stand for fair play against bigotry, and I will certainly like to have an administration that projects that. I am not sure that means some [far] reaching legislative agenda. I will find ways to speak out in terms of the need to eliminate the last vestiges of bigotry… I hope to do better on appointments. The problem is that some people are going to measure compassion… by whether you can triple the budget for this account or…this service program. I won't be able to do that.[40]

These remarks were an indicator that Bush would not design an outright pro-civil rights program. It is sheer conservatism that helps explain why several civil rights groups were worried about his record on civil rights reforms. These skeptics were wrong.

Bush's attention to the civil rights agenda stood above that of Democratic presidents Carter and J. F. Kennedy. It was far ahead of his Republican colleagues Nixon and Reagan.[41] Bush spoke again and again on the need for fair play on issues affecting minorities. What seems to have distorted the president's feelings was his near obsession with internationalism and his general inertia in focusing on the particular interests of African Americans. The administration's handling of the Civil Rights Act of 1991 was a symptom of this inertia.

Bush was against quotas and vetoed the first version of the Civil Rights Act of 1990, a statute about discrimination in employment.[42] Bush, besides agreeing to amended legislation in the Civil Rights Act of 1991, was supportive of the Supreme Court ruling in *U.S. vs. Fordice* in which the court ruled that all vestiges of segregation in Mississippi's higher education system be scrapped.[43]

African American community leadership showed its disapproval of Bush when it criticized him for nominating Judge Thomas in October 1991 to replace the late Thurgood Marshall, who had retired as a Supreme Court justice. Thomas was African American, just like Marshall, but they differed on their world views of civil liberties. They also differed in their definitions of "the African American predicament and the responsibility of government regarding it."[44] After lengthy and unpleasant hearings involving Judge Thomas and Anita Hill's accusations of sexual harassment, the Senate confirmed Thomas, but the Senate decision left many African Americans disappointed. Thomas had been seen in the eyes of several African American civil rights groups as a "house black," since he vehemently opposed affirmative action programs. Thomas believed in moral persuasion rather than quotas. Thomas's position that blacks should have separate schools and that integration was not sensible alienated him from many black groups.[45] Thomas's judicial record was scant, but his speeches, writings, and prior government service reflected his conservative leanings.[46] Groups such as the NAACP, the AFL-CIO, and the Leadership Conference on Civil Rights, as well as eighteen out of nineteen black members of Congress, opposed the Thomas nomination. Civil rights activist Jackson was critical of Thomas on the grounds that he had benefited from affirmative action, yet he opposed it for others in favor of self-help and individual initiative.[47]

The National Association for the Advancement of Colored People (NAACP), through its Executive Director Sidney Hook, wanted President Bush to nominate a black person "who embodies many of the attributes Justice Marshall so ably articulated."[48] Thomas's hearing was the closest Supreme Court confirmation vote in more than a century. Although Thomas was not popular among black groups, he was able to play the race card well by countercharging that he had been subjected to high-tech lynching, a kind of harassment that "uppity blacks who in any way deign to think for themselves" experience time and again.[49] Bush's nominee won the day. Even then it was not clear that Thomas would participate in reversing the gains of the 1960s. Thomas's ideas may not have been well taken among blacks in general, but he symbolized Bush's plan for including minorities in his politics.

The Bush administration received additional wrath from civil rights activists when he did not strongly denounce the perpetrators of the Los Angeles riots in early March 1991. Widespread riots engulfed Los Angeles after black motorist King had been beaten in broad daylight by white police officers. When the officers were charged, the verdict was considered racist because of the acquittal of most of the white officers, even when more than fifty people were dead and considerable loss of property had resulted from the riots. Jackson castigated Bush for having campaigned together with Los Angeles Police Chief Daryl F. Gates.[50] It was inconceivable that Bush would provide accolades to a police chief unable to perform his duties to the satisfaction of all races living in Los Angeles. In unveiling the Crime Bill, Bush thought it wise to congratulate Chief Gates, but his timing was, in the view of many civil rights activists, unpalatable, especially because racial tension was high following the riot protesting the beating of King.

Health Politics

True to his promise of including African Americans in his Cabinet, the president appointed Dr. Louis W. Sullivan as secretary of the Department of Health and Human Services. Health care had been a high priority in African American politics. Most Americans have had problems with access to health services, particularly the uninsured and underinsured, but access problems were more severe in predominantly minority communities.

These problems were compounded by fiscal constraints created by the Reagan tax cut and the deficit growth era. The Bush team attempted to float several policy options to undo the sectors' key problems. Attempts to promulgate a full-scale national health insurance program yielded little success. No consensus was reached in the Bush era and state and local government authorities were left to unveil their health policy strategies. The Bush administration did not offer a health plan blueprint for America, although there was commitment to meet the health needs of the American people.

Bush was misconstrued when he nominated celebrated national basketball league hero, Earvin "Magic" Johnson, to sit on the National Commission of AIDS. The president intended to promote AIDS awareness in the country. The appointment was initially seen as politicking unfavorable to minorities who thought that Bush was unfairly linking the disease to minorities. Magic's role was to provide emotional support to the needy. When Bush met Magic in January of 1992, he told the press that his intention was to project the idea that AIDS was a health problem for all of society to confront. It was in that spirit that Magic accepted his appointment to the commission, despite efforts to persuade him to shun it.[51]

EDUCATION AND THE PRESIDENT

"I want to be the education president."[52] When Bush uttered these words as he campaigned for the presidency, he was overstating the fact that there was something amiss with the educational system. Upon becoming president, Bush repeated this message, albeit differently, when he pledged to work together with Congress to solve the education mess.[53] There was widespread fear that America's global intellectual lead would erode if education was ignored. James Fallows identified reforms in America's education system as one way of ensuring individual upward mobility and rejuvenation.[54] Bush clearly saw the writing on the wall.

The expectation of America was that the Bush administration would institute programs to get more disadvantaged youngsters into preschool.[55] Reforms were needed in matters such as the quality of education as well. Bush retorted that as the "education president,"

> I will focus national attention on the challenge of improving our schools and the education of every child. Although most of my national agenda for education must happen at the state and local levels, the federal government should act as a catalyst for excellence in education, providing incentives and encouraging local experimentation with new ideas.[56]

Bush unveiled a six point national education strategy whose highlights follow:[57]

1. Rewarding successful students, teachers, and administrators. Create merit schools with up to US$500 million in federal funds;
2. Expanding choice in education to create magnet schools and encourage innovation and experimentation in public schools;

3. Focusing federal assistance on at risk students, providing more assistance to these children in their early years through such programs as Head Start initiatives. In this program, all eligible four year olds can attend school. In launching this program, Bush remarked, "Not everyone can have a caring parent, but everyone should have a teacher who cares."[58]
4. Infusing moral values and family participation into the U.S. educational system. Bush believed that values and morality could be taught. He wanted the "puritan values" that were taught to him in his youth such as fairness, honesty, self-discipline, and respect for the law to be reintroduced in the school systems.[59]
5. In tandem with values such as differentiating right and wrong and how to say no to drugs and teenage pregnancy, the education package entailed preparing American youth for the challenges of the twenty-first century. This meant improved training in technical and vocational skills. The president's plan was based on his conviction that "if we want America to remain a leader, a force for good in the world, we must lead the way in educational innovation."[60]
6. The sixth point was encouraging American industry and researchers to work together to ensure that not even one person was denied college education because of financial need.

The Bush education vision was not insensitive to the plight of disadvantaged Americans. Bush began his education war by appointing a Hispanic, Lauro Cavazos, as secretary of education to his Cabinet. However, it was suggested that Cavazos was one of the weakest cabinet members.[61] Cavazos had been a former college administrator, but his mediocre performance made Bush convince only a few Americans that he was truly the education president. Cavazos resigned abruptly in December 1990.

The Bush administration, one would assume, would have had sweeping reforms to match their campaign rhetoric. In the pre-Bush era, discussions of education focused on the equality agenda. America's education system faced challenges brought about by cutbacks in federal financial support; overcrowding, particularly at the lower grade levels; and broad curriculum problems that led to poor performance in tests, such as the Scholastic Assessment Test (SAT). According to the American Federation of Teachers, standards had fallen, in part because the United States ranked thirteenth out of fifteen industrialized countries in education funding.[62]

The Bush administration did not match its rhetoric with federal funds. Bush opposed any expansion in federal support toward school budgets. Traditionally, federal support amounted to about only 6 percent. Since the federal government's failure to increase school dollars was a manifestation of an ongoing debate on the dynamics of American federalism, Bush's criticism of the education system was symbolic.[63] Bush, by talking about education in America, triggered debates for reform. The Bush administration ushered in a countrywide self-evaluation of education projects. Without providing additional funds, Bush's rhetoric encouraged state and local reforms. For example, in St. Paul, Minnesota, a school board promised to retire if the school dropout rates did not fall by 25 percent.[64] In Kentucky, the entire education system was overhauled. Although the initial catalyst was a lawsuit over funding inequities, it was the state legislature that enacted a bill that guaranteed almost $2,500 per pupil in state aid while the poorest districts were given 25 percent more.[65]

THE SAVINGS AND LOAN SCANDAL

President Bush inherited several national problems from the Reagan era, and he could not avoid the savings and loan scandal. American savings and loans institutions were already decaying, and most were threatening to disrupt the federal coffers. Loss of over $170 billion in assets of ailing institutions negatively impacted the United States' already fragile budget deficit.[66] President Bush felt uneasy about the political implications of America's failing savings and loan scandal. He blamed it on his predecessor, Reagan, a criticism that many right-wing Republicans detested.[67]

The savings and loan crisis began in the late 1970s and ran through the 1980s. The crisis was unearthed by federal regulators upon realizing that several institutions were collapsing. In 1988, for example, the Federal Savings and Loans Insurance Corporations were in desperate straits. There were losses on the federally insured thrifts whose deposits it had guaranteed. There was no political will to redress this situation as it was an election year.

The scandal assumed a potentially explosive proportion when a number of politicians were implicated. Even after deregulation of the industry at the start of the decade, some unscrupulous operatives outright mismanaged these institutions as politicians looked the other way. A number of savings and loan groups financed countless condominium blocks and office buildings that were never to be occupied for long durations. A number of these companies and savings and loan groups also invested heavily in junk bonds. A number of entrepreneurs used these bonds to artificially shore up these thrifts. Federal investigators zeroed in on groups such as Silverado, Charles Keating's Lincoln Savings and Loan, and Centrust Bank, as well as San Jacinto Savings based in Texas.

One of the then directors of the Denver-based Silverado Savings and Loan was President Bush's third son, Neil. Neil Bush, it would appear, was manipulated into accepting this position by shrewd businessmen who wished to gain political protection from federal regulators. Neil resigned upon realizing that his association with the group would place his father's presidential ambitions in jeopardy. He was, however, considered negligent in this affair.

The dealings were political in the sense that key players in the scandal, such as Kenneth Good, a Denver-based real estate investor, had defaulted on $30 million in loans from Silverado. Good had contributed large sums of money to the Republican Party's 1988 campaign. This contribution was for purposes of buying influence with the Bush administration. Another developer, Larry Mizel, used the Silverado Company as his piggy bank and received loans in exchange for undesirable land. Mizel directed a steady flow of financial resources to state and national politicians, including backing Michigan senator Don Riegle. Riegle was one of the senators dubbed the "Keating Five" under federal investigation. A July 1990 poll, however, exonerated the president from the problems in the savings and loan crisis.[68] A major question for the president and Congress was how to bail out the savings and loan thrifts decisively without adversely affecting the U.S. economy. Bush moved fast to initiate changes in the entire saving and loans sector by ordering a cleanup exercise. He sought congressional support in his attempt to mop up the failed savings and loan institutions. Bush's rescue plan included a costly bailout scheme involving the liquidation or merging of the insolvent savings and loan.[69] Underperforming thrifts were sold. However, media accounts show that the American public, particularly elements in the Democratic Party, thought the operation was too expensive.[70] The savings and loan scandal was about thrift managers defrauding the government and depositors of millions of dollars.

Bush was praised for his swift action, but his appointee, William Taylor, chairman of the Federal Deposit Insurance Corps, was unable to complete the cleanup operation by the 1992 elections. The choices were indeed costly and attracted harsh criticism in the U.S. media. Some lobbyists thought the Bush savings and loans plan did not count much to reducing the budget deficit and would hurt the better firms in the savings and loan sector. Yet they cheered his administration's indictments against the offenders.[71] Bush's actions underlined his resolve and desire to remedy a problem brought to the forefront by the preceding administration.

BUDGET PROBLEMS REVISITED

The budget deficit was the Bush presidency's largest domestic problem. It was not his administration's making, but it was his top priority. Bush adopted an everything's-on-the-table approach to solving the budget deficit problems and the engulfing economic recession. Bush had campaigned on a no-tax ticket. Increasing taxes made economic sense but little political sense. Several commentators thought the U.S. Congress and the president had let down the public in attempting to solve the budget deficit without raising taxes.

Bush was seen as indecisive in the budget debate.[72] Bush's indecisiveness resulted in a full point drop in opinion poll ratings.[73] He had compromised on the no taxes pledge, thereby playing into the hands of the Democrats. Further, Bush was unable to organize the Republican Congress to back his budget proposals that lowered his leadership credibility. In addition, he continued to downplay the existence of a recession, calling it an economic slowdown, until early January 1991 when he conceded that some areas had a recession and insisted it would be short and mild.[74] Bush blamed Congress for not working hard enough to create an environment for the United States to create jobs and increase consumer confidence. The hard times were blamed on the Federal Reserve Board for doing a poor job.[75] Poor economic performance was blamed largely on external factors, such as negative economic growth and the decline in American manufacturing, plus the diminished demand for American housing, vehicles, and other consumables. All of these were traced back to Reaganomics.

In discussing Bush's domestic record, his managerial competence was under scrutiny. Critics contended that Bush neglected economic policymaking and was disinterested in designating a manager with clear instructions to show the way. Even Secretary of the Treasury Brady was denied full coordinating power.[76] Bush was further blamed for having little interest in the mismanagement of the Department of Housing and Urban Development. A Senate committee revealed that the Office of Management and Budget (OMB) could have uncovered some of the scandals that wrecked HUD[77] and directly challenged Bush's presidential management style. Historically, a president is often evaluated for his supervision of the Executive Office of the President (EOP). Recall, for example, when F. D. Roosevelt introduced the concept of presidents as chief managers of the federal government when he pushed through his New Deal initiatives and introduced a large presidential bureaucracy. Bush performed poorly on this score. He did not enlist a versatile management team to rebuild HUD. His appointment of Kemp and his public rhetoric of waging a war on poverty on the housing front was not well received, particularly by the poor.

THE ENVIRONMENTAL PRESIDENT

Environmental policy and climate change issues have been in the limelight for the greater part of the 1980s and early 1990s. Presidential activism in environmental matters is not new in studies of the American presidency. For example, in 1963 President J. F. Kennedy traveled across the country to talk about conservation. During the 1960s and 1970s, the environment became a legitimate policy issue in national politics. Much like other policy areas, environmental policy activism involved key actors in the American political system including the president, Congress, and interest groups, as well as citizens, who all voiced concerns about the sustainability of programs to conserve and protect the environment.

In terms of presidential action, ideological approaches to environmental program management were more profound in the Nixon years. The Nixon presidency's "new federalism" approach influenced policy implementation in a more significant way than ever before. Nixon's administration, with a few exceptions, had hoped state governments would become more involved in managing the environment.

In the late 1980s and early 1990s the federal government took more direct interest in addressing global warming issues, in part because the problem was widely considered to be in the realm of international politics and foreign policy. In the 1988 campaign, Bush tried hard to distance himself from Reagan's environmental policies and to portray himself as a friend of the environment. "The environmental presidency" translated into a campaign theme for Bush. The Bush administration was given credit for signing the Clean Air Act Amendments of 1990 (P.L. 101–549) and the Energy Policy Act of 1992 (EPAct). The Clean Air Act Amendments were the most significant environmental legislation since the enactments of the Clean Air Act of 1970 and the Clean Air Act Amendments of 1977. The 1990 amendments created a wide range of new regulatory requirements that included the installation of advanced pollution control equipment in industries and reductions in emissions of air pollutants.

The EPAct of 1992 established new standards aimed at increasing clean energy use in the country. The Bush administration directed the federal government to increase conservation in federal buildings whenever feasible. The legislation established a comprehensive energy efficiency program that provided incentives for energy conservation and created new standards for appliances in industry. Title XXII authorized tax incentives for renewable energy technologies to encourage local production and lessen dependence on imported energy. The legislation amended the Public Utility Holding Company Act of 1935 to help smaller utility companies survive competition for the larger corporations. According to Professor Jacqueline Vaughn Switzer, these legislative successes "represented a break in the legislative gridlock that had characterized Congress under Republican administrations."[78]

The administration achieved limited success in other areas of environmental protection. In the area of biodiversity politics, President Bush gave support to the development of genetically engineered plants, having declared them as equal to natural plants. Although this was a bold decision, a fraction of environmentalist farmers and consumers opposed this position, contending that it was meant to appease the president's business associates, especially those with links to corporations, such as Monsanto, that developed and sold genetically modified seeds.[79] On Bush's watch, the list of endangered species was expanded, albeit amid charges that he dismantled the Endangered Species Act of 1973. The bill had been enacted at the behest of President Nixon to protect endangered species from extinction, as well as protecting their enabling ecosystems. Still, the Department of the Interior did not protect some critical habitats. Part of the problem was that officials in the Bush administration grappled with an onslaught of litigation that made it harder to protect endangered species. For example, the influential Sierra Club litigated against the administration for approving new logging activities in Oregon. The Sierra Club claimed that logging activities threatened some animal species, including the rare spotted owl. Tens of other groups and individuals printed and distributed protest stickers and ran newspaper advertisements with adverse slogans, such as one from the Wilderness Society that read, "Don't Let One Bush Kill the Whole Forest."[80] U.S environmental groups that disapproved of his leadership included the Friends of the Earth, National Wildlife Federation, and the National Audubon Society.

The Wetlands

On wetlands issues, critics charged that Bush watered down the no-net-loss-of-wetlands policy that he promised to support. Although the president's commitment to environmental protection has been widely questioned, President Bush signed into law a bill that settled the long-debated issue of whether the U.S. Department of the Interior had the right to buy water rights originally designated for Bureau of Reclamation irrigation projects and use them to maintain wetlands. Public Law 10–618 gave the Department of the Interior that authority and granted discretion to the secretary of the interior to take actions to prevent deterioration of water quality, as well as preserve wildlife habitat conditions connected to wastewaters from irrigation projects.

Internationally, the United States slipped from being a key player in environmental protection to being isolated from a group of several world elite nations during the June 3–14, 1992, Earth Summit held in Rio de Janeiro, Brazil. Bush had originally pledged to convene an international climate change conference during his first year in office, but he backtracked on this pledge and left the job to the UN. Bush even threatened a boycott of the conference until he received certain assurances on emissions. While Bush attended the UN conference, he declined to sign the biodiversity agreements, or treaty, which all major powers including Britain, Japan, and the European Community

(EEC) signed. Bush's international image was tainted when a memo written by Environmental Protection Agency Chief William Reilly to the president urging him to sign the biodiversity treaty was leaked to the media.[81] This brought to light conflicts over the Bush administration's commitment to global environmental protection. Uday Desai thought Bush was merely underscoring the basic fact that individual states are mandated to tackle environmental problems.[82]

Bush seemingly succumbed to the neoconservatives in his party to deny the world American leadership in managing climate change and environmental protection. He was heavily criticized for deciding to attend the Earth Summit at the last minute and then not showing any "clear leadership or vision while there."[83] The international media and environmental community blamed President Bush for his lack of poise and leadership.[84] Many attendees argued that Bush's actions contributed to anti-American sentiments. Within the United States, Al Gore criticized the president for refusing to sign one of the important documents of the Earth Summit—the Biodiversity Treaty.[85] Then a senator, Gore was chairman of the U.S. Senate delegation to the United Nations Conference on the Environment and Development.

Evidently, environmental politics have more to do with influence from the big industrial corporations and their think-tank supporters. For example, conservative Competitive Enterprise Institute (CEI), and other groups allied with big business, regarded Bush's presence at Rio as unnecessary. For these groups, presidential presence would publicize anti-Western and antifreedom agendas, especially from left-leaning groups. At no time would these corporations endorse an environmental agenda or support treaties that were detrimental to their interests.

While President Bush saw U.S. leadership in environmental conservation as necessary, his prescription was conservative to the core. When asked what he had wanted from the Earth Summit, President Bush's response was that the best way to protect the environment was through market-based approaches.[86] His departure from left-leaning environmentalists was illustrated in his remarks—"I am determined to protect the environment, and I am also determined to protect the American taxpayer. The days of the open checkbook are over."[87]

Having said this, and recognizing the importance of the market, Bush noted that there was danger that the biodiversity treaty would discourage technological initiatives by the private sector. In his numerous speeches on this subject, Bush saw the United States as a partner to the developing world's development process. However, like other conservatives, he argued that developing countries had to develop in an environmentally sensible and sustainable way. Several conservative groups argued against establishment of new bureaucracies to regulate the management of the environment and establishment of a global fund to help underwrite antipollution efforts in developing countries. It is widely believed that the administration was not ready to entertain demands from poor countries seeking handouts for various environmental protection programs. The conservatives did not favor provision of increased development assistance in that direction.

President Bush rejected the idea of the United States signing treaties with targets and timetables in their action plans to reduce greenhouse gas emissions and other pollutants that caused global warming. In fact, his initial reluctance to travel to Rio de Janeiro had been attributed to discomfort about the conference fixing timetables and targets for controlling emissions.[88]

At the end of the summit, President Bush symbolically toured a section of the rainforests near Rio de Janeiro. However, his critics disapproved of his performance in Rio de Janeiro. President Bush dismissed his critics saying that Americans are leaders, not followers, on environmental issues and would implement the Rio de Janeiro accords as necessary.[89] Bush continued to claim he was still the "environmental president"[90] and the U.S environmental record was "second to none."[91]

Among Bush's accomplishments at Rio de Janeiro was an agreement on principles for preserving forests. The administration announced a $1.4 billion fund to monitor climate change and invest in biodiversity studies. In his mind, the media had ignored or given insufficient coverage to his positive accomplishments in the area of environmental protection.[92]

In summary, there were two distinct public expectations when the Bush agenda replaced the Reagan agenda. While conservatives expected Bush to continue Reagan's domestic agenda, Democrats disagreed. Most observers agree that the middle-ground approach produced an outcome that undermined Bush's political capital. In the end, the domestic front proved to be the president's Achilles' heel. Interestingly, Bush's failure to fulfill domestic policy promises resulted from his priorities rather than conflicts with an opposition-controlled Congress.

This chapter has provided a brief overview of the complexities in managing domestic policies. The complexities included the difficult balancing act that involved leading the world's efforts to manage problems associated with global climate change. This was an area in which domestic interests were at odds with global public opinion. Internationally, there was consensus that the ultimate success or failure of addressing environmental problems was a function of the president's focused interest in the matter. This discussion is included to demonstrate the linkages between domestic issues and the global outreach of the presidency. Thus, the demands on the presidency must be considered as a variable in understanding his total leadership capacities.

Notes

* Theodore White, *The Making of the President* (Athenaeum, NY: Scribner, 1972), xiii.
1. Before Bush assumed the presidency, various international news reports had predicted that he would have had to cultivate rapport with several interest groups to be as popular. "Bush Takes His Turn," *The Economist*, August 20, 1988, 21–23. Also see, Eleanor Clift, "The 'Carterization' of Bush: Problems With Oil, Recession, Hostages," *Newsweek*, October 22, 1990, 28.
2. Thomas M. DeFrank, Mark Muller, and Steven Waldman, "Goodbye to the Gipper," *Newsweek*, January 9, 1989, 20.
3. John Barry and Tom Morganthau, "The Defense Dilemma," *Newsweek*, January 23, 1989, 12.
4. Lee Smith, et al. "Politics and Policy, An Agenda for President Bush," *Fortune*, January 16, 1989, 82, http://money.cnn.com/magazines/fortune/fortune_archive/1989/01/16/71520/index.htm
5. Ibid.
6. Inaugural address of George Bush, The Avalon Project at Yale Law School, Yale University, http://www.yale.edu/lawweb/avalon/presiden/inaug/bush.htm
7. USIS, Madras, India Background Information, January 1989.
8. Peter F. Drucker, *Post-Capitalist Society* (New York: Harper Collins, 1994), 159.
9. Ann McDaniel, Evan Thomas, and Howard Fineman, "The Rewards of Leadership: Bush's War Role Earns Him the Nation's Gratitude," *Newsweek*, March 11, 1991, 30.
10. Ibid.
11. Ibid.
12. Charles W. Dunn and David J. Woodard, *American Conservatism From Burke to Bush: An Introduction* (New York: Madison Books, 1991), 31.
13. Ibid., 16–17.
14. Ibid., 18.
15. Clinton Rossiter, *Conservatism in America* (New York: Alfred A Knopf, 1955), 47.
16. Ibid., 48–49.
17. Thomas Ferguson and Joel Rogers, "The Myth of America's Turn to the Right," in *American Politics, Classic and Contemporary Readings*,

ed. Alan J. Ciglar and Burdett A. Loomis (Boston: Houghton Mifflin, 1989), 198–199.
18. Ibid.
19. "Conservatives Among the Crawfish," *The Economist*, August 20, 1988, 22.
20. John W. Mashek, "Gauging Effect in Congress of Bush's Limited Clout," *The Boston Globe*, March 6, 1989, 7 and Dan Balz, "Bush Given Painful Lesson About Divided Government," *The Washington Post*, March 10, 1989, A1.
21. Nina J. Easton, *Gang of Five: Leaders at the Center of the Conservative Crusades* (New York: Simon & Schuster, 2000) and Michael A. Viguerie and David Franke, *America's Right Turn: How Conservatives Used News and Alternative Media to Take Power* (New York: Bonus Books, 2004).
22. Mashek, "Gauging Effect in Congress of Bush's Limited Clout," 7.
23. Shirley A. Warshaw, *The Domestic Presidency: Policy Making in the White House* (Boston: Allyn & Bacon, 1997), 111.
24. Amy Moritz (Ridenour), of National Center for Public Policy Research, gave several public speeches on conservative talk shows in his support.
25. Greg Mueller, "Conservative Leaders Congratulate Bush," *PR Newswire*, November 15, 1988.
26. Mathew Rees, *From the Deck to the Sea: Blacks and the Republican Party* (Wakefield, NH: Longwood Academic Press, 1991).
27. Jeffrey E. Cohen, "The Dynamics and Interactions Between the President's and the Public Civil Rights Agendas: A Study in Presidential Leadership and Representation," *Policy Studies Journal* 21, no. 3 (1993): 524–521. A further explanation can be discerned from the fact that Johnson's election of 1964 was basically about the rights and welfare of blacks. See Joshua Muravchik, "Why the Democrats Lost Again," *Commentary Magazine*, American Jewish Committee, February 1989, 128.
28. Lucius J. Barker, "Limits of Political Strategy: A Systematic View of the American Experience," *American Political Science Review* 88, no. 1 (March 1994): 5.
29. Steven A. Shull, *A Kinder, Gentler Racism?: The Reagan-Bush Civil Rights Legacy* (Armonk, NY: M.E. Sharpe, 1993).
30. Ibid.
31. Ibid., 6.
32. Ibid.
33. Lucius Barker, *New Perspectives in American Politics* (New Brunswick, NJ: Transaction Publishers, 1989), 329.
34. Ibid., 385.
35. Barker, "New Perspectives in American Politics," 6.

36. Augustus J. Jones Jr., "Kinder, Gentler? George Bush and Civil Rights," in *Leadership and the Bush Presidency: Prudence or Drift in an Era of Change?*, ed. Ryan Barilleaux and M. Stuckey (Westport, CT: Praeger 1992), 177–190.
37. James D. King and James W. Riddlesperger Jr., "Presidential Leadership of Congressional Civil Rights Voting: The Cases of Eisenhower and Johnson," *Policy Studies Journal* 21, no. 3 (1993): 553.
38. Margaret G. Warner, "Bush Battles the 'Wimp Factor,' A Searching Look at the Vice President's Most Persistent Political Liability," *Newsweek*, October 19, 1987, 35.
39. Ibid., in the 1990 Senate race between David Duke (a former Ku Klux Klan and American Nazi member) and Bennett Johnston in Louisiana, Bush openly campaigned against Duke. Also see Michael W. Giles and Melanie A. Buckner, "David Duke and Black Threat: An Old Hypothesis Revisited," *Journal of Politics* 55, no. 3 (August 1993): 702–713.
40. Jonathan Alter, "The Inauguration: Bush Reaches Out," *Newsweek*, January 30, 1989, 22.
41. Jeffrey E. Cohen, "The Dynamics and Interactions Between the President's and The Public Civil Rights Agendas: A Study in Presidential Leadership and Representation," *Policy Studies Journal* 21, no. 3 (1993): 516.
42. Stephen L. Wasby, "Transformed Triangle: Court, Congress and Presidency in Civil Rights," in *Policy Studies Journal* 21, no. 3 (1993): 571.
43. Ibid., 569.
44. Lucius J. Barker, "Limits of Political Strategy," 6.
45. Maureen Dowd, "Conservative Black Judge, Clarence Thomas, Is Named to Marshall's Court Seat," *New York Times*, July 2, 1991, A1.
46. Historical Documents of 1991, Cumulative Index 1987–1991, *Congressional Quarterly Inc.*, hearings on Clarence Thomas's Supreme Court Nominations, Washington DC, September 10–13 and October 11–15, 1991, 551.
47. Ibid., 552.
48. Ibid.
49. Ibid., 553.
50. Jesse L. Jackson, speech delivered at African Methodist Episcopal Church in Los Angeles, April 7, 1991.
51. Office of the Federal Register, National Archives and Records Administration, *Weekly Compilation of Presidential Documents* 28: 87–88, January 14, 1992. Washington, DC: U.S. Government.
52. "Poor George," *The Economist*, August 13, 1988, 11–12.
53. Tamara Henry, "Campaign '88—The Issues Candidates Stress Importance of Education," *United Press International*, October 22, 1988, and

Christopher Connell, "Bush to Students, Parents and Teachers: Our Schools Are in Trouble," *The Associated Press*, September 3, 1991 (Wires Services available at Lexis Nexis).
54. James Fallows, *More Like Us: Putting America's Native Strengths and Traditional Values to Work to Overcome the Asian Challenge* (Boston: Houghton Mifflin, 1989), 4.
55. Phi Delta Kappan LXX, "Excellence," *Education Digest*, January 1989, 1. Also see "Politics and Policy, An Agenda for Bush," *Fortune*, January 16, 1989, 85.
56. Ibid., 5.
57. Ibid.
58. Ibid.
59. Congress of the United States, "Bush on Education Strategy," Historic Documents of 1991, Washington, DC, April 18, 1991, 222.
60. Ibid.
61. John W. Mashek, "The Circle in the Oval Office; From a Big Network, Only a Few Advisers Have Bush's Attention," *The Boston Globe*, May 28, 1990, 3. Also see, Carol Innerst, "Cavazos Fired From Cabinet," *The Washington Times*, December 13, 1990, A1.
62. Connie Leslie and Debra Rosenberg, "Hear America Scratching," *Newsweek*, November 12, 1990, 88. Also see Diego Ribadeneira, "Teachers Say U.S. Education Investment Falls Short," *The Boston Globe*, July 3, 1990, 3 and Fred A. Baughman Jr., "Who's To Blame for Poor Education?," *The San Diego Union-Tribune*, June 23, 1990, B-11.
63. Deidra Wright, "States Reform Educational System," *PA Times* 13, no. 12 (December 1990): 1 and 36.
64. Larry Martz and Rich Thomas, "Bush League Between Their Flips and Flops Over the Budget, the President and Congress Looked Like a Bunch of Stumble Bums," *Newsweek*, October 22, 1990, 67.
65. Wright, "States Reform Educational System." Also see Jonathan Walters, "The Most Radical Idea in Education: Let the Schools Run It," *Governing* 4, no. 4 (January 1991): 41–45.
66. Major Garrett, "Deficit Sets Record at $ 282.2 Billion," *The Washington Times*, July 16, 1991, A5; Don L. Reed, "Consequences of Greed," *St. Louis Post-Dispatch*, January 27, 1989, 2B; Warren T. Brookes, "S & Ls Don't Deserve Bail Out by Taxpayers," *The Oregonian*, November 11, 1988, E 07; and William M. Isaac, "Cuomo Wrong About Bush and S & Ls," *The American Banker*, August 6, 1992, 4.
67. Lucy Howard and Gregory Cerio, "Is Bush Ignoring Reagan," *Newsweek*, January 14, 1991, 6.

68. George C. Edwards III, "George Bush and the Public Presidency: The Politics of Inclusion," in *The Bush Presidency: First Appraisals*, ed. Colin Campbell and Bert Rockman (Chatham, NJ: Chatham, 1991), 140.
69. Steven K. Wilmsen, *Silverado: Neil Bush and the Savings & Loan Scandal* (Washington, DC: National Press Books, 1991).
70. Rod Smith, "Most Local Financial Execs Angered by Bush's Plan to Bail Out Thrifts," *Pacific Business News* 26, no. 48 (February 13, 1989): A10.
71. Ibid., and *U.S. News and World Report*, May 21, 1990, 34.
72. Martz and Thomas, "Bush League: Between Their Flips and Flops over the Budget, the President and Congress Looked like a Bunch of Stumble Bums," 20–22.
73. Ibid. Also see Robert J. Samuelson, "Bush's Capital Gains Obsession: It Is a Huge Distraction From Reducing the Deficit," *Newsweek*, October 1, 1990, 32.
74. Mark Memmott, "Bush Concedes 'Downturn,' Says It'll Be Short," *USA Today*, November 16, 1990, 1B, and Robert Akerman, "Bush Should Have Acted To Head Off Trouble," *The Atlantic Journal and Constitution*, November 13, 1991, 12.
75. Walter Williams, "George Bush and Executive Branch Domestic Policy Making Competence," *Policy Studies Journal* 21, no. 4 (1993): 700–717.
76. Ibid., 709.
77. Ronald C. Moe, "The HUD Scandal and the Case for an Office of Federal Management," *Public Administration Review* 51, no. 4 (July/August, 1991): 298.
78. Jacqueline Vaughn Switzer, *Environmental Politics: Domestic and Global Dimensions* (Belmont, CA: Wadsworth/Thomson, 2004), 22.
79. Andrew Mushita and Carol B. Thompson, *Biopiracy of Biodiversity Global Exchange as Enclosure* (Trenton, NJ: Africa World Press, 2007), 45.
80. Nicholas Schoon and David Osborne, "Bush Aims To Divert His Critics," *The Independent*, June 12, 1992, 11.
81. Peter Pizor, "Rio Hosts Ground Breaking International Conference," *PA Times* 15, no. 7 (July 1992): S-1.
82. Uday Desai, "Introduction to Symposium on Comparative Environmental Policy," *Policy Studies Journal* 20, no. 4 (1992): 621.
83. Sam Parry, "Bush's Environmental Blow-Up," *Consortium News*, http://www.consortiumnews.com
84. Ranee K. L. Rance Panjabi, Arthur H. Campeau, and Maurice F. Strong, "The Earth Summit at Rio: Politics, Economics, and the Environment" (Boston: Northeastern Press, 1997).

85. Isabel Vincent, "Stand Unfortunate, Senator Says," *The Globe and Mail*, June 6, 1992.
86. "Bush and the Earth Summit," *USA Today*, May 28, 1992, 13A.
87. Schoon and Osborne, "Bush Aims To Divert His Critics," *The Independent*, June 12, 1992, 11.
88. Jessica Lee, "Advisers Split Over Attendance," *USA Today*, April 22, 1992, 2A.
89. Michael Wines, "The President Leaves Rio With Shots at Foreign and U.S. Critics," *New York Times*, June 14, 1992, 10.
90. Ann Devroy, "Bush Lashes Out at Critics: President Praises Results of Troubled Trip," *Washington Post*, June 14, 1992, A1.
91. Jessica Lee and Linda Kanamine, "Bush Defends Environmental Policies: Bush Stands Tough, but Alone, in Rio," *USA Today*, June 12, 1992, 1A.
92. Ibid., see Carnegie Endowment National Commission, *Changing Our Ways, America and the New World* (Washington, DC: Brookings Institution Press, 1992), 8.

Chapter 9

The Reelection Debacle

We have fought the good fight and we've kept the faith and I believe upheld the honor of the presidency of the U.S.
—George Bush*

This chapter is about the failed reelection and end of a presidency. The end of a presidential term signifies a change in the nation's political order. The fundamental question is why did President Bush lose the election in 1992? Explanations on why presidents lose elections vary. On that score, the extent to which a president is perceived to have underperformed in any one major area of responsibility can contribute to an election failure. We have previously alluded to Bush's unmaking by observing the president scored very highly on foreign policy but dismally on domestic policy. This was not to overstate Will's warning that foreign policy is among the most important subjects for presidents, but it does not win votes.[1] Will argued that foreign policy considerations were unlikely to count in the larger scheme. In this chapter, we argue that Bush did not internalize this message as seriously as necessary. If he did, it was too late.

A critic berated Bush for not sustaining Reagan's vigorous economic growth targets and doing little to stop the disintegration of Reagan's Republican coalition.[2] Most voters were not enthusiastic about the return of Bush, as he reversed the Reagan policies, contrary to his ideological ticket. Bush betrayed Americans over the no tax pledge when he increased taxes.[3]

Bush's use of veto powers caused considerable political tension among the population despite the fact that he had every one of his thirty-five vetoes upheld.[4] A case in point was his veto of the Civil Rights Act of 1990, which cast doubt on his commitment to moderate and centrist policies.[5] Bush vetoed the continuing resolution providing temporary funding for the government and, as a result of this veto, shut the government down.[6] Barbara Sinclair argued that Bush frequently used the veto threat to push his agenda. This, she noted, was a sign of weakness rather than strength.[7] An assessment of the president's use of the veto power does not indicate an abuse of the powers granted in the Constitution. Therefore, his use of veto powers as an element of political failure did not account for his loss in the election.

From the standpoint of electoral politics, other variables were at play. The unmaking of the president was a result of his betrayal of Reagan's core supporters, thus losing an important and influential set of supporters. This betrayal was reflected in his appointment of loyalists and acquaintances rather than Reagan conservatives.[8]

This betrayal was reinforced by the Bush administration's alleged mistreatment of former President Reagan. The Bush team was seen as ungrateful to Reagan, whose leadership of the conservative wing of the Republican Party had been hailed as instrumental in Bush's 1988 victory. In 1992 the conservative wing's support was lukewarm if not absent. Bush's supporters were seen to have given no credit to the highly popular Reagan, thus losing important support from the religious right. The 1988 victory, won by President Bush with 54 percent of the popular vote did not repeat itself.[9] Clinton was clearly no Dukakis whom Bush had previously defeated. No doubt, a section of Republicans underestimated Clinton, thinking they would apply the same tactics used for Dukakis.[10]

In the campaign rhetoric of 1992, Bush did not think that Clinton and Gore would be the best persons to guide the United States for four more years to promote world economic recovery. After the 1988 elections, Bush remarked that the people have spoken. The Republicans had been in office for twelve consecutive years and the Bush campaign team overestimated the powers of incumbency. Bush made a last-minute Cabinet reshuffle to place his close friend, Secretary of State Baker, in the key position of campaign manager. Baker was not new to campaign management. He had campaigned for Bush during 1980 when he was a running mate to Reagan. He had also done the same for President Ford and was instrumental in the process. Baker was also a highly successful secretary of state and had done well in promoting the ideals of Bush's new world order. A brief review of the campaign's strategy shows that despite Baker's illustrious public service, he could not turn the anti-Bush tide. Baker's campaign strategies were ineffective. For example, the idea of planting doubts about Clinton's ability, the mudslinging about Clinton's anti-Vietnam war stance, and draft dodger characterization, were unconvincing to the majority of the voters.

Campaigns face many challenges and often draw on past experiences to win votes. Republican campaign managers struggled to attract new voters. The 1992 reelection campaign was an uphill task as many pundits demonstrated. Its major characteristics have been articulated comprehensively by Betty Glad, Nelson Polsby, and Aaron Wildavsky, among other authors.[11] Rarely do presidential scholars describe the Bush campaign as having been well organized.

For his part, Clinton built a strong coalition of interests mustering over 40 percent of the Caucasian vote, 84 percent of the African American vote, and 61 percent of the Hispanic vote. Clinton received 52 percent of votes of persons aged 60 years and above and 47 percent of voters between 18 and 24 years of age. A majority of women and 51 percent of single persons also voted for Clinton, as did 73 percent of the gay community nationally. There was evidence that ideologically moderate individuals—the "Reagan Democrats"—turned out in large numbers for Clinton. In a nutshell, as prominent TV anchor Dan Rather stated, "he did very well with every group he needed to do well."[12] In addition, Clinton's campaign spokesman, Mickey Kantor, expressed the following opinion:

> We were delighted with it, of course, because it was a victory across the country. It was broad. It was deep. It covered all demographic groups as well as many, many states in all regions of the country, and that's important—not only to Governor Clinton and Senator Gore, but to the country itself, to bring us together, and not to be a victory of one region over the other, or one group over the other.[13]

While Clinton's campaign focused on the message of a reversal of rising federal deficits and economic progress, Bush was presented in the media as out of touch. Bush continued to state there was no recession in the country and rendered himself vulnerable after he was photographed playing golf and riding in speedboats.[14]

Several observers saw the Bush campaign as ineffective since it emphasized emotional issues such as religion, race, patriotism, and Clinton's character rather than reflecting on matters of substance. Later, studies showed that attacking an opponent's character was exaggerated as a means for winning votes.[15] The Bush campaign had continuously run negative advertisements, including the attempt to negatively depict Hillary Clinton as a career woman and to castigate Bill Clinton's moral standards.

Clinton brought resourcefulness and energy to the campaign that the Bush campaign failed to match. There was strong evidence that Clinton had superior campaigning skills. On the eve of the elections, Clinton traversed through vital constituencies to grab the key headlines from the incumbent. There is considerable evidence that Clinton's campaign was one of the best in American history. The media described his campaign efforts as tireless, resilient, and that Clinton was a candidate who never slept. Clinton's personality allowed him to shake more hands than his opponent, and he always worked the crowd before focusing on his message. In one account, the media reported that "…in the downpour,

Clinton never looked behind him for an umbrella. As everyone but Secret Service retreated, he stood soaked in the twilight shaking every hand, meeting every pair of eyes, taking care of business."[16]

The Bush campaign was criticized on the international front when they credited President Bush with ending the cold war. Although the cold war ended under the administration of Bush, how it ended remains a contentious and widely debated issue. While conservatives have traditionally credited Reagan for his military build up and tough talk, the centrist explanation regarded the end of the cold war as a product of bipartisan support for containment through diplomatic and military policies.[17] The Democrats dismissed the assertion that Bush was a major player in the cold war game by providing evidence that Bush did little to help the Soviet Union establish a market economy. Bush was also criticized for not doing enough to stop Serbian aggression in Bosnia. On the domestic level, the attempt by the Bush campaign to blame Congress for the unresolved economic crisis was summarily dismissed. The Bush campaign focused on issues that did not resonate with the interests of a vast majority of American voters. Republican strategist Ed Rollins stated it well, "Americans time after time and poll after poll since the convention said they didn't care about the draft, they didn't care about allegations of marital infidelity. What they cared about was where this country was going to go."[18]

For his part, Clinton had taken a keen look at polls and tailored his rhetoric to the needs of his core supporters and the "swing voters." Other analysts focused on the role played by Independent Party candidate, Ross Perot. Although Perot challenged both parties, his relentless attacks on Bush stood in Clinton's favor. His United We Stand America (UWSA) grassroots organization had a populist agenda that undermined the two-party electoral structure. Perot emphasized change, much to the advantage of Clinton. At the campaigns, Perot spoke against Washington insiders, especially wasteful spending and insider politics. In the end, Perot took more votes from Bush than Clinton.[19] Although the media were unfavorable to Perot, he received the highest number of votes among third-party candidates in modern election history.[20]

Clinton's message of injecting new blood into Washington, economic recovery, and health care reforms resonated with a vast majority of voters nationally. In addition, Clinton's bus trip, especially after the July convention, gave the candidate a populist appeal among the voters. Undecided "swing voters" jumped on board rejecting the Republican Party's characterization of Democrats as "tax-and-spend liberals." The Republican campaign strategy failed to persuade voters.

Attempts to adopt the Nixon-Agnew style of emphasizing international successes also failed to impress voters. Nixon, with Kissinger's help, had been a highly successful internationalist, but Bush could not articulate his successes as eloquently as Nixon articulated his. The Bush team had very little to talk about in the wake of a poorly performing economy. Bush ignored domestic issues such as unemployment, and the few times he attempted to discuss them, he received insignificant public support. The public was hardly convinced that another Republican administration would mean more jobs or a restoration of the jobs already lost in the recession. The U.S. economy had failed to rebound after the 1990 recession. According to the Chairman of the Joint Economic Committee of Congress Rep. Lee Hamilton, D-In., in December 1990, the national unemployment rate reached 5.9 percent while U.S. output of goods and services shrunk by almost 1 percent. There were fears that unemployment would peak at 6.4 percent in 1991, leading to a prolonged slump and recession.[21] Economists further argued that the war in the Persian Gulf negatively impacted gas prices.

The picture of compartmentalized state and local unemployment rates from the Department of Labor showed that some areas faced a serious economic downturn. For example, the unemployment rate in Massachusetts was 6.6 percent, 6.8 percent in New Hampshire, and 6.5 percent in New York. In the west, California's jobless rate was 6.5 percent, up sharply from 4.9 percent in November 1989.[22]

The Democrats, this time around, were enjoying the support of the unemployed and low-income Americans who cared little about Clinton's lack of international credentials. Political pundits and economists emphasized the importance of leadership during crisis situations. According to one school of thought, it was not so much the recession that cost Bush the presidency, but instead, it was Bush's failure to articulate and enforce a blueprint for recovery. Such a blueprint design might have spurred economic growth and boosted employment.

A number of analysts also felt that Reagan's recession was much more severe than Bush's recession. Reagan became president at a time when the Federal Reserve decided to reduce double-digit inflation and pushed the economy into a recession. The impact on low-income communities had been worse under the Reagan deficits, and Bush inherited an economy on the decline.[23] Therefore, it appeared that, all things being equal, Bush could have been returned to the White House if the sole criterion was managing the recession. As is well established, presidential actions alone do not run the economy or, for that matter, determine its performance. The key players in most years are the financial markets, members of the public as consumers, and the Federal Reserve Board.

From another perspective, Bush suffered from complacency until it was too late. Bush's strategies should have reflected more on the fact that the powers of incumbency were generally exaggerated.[24] Bush was just like Carter,[25] lacking a strong enough base to enjoy the benefits of incumbency. The Bush presidency was branded as having failed. Perhaps the biggest problem was that of failed trust. Bush's supporters saw him as having broken his campaign promise not to bring new taxes to the people.[26]

In a campaign speech, Bush told Americans that they should elect a president who would have the right vision to "get us from here to there" and who would be trusted with American lives.[27] The criteria were the ones by which the Bush presidency was evaluated. First, from the start of his presidency, Bush had been portrayed as lacking a vision, particularly in domestic affairs. For many Americans, this image persisted. Second, Bush's leadership took America to war in the gulf and consolidated the country's stature as a premier global policeman of the new world order. Fellow Republicans wondered whether the American adventurism that Bush promoted was a better option than the isolationist strategies of the past. Third, Bush's presidency was focused on security and transition from the cold war. The changed global balance of power ushered in uncertainty, especially the use of dirty bombs by terrorists and rogue states. Bush's leadership offered only some security, essentially, because he negotiated with the Russians over nuclear arsenals.

The question is whether President Bush did enough. Certainly the 1992 reelection campaign declared him a failure. Bush, it was argued, failed in his performance as a manager of the U.S. economy. He failed on tax strategies and deficit management. This was a major part of domestic affairs that he felt could "pretty much run on its own."[28] Norquist asserted that President Bush's "most serious mistake was to reverse the Reagan economic policies seen in the budget deal negotiated with Congress in 1990."[29] The president's decision to work with congressional Democrats to raise taxes, despite his earlier campaign pledge, alienated many members of his Republican Party.

Bush was also considered a poor manager of presidential staff and was not viewed as presidential enough when he let his abrasive Chief of Staff John Sununu lead him on a war path with Congress.[30] Bush had been unable to strike a deal with the Democrats who controlled Congress. After an outpouring of complaints from many Republican colleagues and a national outcry over Sununu's style of managing state affairs, Bush reluctantly impressed upon Sununu the need to resign. Sununu resigned in disgrace.

Sununu resigned just as the 1992 elections were nearing. The chief of staff, it has been argued, is "a systems manager…without his backing and evident support of it…the White House is in chaos."[31] Many argued that Sununu got the president to be unpopular because of his personality.[32] The point was that Bush started getting less presidential in his office, thus worsening government program management. In Machiavellian terms, a leader is judged by those around him, and certainly Sununu was a liability. In this particular case, as 1992 advanced, Bush was presented as managerially incompetent. Bush could have been better served, suggested Theodore C. Sorensen, if he had appointed nonpartisan technocrats to boost his managerial capacity.[33] The idea was not unprecedented. Lincoln had done so by nominating Democrat Andrew Johnson to be his vice president in 1860 to save the Union.[34] The point is that the principle and not necessarily the competence of the nominee was at issue.

A president must, in all cases, appear as a unifier of all Americans. A group of *New York Times* syndicate writers observed that

> When any president steps out of his role as a national symbol and unifier and speaks out as a partisan leader in favor of or against particular solutions to domestic problems, he seems, to many Americans, to have abandoned his right character and to have demeaned his office. He becomes a politician.[35]

Bush fit this profile. He spoke of Democrats frustrating his budget proposals, his crime bill, and general domestic policy plans. Bush played politics and ran into deep waters. Bush was not unifying enough. He gave his nominees and appointees too much backing and took his time to release them, even when the signs were clear that they were liabilities. The Sununu case was exemplary.

It may, however, be erroneous to single out a single member of the Bush administration for blame. There was conventional wisdom of executive office responsibility, but in the final analysis, the president took all the blame. For opinion polling, some presidential actions placed Bush quite high on the politically correct scale. After the Gulf War victory, initial polls showed Bush to be unbeatable in the pending elections. The victory in Desert Storm led to a public approval rating of over 80 percent. By 1992 this figure was dropping and reached as low as 43 percent as the elections were around the corner.[36]

Although several tracking polls reported Bush ahead of Clinton, the general consensus was that the successful conduct of the war effort was an insufficient tool for shaping his campaign strategy. Bush's popularity during Operation Desert Storm was "not great enough to outlast time and the erosion of artificially high popularity—especially in the recession."[37] There was evidence that Bush's high ratings began to fall upon the revelation that he was a party to the Iran-contra scandal.

As for the minorities, African American voters voted overwhelmingly for Clinton due to worsening economic conditions. By various accounts, minority groups countrywide preferred a Democratic Party leadership to the GOP and received his victory with a sigh of relief.[38] Perhaps, on a broader level, politics of the economy more than ethnic or racial politics were the cause of the 1992 Bush reelection debacle.

It was not the decision of Jackson to step down that boosted Clinton's chances.[39] After all, Clinton had been an underdog in the Democratic Party's primaries. The frontrunners included Mario Cuomo of New York, John Silber of Massachusetts, and Bob Kerrey of Nebraska. Besides the competitive nature of the pool of candidates, the nation's first African-American elected governor Douglas Wilder posed an additional challenge to Clinton's nomination.[40] Clinton was a beneficiary of a break in the Republican wave started in the Nixon era, broken slightly by Carter. Bush was rejected by Reagan's supporters who thought he was not neo-conservative enough.

In a sense, Baker was right to assert that Clinton won through coalition politics, as Clinton appealed to some Reagan Democrats.[41] Clinton, though a Democrat, was cautious when adopting policies disfavored by Republicans. His era was complicated by the resurgence of Republican control of Congress. It was ironic that Clinton's campaign received the blessing of disgruntled Republicans who weakened Bush's party base. In an interview, Ed Rollins, architect of President Reagan's 1984 landslide victory, poignantly summarized this scenario by noting that

> Reagan and Bush voters defeated George H. W. Bush. It wasn't Bill Clinton. Twenty-eight percent of the Republicans voted for someone other than George Bush. Literally, one out of five Democrats who had supported George Bush also supported him this time. The rest went back home.[42]

This event confirmed the demise of Bush's "political tribe" of moderate Republicans in 1992. His attempt to play Reagan was betrayed by his moderate approach to resolving issues that a core conservative segment in the party had rejected. Bush just could not be a clear "member of the red-meat right" to reiterate Margaret G. Warner's characterization of the president.[43] Bush's reelection was in doubt.

The 1992 reelection failure was a blessing in disguise for Republican renaissance, a period where the party went back to the drawing boards. Loss of the White House was replaced by the gain of Congress. The emergence of Newt Gingrich and other right-wing Republicans in 1994 gave Republicans an obvious edge in the management of American public affairs. The party's core ideology found a more assertive voice in the emergent leaders.

In the final analysis, Bush lost because Americans did not support his domestic policies. To a large extent, Bush had inherited these policies from the Reagan era, but Americans chose to deny him the opportunity for a second term.

Close observers of the presidency contend that at the end of his stint in the Oval Office, Bush thought he was misunderstood. In numerous interviews, he craved the vindication of a second term. He told friends that he had been convinced that he could pull off an upset victory, but his campaign was badly managed.[44] His wife Barbara thought Baker had done a bad job this time around.[45] In reference to his defeat, Bush spoke of having received "the order of the boot"—the same one dished out to Winston Churchill of England.[46]

The media reverted to old titles and labeled him as another lame duck president.[47] There were public comments about his defeat by the young Clinton, who, at 46 years old, was a contemporary of Bush's baby boomer son, George W. Bush. It is hard not to underestimate the "youth" or "generational bump" factor in the 1992 elections.[48]

In conclusion, President Bush was a statesman and gracefully handed over the mantle to President Clinton. In the end, Bush was gracious in defeat. "There is important work to be done and America must always come first. So we will get behind this new president and...wish him well."[49] One can summarize Bush's attempt to win a second term in his own words,

> We have fought the good fight and we have kept the faith and I believe I have upheld the honor of the presidency of the United States ...And I would like to thank so many of you who have

worked beside me to improve America and to literally change the world.⁵⁰

There is much to be learned about presidential elections and the end of a presidency. The academic interpretation of the president's failed election is replete with interpretations. Yet the explanations of the end of this one-term presidency are remarkably similar to theoretical assumptions in the literature. By not adequately focusing on pressures from the domestic front, the first post–cold war presidency ended unceremoniously. The belief in the association between economic performance and electoral votes seemed to have been realized. In that sense, able presidential leadership in international politics was at odds with political management in domestic politics.

In this chapter, we provided only a few reasons that lead to the failed reelection of President Bush, and we described how Governor Clinton won the 1992 elections. Certainly, other issues and factors not included here may have contributed to President Bush's failed reelection. It will suffice to note that the unmaking of the Bush presidency provided an opportunity to examine the enduring features of his legacy. In view of the important changes that occurred in international politics, our purpose has been to demonstrate the importance of changes in the presidency and emerging U.S. leadership in global political affairs. Scholars can revisit the president's legacy to evaluate the degree to which the successor administrations upheld his values and achievements.

Notes

* George Bush, concession speech, cited in "Bush: Time to Support the Winner," *The Boston Globe*, November 5, 1992, 27.
1. George F. Will, *The New Season: A Spectator's Guide to the 1988 Election* (New York: Simon & Schuster, 1987), 52.
2. Grover G. Norquist, "The Unmaking of the President: Why George Bush Lost," *Policy Review* 63 (winter 1993): 10–25. Also see Coral Bell, *The Reagan Paradox: U.S. Foreign Policy in the 1980s* (New Brunswick, NJ: Rutgers University Press, 1989), 156.
3. Norquist, "The Unmaking of the President, Why George Bush Lost," 10.
4. Ibid., 13.
5. David Gergen, *Eyewitness to Power: The Essence of Leadership Nixon to Clinton* (New York: Simon & Schuster, 2000), 160.
6. Barbara Sinclair, "Governing Unheroically (and Sometimes Unappetizingly): Bush and the 101st Congress," in *The Bush Presidency: First Appraisals*, ed. Colin Campbell and Bert Rockman (Chatham, NJ: Chatham, 1991), 178–180.
7. Ibid., 170–171.
8. Norquist, "The Unmaking of the President, Why George Bush Lost," 14.
9. Jane Mayer and Doyle McManus, *Landslide: The Unmaking of the President, 1984–1988* (Boston: Houghton Mifflin Company, 1988), 395.
10. Edward (Ed) Rollins, interview on CNN, *Larry King Live*, November 6, 1992.
11. Betty Glad, "How George Bush Lost the Presidential Election of 1992," in *The Clinton Presidency: Campaigning, Governing, and the Psychology of Leadership*, ed. Stanley A. Renshon (Boulder, CO: Westview Press, 1995), 13–15. See Nelson W. Polsby and Aaron Wildavsky, *Presidential Elections: Strategies and Structures in American Politics* (Chatham, NJ: Chatham House, 1996), 60.
12. Campaign '92 election night, "A Look at How Clinton Won Election," CBS News transcripts, Dan Rather, November 3, 1992.
13. Paula Zahn, CBS reporter, interview, "Mickey Kantor Discusses How Clinton Won the Election," *CBS This Morning*, November 4, 1992.
14. William A. Rusher, "Clinton's First Year," in *Consequences of the Clinton Victory: Essays on the First Year*, ed. Peter W. Schramm (Ashland, OH: Ashbrook Press, 1994), 4.

15. Ibid. Also see Kathryn M. Doherty and James G. Gimpel, "Candidate Character vs. the Economy in the 1992 Election," *Political Behavior* 19, no. 3 (1997): 117–196.
16. Bill Nichols, "How Clinton Won, Tireless Clinton Never Stopped, Never Lost Hope," *USA Today*, November 4, 1992, 4A.
17. John Tirman, "How We Ended the Cold War," *The Nation*, November 1, 1999, 1 and Mary Tillotson, "U.S. History: George H. W. Bush's Presidency Saw End of Cold War," radio broadcast, *Voice of America*, July 18, 2007.
18. Rollins, interview, November 6, 1992.
19. R. Richard Alvarez and Jonathan Nagler, "Economics, Issues and the Perot Candidacy: Voter Choice in the 1992 Presidential Election," *American Journal of Political Science* 39, no. 3 (August 1995): 714.
20. Paul F. Boller Jr., *Presidential Campaigns* (New York: Oxford University Press, 1996), 387. For more details on the role of the press, see Mark J. Rozell, *The Press and the Bush Presidency* (Westport, CT: Praeger, 1996).
21. Mark Memmott, "Congressman: Jobless Rate Could Hit 8%," *USA Today*, December 28, 1990, 1B.
22. Mark Memmott, "Fewer Jobs on East, West Coasts," *USA Today*, January 16, 1991, 6B.
23. Mark Memmot, "Economists Give Clinton Passing Grade," *USA Today*, January 23, 1995, 4B.
24. Albert R. Hunt, "The Campaign and the Issues," in *The American Elections of 1980*, ed. Austin Ranney (Washington, DC: American Institute for Public Policy Research, 1980), 161.
25. Ibid., 142.
26. Craig Unger, *House of Bush, House of Saud: The Secret Relationship Between the World's Two Most Powerful Dynasties* (New York: Scribner, 2004), 191.
27. United States Information Services, library, Nairobi, videotape; Bush Profile, no. 320: III (audio recording of campaign speech).
28. Colin Campbell, *The U.S. Presidency in Crisis: A Comparative Perspective* (New York: Oxford University Press, 1998), 68.
29. Norquist, "The Unmaking of the President, Why George Bush Lost," 11.
30. Thomas Frank, "From Pit Bull to President: Bush Changes Tactics—But Still Will He Change Staffs?," *Newsweek*, November 12, 1990, 30. Also see John Newhouse, "Profiles, The Tactician, Profile of James Addison Baker III, Secretary of State and Close Friend of President George Bush," *The New Yorker*, May 7, 1990, 58.

31. "Sununu's Job, More Than Flights of Fancy," *PA Times* 15, no. 1 (January 1992): 1.
32. Ibid. Also see Bradley H. Patterson, Jr., *The Ring of Power: The White House Staff and Its Expanding Role in Government* (New York: Basic Books, 1988), 1.
33. Theodore C. Sorenson, *A Different Kind of Presidency: A Proposal for Breaking Political Deadlock* (New York: Harper and Row, 1984), 64.
34. Ibid., 61–64.
35. Harold Faber, *The Road to the White House* (New York: Berkley Publishing, 1966), 291.
36. Jon R. Bond and Richard Fleisher, "Clinton and Congress: A First Year Assessment," *American Politics Quarterly* 23, no. 3 (July 1995): 355.
37. Paul Brace and Barbara Hinckley, *Follow the Leader: Opinion Polls and the Modern Presidents* (New York: Basic Books, 1992).
38. Bill Lambrecht, "Clinton Picked Up GOP Pieces," *St. Louis Post-Dispatch* (Missouri) November 5, 1992, A1 and Jason DeParle et al., "The 1992 Elections: State by State," *New York Times*, November 5, 1992, B11.
39. Lucius J. Barker, "Limits of Political Strategy: A Systematic View of the American Experience," *American Political Science Review* 88, no. 1 (March 1994): 6. Barker maintained that Jackson's decision to withdraw from the race helped Clinton's election.
40. Larry Martz and Rich Thomas, "Bush League," *Newsweek*, November 12, 1990, 35.
41. Lucius Barker, "Limits of Political Strategy: A Systematic View of the American Experience," 6.
42. Rollins, interview, November 6, 1992.
43. Margaret G. Warner, "Bush Battles the Wimp Factor, A Searching Look at the Vice President's Most Persistent Political Liability," *Newsweek*, October 19, 1987, 29.
44. Stephen Labaton, "The Transition: The President; Friends Describe a Melancholy Bush," *New York Times*, November 15, 1992, L36.
45. Ibid.
46. Ibid.
47. *The Sun Herald*, cited in the *New York Times*, November 17, 1992, A19.
48. *The New Yorker* used the concept of "generational bump" to discuss the Republican Party's strategy of picking Dan Quayle as running mate to George Bush. The party needed a younger vice president to attract youthful voters. See *The New Yorker*, May 7, 1990, 73.
49. Bush, in an address to his supporters in Houston, Texas, November 3, 1992.
50. Ibid.

CHAPTER 10

THE BUSH LEGACY AND CONCLUSIONS

> *Bush is entitled to a place as the president who guided the ship of state through some perilous waters and helped some of his fellow chiefs of state to find new routes to the safer.*
>
> —Raymond Moore*

This final chapter describes the legacy of the Bush presidency based on an evaluation of the aggregate performance of his administration. This chapter acknowledges the staying power of Bush's ideals and recognizes his contributions to the new world order. This chapter recognizes Bush's imprint upon America and world politics.

Presidential scholars have observed that presidents stake their places in history on specific ideas, actions, and programs. Frequently, presidents focus more on international events. Sometimes a president pegs his legacy on issues that are predominantly domestic in nature. Other times presidents attempt to balance international and domestic agendas, often with mixed results. For example, F. D. Roosevelt tackled the Great Depression while focusing attention on international balance of power issues. Johnson gambled his Great Society ambitions in the wake of the ravaging Vietnam War. Bush grappled with a host of international concerns as the domestic economy faced a recession.

The aim of this book is to analyze presidential leadership at a time when the global political and economic conditions had been reconfigured. President Bush was held responsible for practically every aspect of managing the post–cold war global world order. Consequently, the actions Bush took to establish U.S. global leadership came under scrutiny in presidential scholarship and popular media debates and analyses.

Shaping a New World Order and Democratic Globalism

Bush gave form to the ideological underpinnings of the new world order, defined as the post–cold war period, with the United States at the apex and serving as the sole superpower.[1] In 1989 Bush witnessed the demolition of the Berlin Wall, which marked the beginning of freedom, enlargement of democracy, free markets, and capitalism in the Soviet enclaves. With ideological communism ending in Europe, ideological violence was less likely to survive elsewhere. As Bush proposed in his 1990 State of the Union speech as the new world order took shape, America stood at the "center of a widening circle of freedom." The new world order entailed a peaceful coexistence of nations sharing the values of freedom and democracy.

It is our book's contention that Bush more than other presidents in the post–World War II era pushed to the forefront the agenda of democratic globalism. In this agenda, America operated as a prefect to monitor human rights abuses, democratic reforms, and economic liberalization, as well as threats to international security that included curbing nuclear arms proliferation and new communism projected by religious fundamentalism and terrorism.

Although the Bush administration upheld the core Wilsonian doctrine of promoting democracy, variations existed. Often the policy was selective diplomacy as the president sought to influence the Caucasus and Central Asian regions that were part of the defunct Soviet empire. Pragmatic caution rather than an outright carrot-and-stick approach was the chosen vehicle to export the virtues of democracy. Initially, the United States opened diplomatic relations with six of the twelve former Soviet republics—Armenia, Belarus, Kazakhstan, Kirgizstan, Russia, and Ukraine.[2] The Bush administration withheld official diplomatic recognition from countries that demonstrated no commitment to democratic governance and free markets. These were the republics of Azerbaijan, Georgia, Moldova, Tajikistan, Turkmenistan, and Uzbekistan. Because some of the republics with which the United States maintained diplomatic ties were nuclear-armed nations, critics contended that selective recognition undermined the larger security goals of arms control. President Bush had no illusion that democracy would flourish overnight.[3]

In Africa, Bush was initially concerned with resolving longstanding conflicts that had been a part of cold war hostilities. These conflicts required further diplomatic consultations with Russia. President Bush adopted a consensus-oriented style in contrast to Reagan's more combative approach. Bush began to cooperate with Gorbachev over ending conflicts in Africa.[4] Bush can be credited with facilitating the settlement of regional civil wars and encouraging reforms in the areas of human rights and market development.

Bush stands out as the most Wilsonian president of the United States, at least in making the continent safe for democracy. The Bush envoys in this region set a precedent by producing more political activists than diplomats in pushing African dictatorships to accept political reforms and improve their human rights records. Although Congress, under the Carter presidency, insisted on linking U.S. foreign policy to development assistance, the major push came in the Bush era.[5] One commentator asserted that Bush clearly articulated the human rights agenda in international forums such as the UN.[6] As an example, in 1991, Bush's administration withheld bilateral aid to countries that abused human rights such as Cameroon, Kenya, and Togo.

The result of the administration's stand on human rights and democracy was that one-party dictatorships, such as in Benin, Cape Verde, Kenya, and Zambia, opened up multiparty elections for the first time in more than two decades. The Bush administration earmarked over $30 million for civic education to enhance democratic traditions. As Thomas Kean observed, long after Bush, the country would reap "the dividends of the peaceful collapse of Soviet Communism; the liberation of Kuwait and Panama; the largely unexpected advance of democracy in Africa, Asia, and Latin America and the free trade agreements with Canada and other nations."[7]

These observations were shared within the international academic community. Korwa Adar concluded that this Bush plan was expanded upon by his successor, Clinton.[8] This action indicated the new world order was one in which democracy reigned supreme. The case of U.S. forces returning Jean-Bertrand Aristide as president of Haiti is illustrative.[9] Aristide had been Haiti's first democratically elected president in two hundred years. After assuming the presidency in February of 1991, Aristide was overthrown in September by armed military forces loyal to army commander Lieutenant General Raoul Cédras. The U.S. government considered Cédras a "thug" and backed his removal. The election of Aristide marked an important milestone in the history of this Caribbean nation and was an example of the march to freedom that President Bush announced. Later, it was the Clinton administration that oversaw the return to electoral democracy in Haiti.

The U.S. invasion of Haiti in August 1994 served to indicate the seriousness of the United States in the promotion of democracy. The Clinton administration, in full support of the Bush project of engaging U.S. and allied forces in problem areas, backed multilateral efforts to intervene in peace resolution processes in disputes in Angola, Bosnia, and Rwanda. The Clinton and Bush administrations encouraged and supported organizations such as the Economic Community of West African States (ECOWAS) in peacekeeping operations in Liberia.[10] Bush's humanitarian intervention in Somalia was unprecedented and an event that will likely be remembered for ages.

REFORMING INTERNATIONAL INSTITUTIONS AND REASSERTING GLOBAL POWER

Under President Bush's leadership, institutions such as the World Bank, NATO, and the UN were reformed. The Clinton administration continued to articulate the same position as a strategy for promotion of global U.S. economic interests. The Bush administration did not intend to do away with agencies such as NATO and played a pivotal role in refocusing its mission in the post–cold war era. Under American leadership, efforts were made to expand NATO's membership. Bush gave the UN Security Council a new lease on life as it became more assertive in conflict resolution on the global level. The new world order, to a large extent, had centered on the UN. Clinton accepted the Bush plan and argued that the United States ought to "pay for its share of the costs of UN peacekeeping operations" and pushed for the creation of a "UN Rapid Deployment Force that could be used for purposes beyond traditional peacekeeping for humanitarian purposes."[11]

The post–cold war international environment created opportunities, as well as challenges, for U.S. global leadership. These could also be seen in terms of costs and benefits. The aftermath of the collapse of the Soviet Union meant the end of the possibility of Pax Sovietica and the rejuvenation of the idea of Pax Americana. At the beginning of the Bush administration in 1989, there was great need for the establishment of confidence in the global political system. The Bush administration was aware of this responsibility and took care to project the deterrent strength of the United States through several initiatives. Presidential authority and responsibility were at the core of exercising this power. This is the lesson Bush sought to provide to the next generation of leaders.

The vacuum created by the loss of Soviet power meant there was need for further reestablishment of U.S. global power. The president was aware that displaying an "arrogance of power" was part of the reason why America lost so many lives during the Vietnam War. Thus, the Gulf War was one of the most important tests of presidential leadership at the global level. Bush seized the moment to assert America's position. In Bush's words,

> Recent events have surely proven that there is no substitute for American leadership. In the face of tyranny, let no one doubt American credibility and reliability. Let no one doubt our staying power. We will stand by our friends. One way or another, the leader of Iraq must learn this fundamental truth.[12]

Although vast amounts of scholarly work have been written about the Gulf War, there is, understandably, scanty work done in the English language from Iraqi perspectives. What is known is that the Iraqi dictator's invasion of Kuwait, on August 2, 1990, was seen as a threat to Saudi Arabia. The Bush administration's goal was to end Iraqi occupation of Kuwait and unconditionally restore legitimate government. The United States' goal of providing security and stability to the Persian Gulf was endorsed by the UN Security Council. President Bush was able to persuade Soviet President Gorbachev to delegitimize Iraq's aggression, thereby successfully ending the possibility of dictators counting on East-West conflicts to "stymie concerted United Nations action against aggression."[13]

In April 1990 Secretary of State Baker told Congress that Iraq was a candidate for the watch list of countries that sponsored international terrorism, as they were developing nuclear weapons. This was long before the invasion of Kuwait. Countries on the watch list would be denied advanced technology, international loans, and agricultural credits. In 1988 the number of terrorism incidents had reached 528, with the bulk of them victims of the bombing of Pan American Flight 103 over Lockerbie, Scotland.[14]

Terrorism was a threat that did not go away with the end of the cold war. The Bush administration encouraged international cooperation and influenced governments not to provide support and sanctuary for terrorist groups.[15] Iraq's invasion of Kuwait was a culmination of actions that placed Hussein's regime in the spotlight. Much as the invasion weakened Hussein's military capabilities and provided the United States with greater leverage in the region.

Therefore, what emerged is that after the 1991 victory in the Persian Gulf, American power and strength increased rather than declined. The president resisted the temptation to appear as if he was taking unilateral action against Iraq. To President Bush, it was better to end illegal occupations and provide a framework for future deterrence through the international system under U.S. leadership. Not only did Bush tell Hussein to withdraw troops from Kuwait, but also his comments were clearly stated and remarkably well-understood and received internationally. The president's actions were reinforced by his diplomatic maneuvers to enlist the support of a broad coalition of friendly nations. The strength of Bush's diplomacy, like his conviction to use force, reinforced the need to establish American standards of democratic practice in countries under similar dictatorships.

A related point was the promotion of freedom and peaceful coexistence among all peoples. The president was averse to those abusing human rights and denying the growth of democracy. Bush faced a series of judgments, especially in his denial of U.S. aid to dictators who had previously benefited from U.S. cold war largesse. President Bush stood strong on the side of democracy and freedom. Bush did well to avoid the appearance of reneging on its promise to reward countries that reformed their political systems. Bush's moral standing directly contributed to democratic enlargement and considerably weakened the evils of dictatorships and brutal abuse of international human rights. Presidential leadership strengthened democratic forces worldwide. Bush established the sense of optimism that masses of humanity had been expecting from the City on the Hill.

KINDER AND GENTLER HOME FRONT

The Bush legacy on the domestic front is exhibited in his presidential style and policy actions. The president's fundamental belief was in the recognition of individualism as a key value in shaping American world views. Wildavsky viewed Bush as a product of patrician values who viewed personal responsibility as an important value for the conservative agenda.[16] Bush believed it was important that society showed a kinder and gentler approach to managing crises such as AIDS. At the same time, Bush believed and supported policies that encouraged family values and stressed the personal responsibility of individuals to avoid behavior that would lead to AIDS.[17] Bush's upbringing had instilled in him the importance of family values, rule-guided behavior, and a high sense of individualism. Therefore, his conduct of national affairs demonstrated his reliance on conservative ideas such as sacrifice, duty, commitment, and patriotism.[18]

Analysis of his presidency reveals that Bush reinforced the conservative mood in the country.[19] Conservatism had been part of the Republican culture, peaking during the Reagan era. The mood became powerful and culminated in the Republican victory in the House and Senate elections of 1994. The Bush debacle and his failure to win reelection in 1992 acted as a catalyst for the consolidation of conservative ideals such as patriotism, high morality, moderation, and the aristocratic spirit.[20] For the first time in several decades, the United States became generally more inward looking as Congress increasingly spoke of isolationism. Congress's actions may appear to be a move away from the internationalist agenda of Bush, but ideologically, it was not. Bush may have preferred to complete the post–cold war transition policies and then turn his energies inward, but American voters disagreed.

Bush, like Reagan in 1984, made the movement to the political right acceptable in the eyes of many Democrats. In the Reagan era, many members of the Democratic Congress backed the budget deficit reduction strategy defined by the Gramm-Rudman Act.[21] The Bush years saw the partial reversal of programs whose history was embedded in F. D. Roosevelt's New Deal and Johnson's Great Society schemes that upheld the big government syndrome. This was exemplified in revisions of welfare and social service policies. As a conservative, Bush was not only moderate but also cautious, especially in the domestic policy arena.[22]

In the area of education, Bush's America 2000 program, for example, improved community involvement by providing quality education programs to American schoolchildren and empowered parents to have greater choices in selecting schools for their children. Bush saw these reforms as a means to reverse the deteriorating standards of education in communities. Bush used a cautious approach to solving the domestic problems the United States faced while the national mood in 1992 called for more aggressive presidential action. Bush had hoped the domestic problems would be solved without much direct presidential input.

Although the reforms Bush promised were not convincing to the electorate, the post–Bush years witnessed a cautious move by the White House to revive aspects of American economic domination of the world, especially in the energy market.

In his international ventures, Bush limited the activities of the new Communists and promoted the cause for global democracy. It is difficult to deny him recognition for the manner by which he steered the world out of the cold war. President Bush had the enormous challenge of establishing global security, which demanded skilled diplomatic leadership and provided the necessary stewardship.

REEVALUATING PRESIDENT BUSH'S LEADERSHIP

Raymond Moore observed that the achievements of Bush were not small by any standards. Moore asserted that Bush is entitled to a place in history as one who helped lay the groundwork for greater global democracy, freedom, and market economies.[23] Moore recognized that the post–Bush era may have had significant ethnic, religious, and nationalist wars, but seen in a broader perspective, Bush was the world's most endowed statesman when great events transformed the world. The irony is that Bush's actions were seldom treated as praiseworthy. In fact, there is disagreement over whether his foreign policy successes were enough. *The New Republic* challenged the conventional wisdom that Bush's "high marks" on foreign policy were unassailable.[24] The journal criticized Bush for not removing Hussein from office and making Gorbachev the center of American diplomacy in the Soviet Union. Of course, events in 2003 proved the journal's critics wrong. To have taken a different path would have endangered the nation's security. The changing nature of global politics required the cautious approaches taken by the forty-first president.

Presidential ratings done by Arthur M. Schlesinger Jr. rated Bush within the average category of presidents. He was placed behind Hayes, Taft, Van Buren, Clinton, Harrison, Adams, and Madison and placed ahead of Arthur, Carter, and Ford in the average group. There are three higher rated categories labeled as high average, near great, and great. The last category was reserved for only three presidents: Lincoln, Washington, and F. D. Roosevelt.[25] Yet none of the presidents within the average category presided over a more momentous world than did Bush, especially as a one-term leader.

Bush's legacy was that he retained the honor of the American presidency and catapulted the nation to further frontiers of global and economic leadership. The debate of a declining America subsided immediately after his electoral defeat in 1992.

Bush made political blunders as well. As Peter Calvert said, "The presidential office is an awe inspiring and powerful one; it is a human institution amenable to the same treatment as any other form of leadership."[26] The Bush record ends with poor performance in leaving behind a culture of unfocused management in the White House. The administration reinforced the position that the presidency was about conducting foreign policy and international relations rather than attacking poverty at home.

Despite his weaknesses, Bush remained the first leader of the new world order in which America's position as premier world power appeared unchallenged. He was the first world president, a position that permitted the United States to virtually determine the course of world affairs unchallenged. Through Bush's stewardship, the United States was able to intelligently sustain the country's security by prudently committing American forces where national interests were threatened. Perhaps better than other Western leaders, Bush was able to counter the emergence of new authoritarian rulers in the former Soviet Union.

The sustainability of this position was, however, constrained by his failures on the domestic front. Indeed, for America to be the respected symbol of freedom and progress, its political leadership ought to have struck a balance between success at home and success in the foreign arena. Bush also lost his reelection bid due to the lack of support from his right-wing colleagues in the Republican Party, as well as his mishandling of the budget deficit and his inability to read the American mood. As Paul Quirk observed, Bush was a strategically competent leader who failed because he could not control or predict the economic forces that bedeviled his term in office.[27]

Bush tried to answer the big question about his leadership of whether he did a good job overall during a dedication of the George Bush Library at Texas A&M University. Bush noted that the facility would "serve to educate future generations of Americans, to give them a broader understanding of how their government responded in the way it did to the challenges it faced at a watershed moment in history."[28] The forty-first president of the United States reminded the audience of his role in helping to preside over the end of the cold war. Michael Beschloss said of President Bush,

> By helping to end the Cold War he caused Americans instead to look to a president like Bill Clinton, who was more emotionally involved in domestic issues and the domestic economy, than a president who was skilled in foreign affairs.[29]

As former President Reagan pointed out, Bush "played a major role in everything we accomplished."[30] This is important because the literature and mass media have often minimized President Bush's role in the political management of the country.

Bush summarized his legacy by concluding that he had a clean administration and a respected office of the presidency. We can add to this list several successes such as his Strategic Arms Reduction Treaty with the Soviet Union, rejuvenation of Sino-American relations by his insistence on granting China MFN status despite the moral condemnation of China's human rights abuses, and his expansion of NATO, as well as his embracing a unified Germany into the alliance.

Michael Sturmer, in writing on changing U.S.-German relations, went further, crediting President Bush for "guiding Germany through troubled waters of European and world politics in 1990."[31] The unfolding events in Europe presented an opportunity for the United States to continue its history of productive cooperation with the new Germany. Much was expected of the United States to help transform Germany's role in the enlarged post–cold war European theater. With its prosperous economy and large population of over 80 million people, the new Germany's position in NATO had to be discussed. Much concern hinged upon resolution to trends, suggesting a Franco-Germany counterbalance to U.S. leadership, as well as Europe's self-interest in managing an emerging Chinese economic block. The Bush administration shared much of Germany's outlook in matters of security, especially the question of antiballistic missiles and biological weapons systems.

Although volumes have been written about the reunification of Germany in 1989, there is still work to be done analyzing the role of American statesmen. Much credit to the successful reintegration of the country has been attributed to the courage and resoluteness of the German people and to the support they received from the international community. Former German Chancellor Helmut Kohl on numerous occasions credited President Bush and former Soviet President Gorbachev for providing the political environment that made reunification a success. German newspapers reported that President Bush gave Germany unconditional support during its reunification. These reports were in contrast to the unenthusiastic support from Britain's Thatcher and France's Mitterrand. Bush is reported to have heard Mitterrand joke that, "I like Germany so much, I think there should be two of them!"[32] In addition, the Bush administration was supportive of Western European integration, which it saw as an important ally.

Bush and Trade Agreements

Bush achieved some limited successes in negotiating trade agreements with Japan and Mexico with whom he signed a free market agreement.

He maintained sanctions against Cuba's Fidel Castro and ensured victory over the Sandinistas in Nicaragua and Manuel Noriega in Panama. Bush's record in Latin America's democratic enlargement was remarkable as was his administration's war against narcotics. The Bush administration launched a review of Latin America's debts strategy. Several Latin American leaders, including Mexico's President Carlos Salinas de Gortari and Venezuela's Carlos Andres Perez, proposed suspension of principal payments on foreign debts.[33] Clinton's policy on the promotion of democracy, debt relief, and trade agreements was a continuation of Bush's policies.[34]

Even though full justice cannot be done in a single book, it is appropriate to conclude that the global setting creates material conditions for understanding presidential leadership. While situational factors are known to shape a presidency, it is also observable that American presidential leadership changes the course of world history. For example, the advent of the World Wide Web[35] in 1990 and the emergent Internet browsers gave new meaning to the global world order that provided the setting for the presidency of Bush. Experts in the telecommunications sector now contend that the Internet not only contributed to the time-space compression of the world but also led to the intensification of the world's conscience.

The examples presented in this book only scratch the surface of presidential leadership within a globalized world. We have illustrated aspects of presidential leadership that contribute to our conception of the emergent global order. In the gulf region, Bush orchestrated Operation Desert Storm to remove the Iraqi occupation from Kuwait and set the stage for demonstrating the power of American leadership in global political management. Consistent with the president's vision, Bush left his mark on the world's democratization process. Recall that during one of his first media interviews as president, Bush stated that he hoped his legacy would provide leadership to result in "a kinder, gentler America as a part of a more peaceful democratic world."[36] There are several indicators to show that this vision was partly realized. In Africa, Bush reduced or virtually ended the personal rule phenomenon of most of the vast continent's political systems. The latter job, though unfinished and often troubled, progressed well and was an irreversible process. Consistent with his diplomatic outreach and efforts, the Bush presidency maintained global dominance in world affairs and established his presidency as the first among the family of nations. And on the home front, policies linked to the global commons, such as the environment or trade, expected leadership from Bush's presidency. In a hierarchical world that was rapidly transitioning, these were no simple achievements.

NOTES

* Raymond Moore, "Foreign Policy," in *The Bush Presidency and Adversities: Triumphs and Adversities*, ed. D. M. Hill and P. Williams (New York: St. Martin's, 1994), 180.
1. Jon Roper, *The American Presidents: Heroic Leadership From Kennedy to Clinton* (Edinburgh, U.K.: Edinburgh University Press, 2000), 165. Also see John Robert Green, *The Presidency of George Bush* (Lawrence: University of Kansas, 2000).
2. C. A. Robbins and L. Robinson, "Diplomatic About-Face; Washington in a Race for Influence From the Caucasus to Central Asia," *U.S. News and World Report* 112, no. 7 (February 24, 1993): 51.
3. Ibid.
4. Donald Rothchild, "The U.S. Foreign Policy Trajectory on Africa," *SAIS Review* 21, no. 1 (2001): 179–211.
5. Korwa G. Adar, "Of the Wilsonian and Moralists Conception of Human Rights: Is the Time Germane for the U.S. Human Rights Foreign Policy in Africa?" (paper presented at the 5th American Studies Association of East Africa Conference, Jinja, Uganda, July 17–20, 1995, 15). Also see John Shattuck, *Promoting Democracy and Human Rights* (Washington, DC: U.S. State Department, April 1, 1994).
6. Adar, "Of the Wilsonian and Moralists Conception of Human Rights: Is the Time Germane for the U.S. Human Rights Foreign Policy in Africa?," 22.
7. Thomas Kean, "Who's Presidential: No Candidate Is Better Than Bush," *New York Times*, March 12, 1992, editorial, 23.
8. Adar, "Of the Wilsonian and Moralists Conception of Human Rights: Is the Time Germane for the U.S. Human Rights Foreign Policy in Africa?," 22.
9. Warren Christopher, address to J. F. Kennedy School of Government, Harvard University, Cambridge, MA, January 20, 1995.
10. U.S. State Department, "U.S. Policy for a New Era in Sub-Saharan Africa," fact sheet 2830, issued January 27, 1993.
11. Francis A. Kornegay Jr., "Africa in the New World Order, U.S. Policy," *Africa Report* (January/February 1993): 16.
12. President Bush, speech to Congress and nation, September 11, 1990.
13. President Bush, speech to Congress and the nation, 9:09 p.m. (EST) in the House Chamber at the Capitol, September 11, 1990, Washington, DC. For a detailed discussion on the war, see Jean Edward Smith, *George Bush's War* (New York: Henry Holt and Co., 1992).

14. Barry Schweid, "Baker Says U.S. to Consider Adding Iraq to Terrorist List," *The Associated Press*, May 1, 1990.
15. "Terrorists Active: After a Decline, Terrorism Still Remains a Threat," *The Houston Chronicle*, May 11, 1993, 12.
16. Aaron Wildavsky, *The Beleaguered Presidency* (New Brunswick, NJ: Transaction Publishers, 1991), 304.
17. Ibid., 304.
18. Ibid., 306.
19. Clinton Rossiter, *Conservatism in America* (New York: Alfred Knopf, 1955), 47–48.
20. Ibid., 48. For details of the president's aristocratic family background, see, Kitty Kelly, *The Family: The True Story of the Bush Dynasty* (London: Doubleday, 2004).
21. Thomas Ferguson and Joel Rogers, "The Myth of America's Turn to the Right," in *American Politics, Classic and Contemporary Readings*, ed. Allan J. Cigler and Burdett A. Loomis (Boston: Houghton Mifflin, 1989), 198.
22. Clinton Rossiter defines a conservative as a moderate. Rossiter, *Conservatism in America*, 49. Also see, Ronald E. Pynn, *American Politics: Changing Expectations* (Dubuque, IA: Brown and Benchmark, 1993), 323.
23. Moore, "Foreign Policy," 180. Professor Green arrived at similar conclusions. See Green, *The Presidency of George Bush* (Lawrence: University of Kansas, 2000).
24. "What Foreign Policy?" *The New Republic* 205, no. 14 (September 30, 1991): 5–6.
25. Arthur Schlesinger Jr., "Rating the Presidents: Washington to Clinton," *Political Science Quarterly* 112, no. 2 (summer 1997): 179–189.
26. Peter Calvert, "Studying the Presidency," in *The American Way, Government and Politics in the USA*, ed. Lynton Robins (London: Longman, 1985), 111.
27. Paul J. Quirk, "Presidential Competence," in *The Presidency and the Political System*, ed. Michael Nelson (Washington, DC: Congressional Quarterly Press, 1998), 189.
28. The George Bush School of Government and Public Service, November 6, 1997, archives, http:// www-bushschool.tamu.edu/
29. Ibid.
30. Reagan mentioned this in his address to the Republican Party's convention in New Orleans, August 1988. See "American Survey," *The Economist*, August 20, 1988, 24.

31. Michael Sturmer, "Germany in Search of an Enlightened American Leadership," in *The Future of U.S.-European Relations in Search of a New World Order*, ed. Henry Brandon (Washington, DC: Brookings Institution Press, 1992), 75–88.
32. Joerg Wolf, "Day of German Unity and German-American Day," *The Atlantic Review* (October 7, 2006), http://atlanticreview.org/archives/435-Day-of-German-Unity-and-German-American-Day.html
33. "Go Easier on Latin Debtors," *Business Week*, January 16, 1989, editorial, 112.
34. David Scott Palmer, *U.S. Relations With Latin America During the Clinton Years: Opportunities Lost or Opportunities Squandered?* (Gainesville: University Press of Florida 2006).
35. Manuel Castells, *The Rise of the Network Society* (Oxford, U.K.: Blackwell, 2000), 50–51.
36. Thomas M. DeFrank and Ann McDaniel, "An Interview With Bush: The Deficit Is the Top Priority for the New President," *Newsweek*, January 30, 1989, 32.

SELECTED BIBLIOGRAPHY

Adar, Korwa. "The Wilsonian Conception of Democracy and Human Rights: A Retrospective and Prospective." *African Studies Quarterly* 2, no. 2 (September 25, 1998), http://Africa.ufl.edu/asq

Aho, C. Michael. "Can America Avoid Decline?" Paper presented at the 9th D.S. MacNaughton Symposium Proceedings, Democratic Governance; America in the 21st-Century, Syracuse, New York, 1990: 57–68.

Ake, Claude. "Rethinking African Democracy." In *The Global Resurgence of Democracy*, edited by Larry Diamond and Marc F. Plattner, 77–81. Baltimore: Johns Hopkins University Press, 1993.

Allard, Kenneth. *Somalia Operations: Lesson Learned, National Defense.* Washington, DC: National Defense University Press, 1995.

Ambrose, Stephen E. *Rise to Globalism, American Foreign Policy Since 1938.* New York: Penguin Books, 1991.

Anderson, James E. "Economic Policy: Comparative Advisory Arrangements." In *Presidential Policy Making: An End-of-Century Assessment*, edited by Steven A. Shull, 224–245. Armonk, NY: M. E. Sharpe, 1999.

Andrade, L., and G. Young. "Presidential Agenda Setting: Influences on the Emphasis of Foreign Policy." *Political Research Quarterly* 49 (1996): 591–605.

Baker III, James A. "America in Asia: Emerging Architecture for a Pacific Community." *Foreign Affairs* 70, no. 1 (winter 1991–1992): 1–18.

Barber, James D. *The Presidential Character: Predicting Performance in the White House.* Englewood Cliffs, NJ: Prentice-Hall, 1972.

Barilleaux, Ryan J. "Presidential Conduct of Foreign Policy." *Congress and the Presidency* 15, no. 1 (spring 1988): 1–22.

Barker, Lucius J. "Limits of Political Strategy: A Systematic View of the African American Experience." *American Political Science Review* 88, no. 1 (March 1994): 1–13.

———. *New Perspectives in American Politics*. New Brunswick, NJ: Transaction Publishers, 1989.

Barone, Michael. "The Presidency: Mamas' Boys and Papas' Pride." *The Washington Post*, national weekly edition, August 8–14, 1988, 26–27.

Beard, Charles, and Mary Beard. *The Rise of American Civilization*. 1930. Reprint. Kila, MT: Kessinger Publishers, 2005.

Beers, Burton F. *World History, Patterns of Civilization*. Englewood Cliffs, NJ: Prentice Hall, 1988.

Bell, Coral. *The Reagan Paradox: U.S. Foreign Policy in the 1980s*. New Brunswick, NJ: Rutgers University Press, 1989.

Berman, Larry, and Bruce Jentleson. "Bush and the Post-Cold War World: New Challenges for American Leadership." In *The Bush Presidency: First Appraisals*, edited by Colin Campbell and Bert Rockman, 93–128. Chatham, NJ: Chatham, 1991.

Black, Earl, and Merle Black. *The Rise of Southern Republicans*. Cambridge, MA: Harvard University Press, 2002.

Blum, John M., et al. *The National Experience, A History of the USA Up to 1877*. New Haven, CT: Harcourt, Brace & World, 1963.

Bond, Jon R., and Richard Fleisher. "Clinton and Congress: A First Year Assessment." *American Politics Quarterly* 23, no. 3 (July 1995): 355–372.

Brace, Paul, and Barbara Hinckley. *Follow the Leader: Opinion Polls and the Modern Presidents*. New York: Basic Books, 1992.

Brady, Christopher. *United States Foreign Policy Towards Cambodia, 1977–92: A Question of Realities*. New York: St. Martin's Press, 1999.

Buchanan, Patrick J. *A Republic, Not an Empire: Reclaiming America's Destiny*. Washington, DC: Regnery, 1999.

———. *Where the Right Went Wrong: How Neoconservatives Subverted the Reagan Revolution and Hijacked the Bush Presidency.* New York: St. Martin's Press, 2004.

Bush, George H. W. *All the Best, George Bush: My Life in Letters and Other Writings.* New York: Scribner, 2000.

Bush, George H. W., and Brent Scowcroft. *A World Transformed.* New York: Knopf, 1998.

Calvert, Peter. "Studying the Presidency." In *The American Way, Government and Politics in the USA*, edited by Lynton Robins, 102–115. London: Longman, 1985.

Campbell, Colin. "The Let's Deal President." In *The Bush Presidency: First Appraisals*, edited by Colin Campbell and Bert Rockman, 185–222. Chatham, NJ: Chatham, 1991.

———. *The U.S. Presidency in Crisis: A Comparative Perspective.* New York: Oxford University Press, 1998.

Campbell, Colin, and Bert A. Rockman, eds. *The Bush Presidency: First Appraisals.* Chatham, NJ: Chatham, 1991.

Carleton, William G. "A New Look at Woodrow Wilson." In *Taking Sides: Clashing Views on Controversial Issues in American History*, II, edited by Eugene Kuzirian and Larry Madaras, 251. Guilford, CT: The Dushkin Group, 1987.

Carnegie Endowment National Commission. *Changing Our Ways: America and the New World.* Washington, DC: Brookings Institution, 1992.

Carothers, Thomas. *Aiding Democracy Abroad: The Learning Curve.* Washington, DC: Carnegie Endowment for International Peace, 1999.

Castells, Manuel. *The Rise of the Network Society.* Oxford, U.K.: Blackwell, 2000.

Chazan, Naomi, et al. *Politics and Society in Contemporary Africa.* Boulder, CO: Lynne Rienner, 1992.

Clark, Jeffrey. "Debacle in Somalia." *Foreign Affairs* 72, no. 1 (winter 1993): 109–123.

Cohen, Jeffrey E. "The Dynamics and Interactions Between the President's and the Public Civil Rights Agendas: A Study in Presidential Leadership and Representation." *Policy Studies Journal* 21, no. 3 (1993): 514–522.

Congress of the United States. "Bush on Education Strategy." *Historic Documents of 1991.* Washington, DC (April 18, 1991): 222.

Cossa, Robert A. "U.S. Foreign Policy in Asia: Churchill Was Right!" *Strategic Review* 23, no. 1 (winter 1995): 74–77.

Cox, Michael. *U.S. Foreign Policy After the Cold War: Superpower Without a Mission?* London: Pinter Press, 1995.

Crandall, Russell. *Driven by Drugs: U.S. Policy Toward Columbia.* Boulder, CO: Lynne Rienner, 2002.

Cronin, Thomas, and M. A. Genovese. *The Paradoxes of the American Presidency.* New York: Oxford University Press, 1998.

Dahl, Robert. *Controlling Nuclear Weapons, Democracy Versus Guardianship.* Syracuse, NY: Syracuse University Press, 1985.

Daniels, Jonathan. *The Man of Independence.* London: Victor Gollancz, 1951.

De Conde, Alexander. *A History of American Foreign Policy, Volume II: Global Power, 1900 to the Present.* New York: Charles Scribner's Sons, 1978.

d'Encausse, Hélène Carrère. *The End of the Soviet Empire: The Triumph of the Nations.* New York: Basic Books, 1993.

Desai, Uday. "Introduction to Symposium on Comparative Environmental Policy." *Policy Studies Journal* 20, no. 4 (1992): 621–627.

Diamond, Larry. "Promoting Democracy in Africa: United States and International Policies in Transition." In *The United States and Africa From Independence to the End of the Cold War*, edited by Macharia

Munene, Korwa Adar, and Joshua Nyunya, 193–220. Nairobi, Kenya: East African Educational Publishers, 1995.

———. "The U.S. Foreign Policy Trajectory on Africa." *SAIS Review* 21, no. 1 (2001): 179–211.

Diclerico, Robert E. *The American President.* Englewood Cliffs, NJ: Prentice Hall, 1983.

Dowd, Maureen. "Biography of a Candidate: Man in the News; Making and Remaking a Political Identity: George Herbert Walker Bush." *New York Times*, August 20, 1992, A1.

Drucker, Peter F. *Post-Capitalist Society.* New York: Harper Collins, 1994.

Dunn, Charles W., and David J. Woodard. *American Conservatism From Burke to Bush: An Introduction.* New York: Madison Books, 1991.

The Economist, "American Survey," August 20, 1988.

Edwards III, George C. "George Bush and the Public Presidency: The Politics of Inclusion." In *The Bush Presidency: First Appraisals*, edited by Colin Campbell and Bert Rockman, 129–154. Chatham, NJ: Chatham, 1991.

Evans Jr., Rowland, and Robert D. Novak, eds. *Nixon in the White House: The Frustration of Power.* New York: Vintage Books, 1971.

Faber, Harold. *The Road to the White House.* New York: Berkley Publishing, 1966.

Fallows, James. *More Like Us: Making America Great Again.* Boston: Houghton Mifflin, 1989.

Ferguson, Thomas, and Joel Rogers. "The Myth of America's Turn to the Right." In *American Politics, Classic and Contemporary Readings*, edited by Alan J. Ciglar and Burdett A. Loomis, 198–199. Boston: Houghton Mifflin, 1989.

Fingleton, Eamonn. "Japan's Invisible Leviathan." *Foreign Affairs* 74, no. 2 (March–April 1995): 69–85.

Foell, Earl W. "Making Sense of the World: New World Order and Disorder." *World Monitor.* Christian Science Publishing, March 1991: 36.

Franklin, Daniel P., and Robert Shepard. "Is Prudence a Policy?" In *Leadership and the Bush Presidency: Prudence or Drift in an Era of Change?*, edited by Ryan Barilleaux and Mary Stuckey, 165–176. Westport, CT: Praeger, 1992.

Friedman, Alan. *Spider's Web: The Secret History of How the White House Illegally Armed Iraq.* New York: Bantam Books, 1993.

Gardner, John W. *On Leadership.* New York: The Free Press, 1990.

Gergen, David. *Eyewitness to Power: The Essence of Leadership Nixon to Clinton.* New York: Simon & Schuster, 2000.

Giles, Michael W., and Melanie A. Buckner. "David Duke and Black Threat: An Old Hypothesis Revisited." *Journal of Politics* 55, no. 3 (August 1993): 702–713.

Gingrich, Newt. *To Renew America.* New York: Harper Collins, 1995.

Gladilin, Anatoly. "Will America Save the World?" *Moscow News* 38 (October 2–8, 1997): 4–5.

Gleske, Leonhard. "The Opportunities and Perils for the United States of European Integration." In *The Future of U.S.-European Relations in Search of a New World Order*, edited by Henry Brandon, 89–110. Washington, DC: Brookings Institution, 1992.

Goldstein, Joel K. *The Modern American Vice-Presidency: The Transformation of a Political Institution.* Princeton, NJ: Princeton University Press, 1982.

Gorbachev, Mikhail. "Bringing Order to the New World Disorder." *Indian Express Hyderabad*, September 7, 1995, 1.

Green, John Robert. *The Presidency of George Bush.* Lawrence: University of Kansas, 2000.

Greenberg, Edward S. *The American Political System: A Radical Approach.* New York: Scott Foresman, 1989.

Selected Bibliography

Greenstein, Fred I. *Presidential Difference: Leadership from FDR to George W. Bush.* Princeton, NJ: Princeton University Press, 2004.

Hagerty, Devin T. "Nuclear Deterrence in South Asia: The 1990 Indo-Pakistani Crisis." *International Security* 20, no. 3 (winter 1995), http://www.mtholyoke.edu/acad/intrel/sasianuk.htm

Hempstone, Smith. *Rogue Ambassador.* Sewanee, TN: University of the South Press, 1997.

Hickey, Dennis. "America's Military Relations With the People's Republic of China: The Need for Reassessment." *The Journal of Northeast Asian Studies* 7, no. 3 (fall 1988): 29–43.

Hughes, Emmet John. *The Living Presidency: The Resources and Dilemmas of American Presidential Office.* New York: Coward, McCann & Geoghegan, 1973.

Hunt, Albert R. "The Campaign and the Issues." In *The American Elections of 1980*, edited by Austin Ranney, 161–176. Washington, DC: American Institute for Public Policy Research, 1980.

Hyams, Joe. *Flight of the Avenger: George Bush at War.* San Diego, CA: Harcourt Brace Jovanovich, 1991.

Hybel, Alex R. *Power Over Rationality: The Bush Administration and the Gulf Crisis.* Albany: State University of New York Press, 1993.

Irish, Marian D. "The President's Foreign Policy Machine." In *The Future of the American Presidency*, edited by Charles W. Dunn, 146. Morristown, NJ: General Learning Press, 1975.

Jones, Charles O. *The Presidency in a Separated System.* Washington, DC: The Brookings Institution Press, 1994.

Jones Jr., Augustus J. "Kinder, Gentler? George Bush and Civil Rights." In *Leadership and the Bush Presidency: Prudence or Drift in an Era of Change?*, edited by R. Barilleaux and M. Stuckey, 177–190. Westport, CT: Praeger 1992.

Jowitt, Ken. "The New World Disorder." In *The Global Resurgence of Democracy*, edited by Larry Diamond and Marc F. Plattner, 247–256. Baltimore: John Hopkins University Press, 1993.

Juster, Kenneth I. "The Myth of Iraqgate." *Foreign Affairs* 94 (spring 1994): 105–119.

Kellerman, B., and Ryan Barilleaux. *The President as World Leader*. New York: St. Martin's, 1991.

Kelly, Kitty. *The Family: The True Story of the Bush Dynasty*. London: Doubleday, 2004.

Kemp, Geoffrey. "U.S. Strategic Interests and Military Options in Sub-Saharan Africa." In *Africa and the U.S. Vital Interest*, edited by Jennifer Seymour Whitaker, 120–152. New York: New York University Press, 1978.

Kennedy, John F. *Profiles in Courage*. New York: Harper and Row, 1961.

King, James D., and James W. Riddlesperger Jr. "Presidential Leadership of Congressional Civil Rights Voting: The Cases of Eisenhower and Johnson." *Policy Studies Journal* 21, no. 3 (autumn 1993): 544–555.

King, Nicholas. *George Bush, A Biography*. New York: Dodd Mead, 1980.

Kingdon, John. *Agendas, Alternatives, and Public Choices*. Boston: Little, Brown, 1984.

Kolko, Gabriel. *Main Currents in Modern American History*. New York: Harper and Row, 1976.

Koo, Youngnok. "East Asian Lobbies in Washington: Comparative Strategies." Occasional Paper, Asia Program. Prepared for a colloquium at the Wilson Center, Washington, DC, May 14, 1985.

Kornegay Jr., Francis A. "Africa in the New World Order, U.S. Policy." *Africa Report* (January/February 1993): 16.

Kuzirian, Eugene, and Larry Madaras. *Taking Sides: Clashing Views on Controversial Issues in American History*. Guilford, CT: Dushkin Publishing Group, 1987.

Ladd, Everett Carll. "On Mandates, Realignment and the 1984 Presidential Election." In *Taking Sides II*, edited by Eugene Kuzirian and Larry Madaras. Guilford, CT: Dushkin Publishing Group, 1987.

Lerner, Max. *America as a Civilization*. New York: Simon & Schuster, 1957.

Light, Paul. *The President's Agenda: Domestic Choice From Kennedy to Carter*. Baltimore: Johns Hopkins University, 1982.

Lipset, Seymour M., and Earl Raab. *The Politics of Unreason: Right Wing Extremism in America, 1790–1970*. New York: Harper and Row, 1970.

Lonnstrom, D. A., and T. O. Kelly II. "Rating the Presidents: A Tracking Study." *Presidential Studies Quarterly* 27, no. 3 (summer 1997): 591–598.

Lowenthal, Abraham F. "Rediscovering Latin America." *Foreign Affairs* 69, no. 4 (fall 1990): 27–41.

———. *The United States and Latin American Democracy: Learning From History*. Boston: World Peace Foundation, 1991.

Macpherson, C. B. *The Real World of Democracy*. New York: Oxford University Press, 1966.

Magdoff, Harry. *The Age of Imperialism: The Economics of U.S. Foreign Policy*. New York: Monthly Review Press, 1968.

Malcolm, Noel. "Project Europe a Rival to U.S.?" *Foreign Affairs* 74, no. 2 (March/April 1995): 54.

Mansfield Jr., Harvey. *Taming the Prince: The Ambivalence of Modern Executive Power*. New York: Free Press, 1989.

Martin, Ralph G. *A Hero for Our Time*. Boston: Ballantine Books, 1983.

Mayer, Jane, and Doyle McManus. *Landslide: The Unmaking of the President, 1984–1988*. Boston: Houghton Mifflin Company, 1988.

Mboya, Tom. *Freedom and After.* Nairobi, Kenya: Heinemann, 1963.

Moore, Raymond A. "Foreign Policy." In *The Bush Presidency and Adversities: Triumphs and Adversities*, edited by D. M. Hill and P. Williams, 162–183. New York: St. Martin's, 1994.

Moe, Ronald C. "The HUD Scandal and the Case for an Office of Federal Management." *Public Administration Review* 51, no. 4 (July/August 1991): 298.

Morris, Milton D. "African Americans and the New World Order." *The Washington Quarterly* 15, no.4 (autumn, 1992): 5–51.

Morris, Roger. *Uncertain Greatness: Henry Kissinger and American Foreign Policy.* New York: Harper and Row, 1977.

Motyl, Alexander. *The Post-Soviet Nations: Perspectives on the Demise of the USSR.* Columbia, NY: Columbia University Press, 1992.

Mushita, Andrew, and Carol B. Thompson. *Biopiracy of Biodiversity Global Exchange as Enclosure.* Trenton, NJ: Africa World Press, 2007.

Myrdal, Gunnar. *An American Dilemma.* New York: Harper and Row, 1962.

Nelson, Michael. *The Presidency and the Political System.* Washington, DC: Congressional Quarterly Press, 1998.

Neustadt, Richard. *Presidential Power and the Modern Presidents: The Politics of Leadership From Roosevelt to Reagan.* New York: The Free Press, 1990.

Nicolson, Harold. *Kings, Courts and Monarchy.* New York: Simon & Schuster, 1962.

Nixon, Richard M. *The Real War.* New York: Warner Books, 1980.

———. *U.S. Foreign Policy for the 1970s: Building for Peace, A Report to the Congress.* Washington, DC: U.S. Congress, 1971.

Norquist, Grover G. "The Unmaking of a President: Why George Bush Lost." *Policy Review* 63 (winter 1993): 10–25.

Nye Jr., Joseph S. "Peering Into the Future." *Foreign Affairs* 73, no. 4 (July/August 1994): 82–93.

———. "What New World Order?" *Foreign Affairs* 71, no. 2 (spring 1992): 83–96.

Odom, William E. "How To Create a True World Order." *Orbis, A Journal of World Affairs* 39, no. 2 (spring 1995): 155–156.

Ohmae, Kenichi. *The Evolving Global Economy: Making Sense of the New World Order.* Cambridge, MA: Harvard Business Review Press, 1995.

Palmer, David Scott. *U.S. Relations With Latin America During the Clinton Years: Opportunities Lost or Opportunities Squandered?* Gainesville: University Press of Florida, 2006.

Palmer, John L., and Isabel V. Sawhill. *The Reagan Record: An Urban Institute Study.* Cambridge, MA: Ballinger, 1984.

Parmet, Herbert S. *George Bush: The Life of a Lone Star Yankee.* New Brunswick, NJ: Transaction, 2001.

Pastor, Robert A. "The Bush Administration and Latin America: The Pragmatic Style and the Regionalist Option." *Journal of Interamerican Studies and World Affairs* 33, no. 3 (autumn 1991): 1–34.

Petras, James. "Gulf War and the New World Order." *Economic and Political Weekly* 26, no. 9/10 (March 2–9, 1991): 482–484.

Pfiffner, James P., and Roger H. Davidson, eds. *Understanding the Presidency.* New York: Longman, 1998.

Phillips, Cabell. *The Truman Presidency, The History of a Triumphant Succession.* New York: Macmillan, 1966.

Polsby, Nelson W., and Aaron Wildavsky. *Presidential Elections: Strategies and Structures in American Politics.* Chatham, NJ: Chatham House, 1996.

Pye, Lucian W. *Aspects of Political Development.* Boston: Little, Brown and Co., 1966.

Pynn, Ronald E. *American Politics: Changing Expectations.* Dubuque, IA: Brown & Benchmark, 1993.

Quinones, C. Kenneth. "Korean Reconciliation—Half Way There." In *Korean Security Dynamics in Transition*, edited by Kyung-Ae Park and Dalchoong Kim. New York: St. Martin's Press, 2001.

Quirk, Paul J. "Presidential Competence." In *The Presidency and the Political System*, edited by Michael Nelson, 136–170. Washington, DC: Congressional Quarterly Press, 2005.

Rainwater, Lee, and William L. Yancey. *The Moynihan Report and Politics of Controversy: A Trans-Action Social Science and Public Policy Report.* Cambridge, MA: The MIT Press, 1967.

Reedy, George E. *The Twilight of the Presidency.* New York: New American Library, 1970.

Rees, Matthew. *From the Deck to the Sea: Blacks and the Republican Party.* Wakefield, NH: Longwood Academic Press, 1991.

Reeves, Richard. *A Ford, Not a Lincoln: The Decline of American Political Leadership.* London: Hutchinson Publishers, 1976.

Richburg, Keith. "Back to Vietnam." *Foreign Affairs* 70, no. 1 (fall 1991): 111–131.

Roper, Jon. *The American Presidents: Heroic Leadership From Kennedy to Clinton.* Edinburgh, U.K.: Edinburgh University Press, 2000.

Rossiter, Clinton. *Conservatism in America.* New York: Alfred A. Knopf, 1955.

———. *The American Presidency.* New York: A Mentor Book, 1962.

Rothchild, Donald. "The U.S. Foreign Policy Trajectory on Africa." *SAIS Review* 21, no. 1 (2001): 179–211.

Rozell, Mark J. *The Press and the Bush Presidency.* Westport, CT: Praeger, 1996.

Rusher, William A. "Clinton's First Year." In *Consequences of the Clinton Victory: Essays on the First Year*, edited by Peter W. Schramm, 1–11. Ashland, OH: Ashbrook Press, 1994.

Rutland, Robert. *The Republicans: From Lincoln to Bush.* Columbia: University of Missouri Press, 1996.

Schatzberg, M. G. "Military Intervention and the Myth of Collective Security: The Case of Zaire." *The Journal of Modern African Studies* 27, no. 2 (1989): 316.

Shattuck, John. *Promoting Democracy and Human Rights.* Washington, DC: U.S. State Department, April 1, 1994.

Schlesinger Jr., Arthur M. "Rating the Presidents: Washington to Clinton." *Political Science Quarterly* 112, no. 2 (summer 1997): 179–190.

Schraeder, Peter. "Removing the Shackles? U.S. Foreign Policy Toward Africa After the End of the Cold War." In *Africa in the New International Order: Rethinking State Sovereignty and Regional Security*, edited by E. J. Keller and Donald Rothchild. Boulder, CO: Lynne Rienner, 1996.

Schulzinger, Robert D. *U.S. Diplomacy Since 1900.* New York: Oxford University Press, 1998.

Schweid, Barry. "Dateline Washington: Warren's World." *Foreign Policy* 94 (spring 1994): 136–147.

Sellers, Charles, et al. *A Synopsis of American History.* Chicago: Rand McNally, 1977.

Shahin, Yossi. "Ethnic Diaspora and U.S. Foreign Policies." *Political Science Quarterly* 109 (winter 1994–1995): 811–841.

Shapiro, Irving S. *America's Third Revolution: Public Interest and the Private Role.* New York: Harper and Row, 1984.

Shepperd, Walt. "A Billion Burgers Sold, Bush's New World Order Means More Business as Usual." *Syracuse New Times*, April 3–10, 1991, 6.

Shull, Steven, A. *A Kinder, Gentler Racism?: The Reagan-Bush Civil Rights Legacy.* Armonk, NY: M. E. Sharpe, 1993.

Shultz, George P. *Endless Turmoil for How Much Triumph?* New York: Charles Scribner's Sons, 1994.

Sick, Gary. "The Election Story." *New York Times*, April 15, 1991, A17.

Silver, Thomas B. "The Reagan Legacy and Liberal Opportunities." In *Consequences of the Clinton Victory: Essays on the First Year*, edited by P. W. Schramm, 13–30. Ashland, OH: Ashbrook Press, 1994.

Simonton, Dean K. *Why Presidents Succeed: A Political Psychology of Leadership.* New Haven, CT: Yale University Press, 1987.

Sinclair, Barbara. "Governing Unheroically (and Sometimes Unappetizingly): Bush and the 101st Congress." In *The Bush Presidency: First Appraisals*, edited by Colin Campbell and Bert Rockman, 178–180. Chatham, NJ: Chatham, 1991.

Smith, Jean Edward. *George Bush's War.* New York: Henry Holt and Co., 1992.

Solarz, Stephen J. "What New Policy Toward Cambodia?" *New York Times*, July 26, 1990, A19.

Sorenson, Theodore C. *A Different Kind of Presidency: A Proposal for Breaking Political Deadlock.* New York: Harper and Row, 1984.

Sperlich, Peter W. "Bargaining and Overload: An Essay on Presidential Power." In *Perspectives on the Presidency*, edited by Aaron Wildavsky, 426. Boston: Little, Brown, 1975.

Stinnett, Robert B. *George Bush: His World War II Years.* Reprint. Washington, DC: Brassey's, 1992.

Sturmer, Michael. "Germany in Search of an Enlightened American Leadership." In *The Future of U.S.-European Relations in Search of a New World Order*, edited by Henry Brandon, 75–88. Washington, DC: Brookings Institution, 1992.

Switzer, Jacqueline Vaughn. *Environmental Politics: Domestic and Global Dimensions.* Belmont, CA: Wadsworth/Thomson, 2004.

Tindall, George Brown. *America: A Narrative History.* New York: W. W. Norton and Company, 1988.

Toner, Robin. "Tactical Governance." In *The Donald S. MacNaughton Symposium Proceedings, Democratic Governance: America in the 21st Century.* Syracuse, NY: Syracuse University, 1990.

Unger, Craig. *House of Bush, House of Saud: The Secret Relationship Between the World's Two Most Powerful Dynasties.* New York: Scribner, 2004.

Uslaner, Eric M. "All Politics Are Global: Interest Groups and the Making of Foreign Policy." In *Interest Group Politics*, edited by A. Cigler and B. A. Loomis, 369. Washington, DC: Congressional Quarterly, 1995.

Walters, Jonathan. "The Most Radical Idea in Education: Let the Schools Run It." *Governing* 4, no. 4 (January 1991): 41–45.

Warner, Margaret G. "Bush Battles the 'Wimp Factor,' A Searching Look at the Vice President's Most Persistent Political Liability." *Newsweek*, October 19, 1987, 29–30.

Warshaw, Shirley A. *The Domestic Presidency Policy Making in the White House.* Boston: Allyn & Bacon, 1997.

Wasby, Stephen L. "Transformed Triangle: Court, Congress and Presidency in Civil Rights." *Policy Studies Journal* 21, no. 3 (1993): 571.

Webb, Stephen Saunders. "Five Centuries of American Empire, 1584–2084." In *Democratic Governance: America in the 21st Century, The 9th Annual Donald S. MacNaughton Symposium Proceedings, November 8–9, 1989*, 175–193. Syracuse, NY: Syracuse University Press, 1990.

"What Foreign Policy? President George H. W. Bush's Leadership: The U.S. Foreign Policy Trajectory on Latin America and Asia," *New Republic* 205, no. 14 (September 30, 1991): 5–6.

Whicker, Marcia Lynn. "Policy Making in the White House: The Best Books on the Presidency in 1991." *Public Administration Review* 51, no. 1 (January/February 1991): 74–79.

Whitehead, Lawrence. "The Imposition of Democracy." In *Exporting Democracy, the United States and Latin America*, edited by Abraham F. Lowenthal, 216–242. Baltimore: Johns Hopkins University Press, 1991.

Wildavsky, Aaron. *The Beleaguered Presidency.* New Brunswick, NJ: Transaction Publishers, 1991.

———. "Two Presidencies." *Transaction* 4, no. 2 (1966): 7–14.

Will, George F. "How Reagan Has Changed America." *Newsweek*, January 9, 1989, 14–18.

———. *The New Season: A Spectator's Guide to the 1988 Election.* New York: Simon & Schuster, 1987.

Williams, Walter. "George Bush and Executive Branch Domestic Policy Making Competence." *Policy Studies Journal* 21, no. 4 (1993): 700–717.

Wilmsen, Steven K. *Silverado: Neil Bush and the Savings & Loan Scandal.* Washington DC: National Press Books, 1991.

Witcover, Jules. *From Adams and Jefferson to Truman and Quayle: Crapshoot, Rolling the Dice on the Vice Presidency.* New York: Crown Publishers, 1992.

Wortman, C. B., E. F. Loftus, and M. E. Marshall. *Psychology.* New York: Alfred A. Knopf, 1985.

Zimmerman, Warren. "A Memoir of the Collapse of Yugoslavia." *Foreign Affairs* 74, no. 2 (March/April, 1995): 2–20.

INDEX

Adams, John Quincy, 13
Adar, Korwa, 213
Afghan rebels, 106
Afghanistan, 27
Africa, 111–123
   Africa's recovery, 145
African-Americans, 48, 54, 70, 114, 121, 130, 143–145, 149, 156–162
AIDS, 204, 157, 162
Alfonsin, Raul, 95
Alkalimat, Abdul, 142
Alliance for Progress, 92
America 2000 Program, 205
America's military-industrial complex, 69
American civilization, 14–15, 21, 25
American Conservative Union, 156
American domination, 136
American Freedom Coalition, 156
American war of independence, 14
ancient Rome, 14
Andover Greenwich County Day School, 39
Angola, 113
   Augustino Neto, 113
   Savimbi, Jonas, 113, 128
   UNITA (União Nacional para a Independência Total de Angola, in Angola), 113, 128
anti-aircraft missiles, 80
Anti-Apartheid Act of 1986, 114, 121
appointment of loyalists, 182
Arab League, 67
Arab oil sheikhs and monarchies, 138

Argentina, 95
   Argentine President Carlos Saul Menem, 95
   ending military rule in Argentina, 95
   Gasoducto (natural gas transmission pipeline), 95
Arias, Óscar (Costa Rica's president), 97
Armenia, 199
arms shipments to Iraq, 80
Asia, 200
   Asian, 178, 199, 211
Australia, 74, 79
authoritarian regimes, 134
Ayatollah's Iran, 83
Azerbaijan, 140, 199

Baghdad, 65, 77, 82–83
Bahrain, 31, 64
Baker, Jim (then Secretary of State), 43, 65, 69–70, 83, 88, 95, 102–103, 108, 125, 127, 140–141, 183, 190–191, 194, 202
balance of power, 16, 65, 135, 139, 146, 188, 198
Barbara Sinclair, 182, 193
Barkley, Albin, 44
Barone, Michael, 40, 56, 216
Barre, Siyad, 32, 116, 119, 123–124
Beard, Charles and Mary Beard, 14, 21
Belarus, 199
Belgrade, 140
Benin, 124, 140

Bentsen, Lloyd, 41, 53
Berlin Wall, xi, 7, 18, 107, 198
Biodiversity Treaty, 172–173
    studies, 173
Bolivian, 97
bombing of Pan American Flight, 103
    over Lockerbie, Scotland, 202
booming oil business, 40
Boren, David, 66
Boris Yeltsin, 63, 147
Bosnia, 140, 148, 185, 200
Boston, 8, 21–23, 34, 40, 87, 108,
    129, 176, 178–179, 193, 212
Brazil, 79, 136–137, 148, 171
Britain, 15, 22, 67, 92, 103, 171, 208
Brookings Institution, 8, 22, 80, 213
Buchanan, Patrick, 18, 22, 145, 149
budget, 3, 7, 17, 28, 43, 48, 51–52,
    55, 151–155, 165–168, 178–179,
    188–189, 204, 207
    No tax pledge, 182
    Office of Management and
        Budget (OMB), 168
Bureau of Reclamation, 171
Burma, 105
Bush as a Jack-of-all-Trades, 42
    Bush Envoys, 70, 199
    Bush, moderate pragmatic
        statesmanship, 84
Bush, Barbara, 191
Bush, Dorothy, 38–39
Bush, Nancy, 42, 56
Bush, Neil, 95, 166, 179
Bush's mentor, 41
Bush's vision, xi, 37, 54, 112

Cable News Network (CNN), 57,
    100, 175, 193
cabinet, 162, 164, 178, 183

cabinet (*continued*)
    Bush's first cabinet, 39
Calhoun, John C., 44
California's jobless rate, 186, 194
Calvert, Peter, 33, 35, 206, 212
Cambodia, 102–103, 105, 109
Cameroon, 124, 200
campaign managers, 183
    campaigning, 41, 112, 184, 193
Campbell, Colin, 13, 21, 32, 35, 129,
    179, 194
Cape Verde, 124, 200
Caribbean Islands, 145
Carleton, William E., 21
Carlucci, Frank, 96
Cartagena, Colombia, 97
Carter, Jimmy, 13, 152, 187, 206
Casey, William, 47
Castro, Fidel, 209
Caucasus, 199, 211
Cédras, Raoul, 200
Central Asia, 140, 199, 211
Central Intelligence Agency, 42, 128
Chairman of the Republican
    National Committee, 41
Chairman of the Senate Select
    Committee on Intelligence, 66
Chairman of the U.S. Joint Chiefs
    of Staff, 69
Chechnya, 20, 140
    sovereignty from Moscow, 140
chemical weapons, 80, 83
Chiapas, 94
Chile, 95
China, 18–19, 40–42, 55, 61, 74,
    100–103, 107, 109, 124, 143, 146, 207
    Chinese Intellectuals, 100
    Chinese People's Liberation
        Army, 100

China (*continued*)
    coverage of the riots in China, 100
    humanitarian Tibet, 101
    post-Mao era, 18
    Tiananmen Square China, 100, 107
Christopher, Warren, 111, 129
Churchill, Winston (of England), 108, 191
citizens of America, 156
city on the hill, 203
civil rights, 27–28, 46, 48, 55, 121, 156–162, 176–177
Civil Rights Commission (CRC), 158–159
Civil war crisis of 1860, 72
    Civil war and Africa, 199
        Angola, 113
        Liberia, 115
        Somalia, 115, 118
    Civil war, Cambodia, 102
    Civil war and new world order, 150
    Civil war, Rome, 14
Clean Air Act Amendments of 1977, 169–170
Clean Air Act Amendments of 1990 (P. L. 101–549), 169
Clean Air Act of 1970, 170
Clinton, Bill, xii, 3, 13, 21
    Clinton's lack of international credentials, 186
    North American Free Trade Agreement (NAFTA), 94–95, 107, 121
Cohen, Herman, 128
Cold War, 9, 11–12, 17–20, 45, 48, 61, 63–64, 102, 104, 106–107, 112–113, 112, 115, 117, 119, 122–123, 127–129, 133–134, 139,

Cold War (*continued*)
    142, 146–147, 153, 185, 188, 192, 194, 198–199, 201–205, 207–208
Colombia, 97
commander-in-chief, 14, 20, 25, 42
Compensation and Liability Act of 1980 (CERCLA, P. L. 96–510)
Competitive Enterprise Institute (CEI) Earth Summit, 172
Congo, 113, 122, 127–128, 142, 172
Congress, 1, 5, 8, 26, 32–33, 39, 44, 54–55, 42, 64, 66, 68, 74–75, 77–78, 81, 84–88, 101–102, 106, 128–129
Congressional Black Caucus, 121, 129, 149, 152, 155–156, 161, 163, 167–170, 188, 190–191, 202, 204, 211–212
Congressional Democrats, 188
conservative, 1, 7
    compassionate conservatism, 6, 28, 152
    neoconservatives, 22, 29, 46, 49, 121, 151, 153–156, 159, 161, 172–174, 176–177, 182, 185, 190, 204, 212
Constitution, 12, 15, 25, 26, 46, 52–53, 77–78, 121
    in South Africa, 158, 179, 182
Contra, 64
    Iran Contra-gate, 80, 89, 97, 189
    See also Iran
Coolidge, Calvin, 27
Costa Rica, 95, 97
Crandall, Robert, 108, 218
Croatia, 140
Croats and Slovenes Seceding, 140
Cuba, 31, 93, 103, 120, 142, 209

Cuba (*continued*)
  Cuban American National
    Foundation, 120, 142, 209
Cuomo, Mario, 178, 190

Dahl, Robert, 15, 20, 23, 218
Dalai Lama, 102
Dangerous mines about Bahrain, 64
De Klerk, Frederick, 31, 114–115
debt crisis, 95–96
debt relief plan, 145
democracy, 6, 9, 13–15, 19–20, 23,
    31–32, 69
  Africa, 111–114, 122–128,
    130, 133–134, 136, 139–141,
    143–144, 148, 198–200, 203,
    205, 209, 211
  Latin America and Asia, 91–105,
    108–110
Democracy: "Freedom Works...
    Freedom is Right," 123
Democratic Republic of Congo
    (DRC), 127. *See also* Congo
Deng Xiaoping, 100
Department of Housing and Urban
    Development, 168
Department of the Interior, 170–171
DiClerico, Robert, 26, 34
Director of CIA, 42, 47, 96, 112. *See
    also* Central Intelligence Agency
  Director William Webster, 66, 81
Dole, Elizabeth H., 39
Dole Robert, 39
Drucker, Peter, 153
Dukakis, Michael, 52–54, 70, 182
Duke, David, 29, 177

East Timor, 105
Eastern Europe, xi, 19–20, 120–121,
    135, 139, 141, 145

Economic Community of West
    African States (ECOWAS), 200
education, 149, 151, 154–155, 157,
    160, 178, 205
  civic education, 200
  education president, 163–165
Egypt, 67–68, 76, 78, 80
elections
  in 1980, 47, 54
  in 1988, 183
  in 1992 (generational bump), 191
  New Hampshire, 186
  reelection, 181
Emir Sheik Jaber al-Ahmed
    al-Sabah, 83
endangered species, 170–171
Endangered Species Act of 1973, 170
Energy Policy Act (EPAct)
    of 1992, 169
Enron, 95
environmental president, 169, 173
environmental problems, 172, 174
environmental protection
    programs, 173
envoy to China, 55
Eritrea, 115
Ethiopia, 115–116, 123, 141
ethnic contradictions, 135
ethnic minorities, 157
ethnic nationalism, 19, 142
ethnic wars, 20
Eurasia, 19
European community (EC), 18, 171
European oil merchants, 138
European Union (EU), 18

Fallows, James, 17, 22, 163, 178
Federal Reserve Board, 168, 187
Ford, Gerald, 13, 42–43, 46, 57, 151,
    154, 183, 206

Fletcher, Arthur, 159
France, 40, 103
Franklin, Benjamin, 40
free market agreement, 208
free markets and capitalism, 198
freedom and democracy, 31, 198
Friends of the Earth, 171
frontier of freedom, 112
Fujimori, Alberto, 98
    President Alberto K. Fujimori's authoritarian rule, 97

Gardner, John, 39, 56
gas emissions, 173
gas prices, 186
Gates, Daryl F. as a "Top Cop," 27, 144
Gates, Robert M., 106
gays and lesbians, 157
Geneva protocols, 78
Georgia, 140, 199
Germany, 4, 140, 146–147, 207–208, 213
    Helmut Kohl, 4
    united, 18
Gingrich, Newt, 11, 59, 191
Glad, Betty, 183, 193
Gladilin, Anatoly, 19, 22
global capitalism, 133, 147
"global cop," 68
global fund, 173
global
    peace, 134
    peacemaker, 28
    power, 2, 11–12, 87, 201
    socialism, 133
    warming, 169, 173
globalists, 146
GNP, 48, 151
Goh Chok Tong, 105

good governance, 134
good neighbor policy, 92
Gorbachev, Mikhail, 12, 17, 19, 63, 68, 76, 140–141, 147–148, 199, 202, 205, 208
Gore, Al, 172, 183–184
Governor Clinton, 184, 192
Governor Douglas Wilder, 190
Governor Dukakis, 53
Gramm-Rudman Act, 155, 204
great civilization, 15
Great Depression of 1930, 12, 198
great nations, 91, 123
"Great Satan"—the United States, 64
Great Society, 3, 46, 153, 155, 198, 204
greenhouse, 173
Greenberg, Edward, 15, 21, 25, 34, 41, 56, 87
guardianship moral, 20, 23
Gulf Sea, 31
Gulf War of 1991, 61, 63, 65, 69, 71, 73–77, 79, 81, 83, 85, 87, 89, 135, 138, 157
    Americanizing the War, 74
    "Arab-ize" or de-Americanize the Gulf War of 1991, 74
    Gulf War victory, 189
    "Third world war," 80

Haig Jr., Alexander M., 44, 140, 148
Haiti, 145, 200
Hamilton, Lee D-IN, Chairman of the Joint Economic Committee of Congress, 186
Hanoi, 103–104
Harding, Warren G., 27
Harrison, 13, 206
HAWK, 80, 118, 184
Hayes, Rutherford B. President, 13, 206

Hinckley, John, 44
Hispanic vote, 183
Hispanics, 156–157
Horton, Willie, 52
Hu Yaobang, 100
HUD, 168–169, 179
Hudson Institute and the Heritage Foundation, 155
Hughes, John, 28, 34
human rights, 9, 16, 78, 98, 100–102, 104, 107, 109, 112–113, 125–127, 133, 139, 141, 198–200, 203, 207, 211
human rights abuses, 16, 101, 104–105, 127, 198
humanitarian initiative, 116
Hussein, Saddam, 27, 65–71, 73–84, 86, 88, 107, 136–137, 139, 148, 153

illiberal medical system, 151
inaugural address, 54, 107, 152, 175
India, 78, 83, 93, 101, 105–106, 109, 130, 147–148, 175
India and Pakistan, 106, 109, 130, 147–148
India and Pakistan for Building Nuclear Bombs, 106
Indian Maya, 94
individual responsibility, 55
Indonesia, 93, 105
Institutional Revolutionary Party, 97
international capitalism, 84
International Counternarcotics Strategy, 96
International Monetary Fund (IMF), 98, 127, 143
international terrorism, 51, 153, 202
Internet blogs and Web sites, 26

invasion of Kuwait, 66–67, 73–74, 80–81, 202
Iran, 31, 35, 46–47, 64–66, 72–23, 78, 80, 82–83, 85, 87
Iran Contragate scandal, 64
Iranian ship, 64
Iran-Iraq war, 64
Iraqgate, 77, 80–82, 188
Islamic Bomb, 106
isolationism, 204
  neo-isolationism, 112, 119, 146–147
Israel conduit, 47
Ivy League, 40, 64

Jackson, Jesse, 39, 77, 133, 144, 148–149, 157, 161–162, 177, 190, 195
Japan, 17–18, 52, 74, 78, 93, 95, 99, 120–121, 138, 146, 171, 208
Japanese model, 17
Jefferson, Thomas, xii, 25, 56–58
Johnson, Lyndon B., 3, 38, 45–46, 71, 73–74, 78, 153, 158, 162, 176–177, 198, 204
Jones, Augustus, 159, 177
Jordan, 80
Jowitt, Ken, 135, 140, 148

Kagwanja, Mwangi, 142
Kashmir, 106
Kazakhstan, 199
Kemp, Jack, 39, 43–44, 129, 169
Kennedy, John F., 8, 14, 17, 21, 30–31, 35, 37, 46, 55, 71, 92, 85, 102, 111, 128, 160, 169, 211
Kenya, 9, 13, 22, 116, 125–127, 142, 148, 200
Kerrey, Bob, 190

Index

Khan, Dr. Abdul Qadeer, 106.
 See also Islamic bomb
Khmer Rouge Maoists, 102
Kim Il Sung, North Korean
 Strongman, Death of, 142
"Kindler and Gentler" America, 152,
 176–177, 203–204, 209
King, Coretta Scott, 39
King, Rodney, 27, 144
Kirgizstan, 199
Kissinger School of Foreign
 Affairs, 55
Kissinger, Henry, 41, 55, 114,
 129, 186
Kurds, 82–83
Kurds in Halabja, 83
Kuwait, 66–71, 73–77, 79–83,
 88, 107, 136, 144, 157, 200,
 202–203, 209

lame duck president, 191
Lasch, Christopher, 15
Lasswell, Harold, 29, 38
Lee Kuan Yew, 105
Leninist dogma, 134–135
Lerner, Max, 15, 22
liberalism, 134, 154
liberties, 28, 160
Libyan "terrorist" threat, 31
Lincoln, Abraham, 12, 25, 29–30,
 58, 158, 188, 206
 preserving the Union, 30
Louisiana gubernatorial candidate, 29
Lowenthal, Abram, 108–109

McDonald, Roderick J., 66
Macpherson, C. B., 19, 23
Madison, James, 13, 206
Maine, 40

Mandela, Nelson, 31, 114–115
manifest destiny, 49
Manuel Noriega, 96–97, 209
Maoist Guerilla Organization—
 Shining Path (*Sendero
 Luminoso*), 98
Marcos, F., 105
Mariam, Mengistu Haile, 123
Marshall Plan, 17
Marxist-Leninist, 17, 123
McDonald's franchises, 136
McGrath, Peter, 86
McPherson, Harry, 153
Medicaid, 51, 157
Mexican President Carlos Salinas de
 Gortari, 96, 209
Mexico, 92–95, 97, 107, 208–209
Middle East, 65, 75–77, 86, 115, 157
minority politics of African
 Americans, 156
Mission of Mercy in Somalia, 111
Mitterrand, François, 4, 68, 70,
 83, 208
Mobutu, Sese Seko, 122, 127–128
moderated British monarch, 13
Moldova, 199
Mondale, Walter, 43
Monroe Doctrine, 92, 108
Monroe's Ghost, 92
Monsanto, 170
Moore, Raymond, 197, 205, 211
Morgenthau, Hans, 15
Moscow, 18, 22, 79, 140–141, 220
most-favored-nation (MFN), 100
Mujahideen Islamic
 Fundamentalists, 106
Mulroney, Martin Brian, Prime
 Minister of Canada, 94
Myrdal, Gunnar, 15, 21

Nairobi, 9, 13, 22, 112, 194
Narco-politics and promotion of democracy, 96
National Audubon Society, 171
National Drug Control Strategy, 97
National Endangered Species Act of 1973 (P. L. 93–205), 170
National Environmental Policy Act of 1969, 169, 179
National Security Council (NSC), 96, 104
national security, 28, 67, 71, 96, 104–106, 110, 119, 198
national security reform directives, 96
National Wildlife Federation, 171
native Indian, 94
NATO, 4, 19, 51, 63, 140, 147, 201, 207–208
naval bases in the Philippines, 105
Nepal, 101, 105
Nevis, Allan, 30
"New Communism" by religious fundamentalists, 153, 198
New Deal, 3, 45, 47, 155, 168, 204. *See also* Franklin Roosevelt
New England, 38
New World Order, xii, 5–7, 22, 52, 63, 121, 130, 133–145
  a billion burgers, 136
  center of a widening circle of freedom, 198
  criticisms of the New World Order, 136–137
  Gulliver, (in New World Order), 146
New York Times, 102, 109
New Zealand, 74
Nixon, Richard, 129, 140, 146, 149, 153–154, 160, 169–70, 186

Nixon, Richard (*continued*)
  Nixon–Agnew, 190, 193
  Nixon's "Vietnamization" of the war, 71
  Watergate Tapes, 31
Noriega, Manuel, 96
Norquist, Grover, 188, 193–194
North American Free Trade Agreement (NAFTA), 94
North Korea, 93, 103–105, 142
North Vietnam, 74
nuclear weapons, 20, 23, 51, 71, 103–106, 146, 202
Nye, Joseph, 86, 139, 148

one-party dictatorships, 6, 200
open-door policy toward Pakistan, 106
Operation Desert Storm, 75, 189, 209
Operation Just Cause (Panama), 97
Operation Restore Hope, 111, 115–117
Oregon, 171
Organization of American States, 98

Pacific Rim and Asia, 99
Pax Americana, 135
Pax Sovietica, 201
Peace Corps, 17, 55
Pentagon, 76, 104
Perot, Ross, 185, 194
Persian Gulf, 63–66, 86, 144, 186, 202–203
Perez, Carlos Andres, 96, 209. *See also* Venezuela
Petras, James, 138–139, 148
Peru, 97–98. *See also* Fujimori
  U.S.-Peru relations, 98
Philadelphia, 40, 70
Philippines, 74, 78, 105

Phnom Penh Leninists, 102
Polsby, Nelson, 183, 193
poor south and rich north, 133
potentates and dictators,113
Powell, Colin, 69, 96
power, xii, 2, 20, 27, 34, 37, 87,
   124, 142
  American global, 193, 198,
    201–209
  presidential power 5, 8, 28,
    34, 151
Prescott and Dorothy Walker Bush, 38
President Carlos Andrés Pérez, 96
President Carlos Salinas de Gortari,
   94, 96, 209
President Corazon Aquino, 105
President Nicanor Duarte Frutos, 98
Presidential agenda, 3, 8, 33
Prime Minister Kiichi Miyazawa, 99
Prime Minister Markovic, 140
Prime Minister Noboru Takeshita, 99
Prime Minister Sheikh Saad, 83
Prime Minister Toshiki Kaifu, 99
protests, Iraq war, 70, 75, 77–79,
  Tiananmen Square protests in
  China, 100
psychological and historical
  anthropological insights, 38
Public Utility Holding Company Act
  of 1935, 170
Pye, Lucian, 19, 23

Quayle, Dan, 43, 53, 56–58, 80, 195
Quinones, Kenneth, 104, 109
Quirk, Paul, 207, 212

ranking of presidents, 12–13, 79
rapid transformation of European
  boundaries, 139

Reagan Ronald administration,
   17, 48, 64–65, 72–73, 96, 98,
   114, 158
Reagan conservatives, 182
Reagan democrats, 183, 190
Reagan doctrine, 84, 113
Reagan Revolution, 17, 22, 49,
   55, 154
Reagan's domestic agenda, 174
Reagan-Casey Plan, 47
Reagan's recession, 187
Special Situations Group, 44
Reedy, George E., 25–27, 34
RENAMO, 115
Republican Party presidential
  nomination in 1980, 112
Republican mood, 54–55
right-wing Republicans, 7, 166, 191
Rio de Janeiro, 171, 173
Rockman, Bert, 13, 21, 35, 129,
   179, 193
Roh Tae Woo, 104–105
Rollins, Ed, 185, 190, 193–195
Roosevelt, Franklin D., 3, 8, 12, 30,
   45, 49, 51, 92, 158, 168, 198,
   204, 206
Roosevelt, Theodore, 26
Rossiter, Clinton, 3, 8, 12, 21, 57,
   155, 175, 212, 226
Russia, 19–20, 63, 79, 101, 103,
   135, 139, 143, 147, 188, 199
Rwanda, 200

San Antonio, Texas, 94
Sandinistas in Nicaragua, 209
Saudi Arabia, 65, 68, 75–76,
   115, 202
Schlesinger Jr., Arthur M., 12, 21,
   206, 212

Schwarzkopf Jr., Norman, 69
Scowcroft, Brent, 96, 150, 217
Secretary of Labor. *See* Elizabeth Dole
Secretary of the Interior, 171
Secretary of State George Shultz, 64
Secretary of the Treasury. *See* Jim Baker
Secretary of the Treasury Nicholas Brady, 168
segregation, 114, 160
Senate Committee, 168
Senate delegation to the United Nations Conference on the Environment and Development, 172
Serbian Aggression in Bosnia, 185
Shah Pahlavi, 64, 82
Shatt Al-Arab Estuary, 67
Shepperd, Walt, 136, 148
Sierra Club, 171
Silber, John, 190
Silverado Savings and Loan Bank, 95, 166, 179
Simonton, Dean Keith, 3, 8, 40, 56–57
Singapore, 100, 105
Sorensen, Theodore C., 188
Soros, George, 141
South Africa, 31, 63, 78, 112–115, 120, 128, 142
Souter, David, 159
South Korea, 74, 93, 104–105, 109, 120
South Korean President Roh Tae, 104–105
South Vietnam, 73–74
Soviet Empire, 199
Sperlich, Peter W., 28, 34

Strategic Arms Reduction Treaty with the USSR, 147, 207
Sino-American Relations, 103, 207
State of the Union, 1990, 198
Sturmer, Michael, 228
Sununu, John, Chief of Staff, 188–189, 195
Supreme Allied Commander of NATO, Alexander Haig, 140

Taft, William Howard, 13, 28, 206
Taiwan Strait, 93
Taiwan, 41, 93, 100, 103, 120
Tajikistan, 109
Thailand, 74, 100
tax-and-spend liberals, 186
Thatcher, Margaret, 68, 135, 148, 208
Theodore H. White, 37
Third World debt, 51, 95, 153
Tibet, 101–102
Togo, 200
trade, 91–95, 97, 99–105, 107, 109, 129, 134, 145, 147, 200, 208–210
Treasury Secretary Brady, Nicholas, 95
treaties, 26
  biodiversity, 172–173
  defense, 81
Trujillo, César Gaviria, President of the Republic of Colombia, 97
Truman, Harry, 16, 29, 31, 44–45, 51, 56–58, 71, 87, 153
Turkmenistan, 199

U.S. banks and petrodollars, 138
U.S. invasion of Haiti in August 1994, 200
U.S. policy in Africa, 123
U.S.-Asia relations, 107
U.S.-Latin America, 92, 107

Index

U.S.-led Unified Task Force (UNITAF), 117
Ukraine, 121, 135, 140, 199
UN Operation for Somalia (UNOSOM II), 117
UN Security Council, 78, 201–202
UN Security Council Resolution 678, 136
Unfinished War Against Drugs (Narcotics), 55, 96–97, 151, 209
United Nation's International Atomic Energy Agency Inspectors, 104
United Nations, 4, 31, 80, 145, 172, 202
Urban League, 28
USAID funds, 145
USSR, 17, 113, 134, 140–141
Uzbekistan, 199

Van Buren, 13, 54, 206
Venezuela, 95, 97, 209
veto powers, 182
Vietnam, 45, 53, 104, 113, 117–118, 127, 129, 142, 158–159, 156, 175, 182–186, 189–195, 200–201, 211–213
Vietnam War, 45, 53, 69, 72, 157, 183, 198, 202
 humanitarian Vietnam, 103
 North Vietnam, 74
Vietcong, 74
voiceless in Africa, the, 111–123

Wall Street, 40
war in the Gulf, 187. *See also* Gulf War
War on Poverty, 153, 169
Warner, Margaret G., 37, 39, 56, 177, 195
Washington, D.C., 11, 43

Washington, George, 12
Weinberger, Casper, Secretary of Defense, 64
Wells, Melissa, 127
Western Alliance, 80, 106
wetlands, 171
White House, 20, 25–26, 28, 44–46, 50, 54, 61, 84, 118, 140, 155–156, 187–188, 191, 205–206
Wildavsky, Aaron, 3, 8, 34, 57, 183, 193, 204, 212
Wilderness Society, 171
Will, George, 48–51, 58–59, 181, 193
Wilson, Woodrow, 6–7, 9, 12–13, 21, 30, 113, 135, 146–147, 211
 Wilsonian doctrine of promoting democracy, 199
 Wilsonianism, 147, 199
Witcover, Jules, 42, 56–58, 230
women's rights, 157
World Bank, 119, 124, 130, 143, 201
World Trade Organization (WTO), 99
World War I, 12
World War II, xi, 17, 31, 41, 77, 114, 138, 146, 198
Wortman, C. B., 40, 56

Yale, 159, 175
Yard, Molly, 77
Youth Entering Service to America Foundation (YES), 55
Yugoslavia, 79, 139–140, 148

Zambia, 200
Zapata Petroleum Corporation, 40
Zapatista National Liberation Front, Guerrilla Movement, 94
Zimmerman, Warren, 139, 148

About the Authors

Eric Otenyo is associate professor of politics and international affairs at Northern Arizona University. He previously taught at Illinois State University, Normal. He holds a PhD from Miami University, Ohio, and an MPA from Syracuse University. Dr. Otenyo's previous publications include *Comparative Public Administration: The Essential Readings* (coedited with Nancy Lind) and *Managerial Discretion in Government Decision Making: Beyond the Street Level* (coauthored with Jacqueline Vaughn). He has published in several journals such as *Public Organization Review*, *Studies in Conflict and Terrorism*, *International Journal of Public Administration*, *Public Resistance*, *African Security Review*, *Public Administration and Management: An Interactive Journal*, and *International Journal of Services Economics and Management*.

…

Nancy Lind is professor of politics and government at Illinois State University. She holds a PhD from University of Minnesota. She is coauthor and coeditor of numerous books, including *Controversies of the George W. Bush Presidency Pro and Con Documents* (with Bernard Ivan Tamas), *Presidents From Reagan Through Clinton, 1981–2001: Debating the Issues in Pro and Con Primary Documents* (with Lane Crothers), *Dynamics of Social Welfare Policy: Right Versus Left* (with Gardenia Harris and Bernard Ivan Tamas), and *Nonviolence and Its Alternatives: An Interdisciplinary Reader* (with Manfred Steger). Dr. Lind has taught courses in public administration and American government for over two decades.